The Coca Boom and Rural Social Change in Bolivia

Linking Levels of Analysis

Emilio F. Moran, Series Editor

Covering Ground: Common Water Management and the State in the Peruvian Highlands   *David W. Guillet*

The Coca Boom and Rural Social Change in Bolivia *Harry Sanabria*

The Coca Boom and Rural Social Change in Bolivia

Harry Sanabria

Ann Arbor

THE UNIVERSITY OF MICHIGAN PRESS

A CIP catalogue record for this book is available from the British Library.

Library of Congress Cataloging-in-Publication Data

Sanabria, Harry.
    The coca boom and rural social change in Bolivia / Harry Sanabria.
        p.   cm. — (Linking levels of analysis)
    Includes bibliographical references and index.
    ISBN 0-472-10313-X (alk. paper)
        1. Coca industry—Social aspects—Bolivia—Cochambamba (Dept.)
    2. Cochabamba (Bolivia : Dept.)—Rural conditions. 3. Social
    change—Bolivia—Cochabamba (Dept.) 4. Peasantry—Bolivia—
    Cochabamba (Dept.)   I. Title.   II. Series
    HD9019.C632B647   1993
    338.1'7374'098423—dc20   93-23794
                                                                  CIP

To my parents, Luis and Adelaida, who waited so long and never lost faith in me; to Karen, who had the courage to wait alongside me; to Picci Alonso, who first stirred my interest in anthropology; and to Héctor Oscar Ciarlo, who always loved to teach and in so many ways inspired his students.

Acknowledgments

This book would not have been possible without the support, cooperation, advice, and especially friendship I have been fortunate to receive from so many over the years.

My parents, Luis and Adelaida, have always had faith in me and have been there when I needed them. For many years Karen was at my side; we shared many experiences together, some good and some bad, but all worth remembering. At the University of Puerto Rico my friend Picci Alonso, convinced that anthropology was an endeavor worth pursuing, presented me many years ago with a special gift—a copy of Ralph Linton's *The Study of Man*. Professor Héctor Oscar Ciarlo of the University of Puerto Rico, whose love for philosophy and his students I will always cherish, inspired me to travel to South America and taught me never to forget to ask some of the most important questions in life.

Many, many years ago Carlos Mario Boccia and Atilio Martínez in Argentina offered me their friendship and taught me much about themselves and their country. "Mama Martínez," who as a member of the Mothers of the Plaza de Mayo courageously spent her last years fighting against oppression and for human decency, will always be an inspiration for me. I hope some day they will understand what it meant for me to have shared their hopes, fears, and frustrations.

At the State University of New York–Binghamton Professors Michael Horowitz, Richard Antoun, and Margaret Conkey provided me with a solid training in anthropology and urged me to continue my graduate studies. Professors Arnold Strickon, William Denevan, Steve Stern, William Thiesenhusen, Aidan Southall, and Katherine Bowie at the University of Wisconsin–Madison guided me during the very earliest stages of this project and the difficult process of writing my dissertation. I am above all indebted to Professor Strickon, chairperson of my doctoral committee, who steadfastly read many drafts of the dissertation, never waivered in his support, and demonstrated unflagging patience with me. "Arnie" and I disagreed on many issues, but he allowed me the freedom to pursue my own thoughts (and make and recognize my own mistakes) and never attempted to impose on me his own particular view of what an anthropology project should consist of. I will always be grateful for this opportunity. A special mention of gratitude is also due to David and Minka de Soto, John Stevenson, and Keith Holden, each of whom offered me their friendship and support when I most needed it.

In New York City many thanks are also due to Bruce D. Johnson and Greg Falkin (Narcotic and Drug Research, Inc.), Edmundo Morales (West Chester University), and Luis Loyola (Manhattan College), who generously offered me their advice, support, and friendship before and after I completed my book. A special word of gratitude goes to my good friend and "partner" Eloise Dunlap (Narcotic and Drug Research, Inc.), who never flinched in her belief that I would complete this book. I gratefully acknowledge the solid financial support for my graduate studies at Madison and field research in Bolivia that I received from the Committee on Institutional Cooperation, the University of Wisconsin-Madison Graduate School and the Fulbright-Hays Dissertation Research Abroad Program.

I will always be indebted to all Pampeños who accepted and continue to accept the "gringuito" in their midst, generously shared with me their moments of grief and of happiness, tolerated my unending questions, and always laughed as I stumbled my way through Quechua. I hope that this volume will in some way convey their hopes, aspirations, and most difficult quest for a better life. My greatest debt and gratitude in Pampa, however, goes to Miguel. Miguel was much more than an "informant": he was my assistant, friend, companion in the field, and drinking buddy. Miguel was always there when I needed him. He seemed always cheerful, eager and willing to teach the "gringu" Quechua, how and when to ask questions, and when to keep quiet. Intensely curious, Miguel and I spent many nights together talking about many things—life in other countries, how is it that humans can travel through space, why is it that stars seem to fall from the skies, and many other relevant matters. And he was often with me when I was too intoxicated to walk by myself, helping me to get home safely and into bed.

In Cochabamba Jorge Dandler, Roberto Laserna, José Blanes, Juan Torres, and Eusebio Solíz of the Centro de Estudios de la Realidad Económica y Social (CERES) offered me much needed assistance in the field. The *padrecitos* of the town of Sacaba, Berto and Luis, unselfishly allowed me unrestricted access to their parish archive. Gunnar Mendoza graciously permitted me to explore the rich holdings of the Archivo Nacional de Bolivia, as did Dr. Fiorilo at the Cochabamba office of Derechos Reales. I owe a great deal to my friends Mike, Aida, Carolyn, and Claudio, who made my stay in Cochabamba a truly enjoyable experience.

Jim Weil and a second (anonymous) reviewer carefully and critically read drafts of this manuscript and suggested many ways of improving it. Many thanks to Emilio Moran and to Joyce Harrison of the University of Michigan Press for their patience and support. Seong-Jin An and Lynn Swartley, graduate students in anthropology at the University of Pittsburgh, carefully checked the numerous tables and the long bibliography.

Finally, I would like to thank my colleagues, and the students and staff, at the Department of Anthropology, University of Pittsburgh, who in many ways made my first year at "Pitt" an enjoyable one.

Series Introduction

The series Linking Levels of Analysis focuses on studies that deal with the relationships between local-level systems and larger, more inclusive systems. While we know a great deal about how local and larger systems operate, we know a great deal less about how these levels articulate with each other. It is this kind of research, in all its variety, that Linking Levels of Analysis is designed to publish. Works should contribute to the theoretical understanding of such articulations, create or refine methods appropriate to interlevel analysis, and represent substantive contributions to the social sciences.

It is just such a study that we present in *The Coca Boom and Rural Social Change in Bolivia* by Harry Sanabria. He shows how the humble coca bush, a plant with deep symbolic underpinnings in ritual and daily life in the Andes, has been torn from its traditional linkages and linked, instead, to a global market for illicit drugs—with princely profits for those controlling the linkages. It is a study of the transformation from one kind of linkage between local producers and regional consumers to a very different, and distant, set of consumers. Unlike traditional distributors using seasonal llama caravans, contemporary distributors are willing to use violence to control the production and distribution of this drug. Unlike less thorough analyses of the cocaine "drug war," the author of this study shows how local producers in Bolivia have fought efforts by "drug lords" as well as the well-intentioned efforts of international law enforcement officials to stop the spread of cocaine. The latter forget that coca growing, in itself, is not the cause of addictions in North America or the crime in our cities, but a means of obtaining a modest livelihood for peasant producers. In the process, these peasant producers are caught between two comparably violent, globally connected sets of institutions. Sanabria shows that the emergence of the cocaine business is linked to other historical processes in Bolivia, such as the development of mining and other commodity markets, the limited success of agrarian reform, and declining living standards—especially in peasant regions.

The author also makes an important critique of recent efforts to stem the flow of cocaine—a process that largely focuses on destroying the plant rather than addressing the fundamental need of rural people in Bolivia to make a decent living. Sanabria engages this issue by reminding us that current policies have led and will continue to lead to levels of violence and bloodshed unknown before. The rural peasant in Bolivia is not a villain in this story but rather a victim of the failure of past development strategies and the contemporary addictions of developed nations. This rich analysis of the profound and historically deep links between coca producers and consumers in the Andes, and the transformation of a simple commodity into an object of warlike conflict and violence deserves careful reading and meditation.

It is my hope that this volume will be widely read, and from reflection of its dissection of linkages in the production, distribution, and consumption of cocaine, will come policies that address the roots of the problem both here and in Bolivia.

Future volumes planned for the series will address topics such as "Diagnosing America," with an agenda for future research on American culture; a political and ecological analysis of environmental destruction in Latin America; and a historical analysis of the rise of inequality. Please contact the series editor or other members of the editorial board about work that may be relevant to the series.

Editor
Emilio F. Moran, Indiana University

Editorial Board
John Bowen, Washington University
Conrad Kottak, University of Michigan
Kathleen Newman, Columbia University
Douglas White, University of California, Irvine

Contents

Chapter 1

Introduction

The escalating sale and consumption of drugs, especially cocaine and its derivative form as "crack," in New York City and other major consumption centers during the past decade has attracted considerable attention from and caused a great deal of alarm in the North American mass media, political establishment, and electorate (see, e.g., Inciardi 1986; Bourgois 1989; Goode 1989; Reinarman and Levine 1989a, 1989b; T. Williams 1989; Johnson, Williams, Dei, and Sanabria 1990; Johnson, Hamid, and Sanabria 1992; Wallace 1990). We are daily reminded of the "war on drugs" currently underway at home and abroad. The political establishment, unable or unwilling to successfully grapple with the deep social, cultural, and economic underpinnings of the consumption of illicit drugs by North American consumers, and the spread of drug distribution networks in predominantly poor urban ghettos, is increasingly directing its war against the Third World "drug-producing" countries. Forced eradication programs, punitive economic measures, and military interventions have already taken place abroad (and will most likely escalate in the near future) in an almost futile attempt to stem the tide of drugs—primarily cocaine and heroin—flowing into North America and to undermine the sophisticated and powerful transnational illicit drug trade (Galloway and Vélez de Berliner 1988), currently the "fastest-growing and unquestionably the most profitable" industry (*Fortune Magazine,* qtd. by Kawell 1989:34).

In Bolivia and Peru the age-old coca shrub, traditionally grown to satisfy consumption within those countries would by the early 1980s be almost exclusively cultivated to satisfy the seemingly unsatiable demand for cocaine by North American consumers. As a result, coca was soon torn from its social and cultural context of production and consumption and linked its producers in novel ways to an expanding global market. Conflicts, cleavages, and competition centering on the control of coca and its by-products in the Andean countries soon followed and intensified as well as social and economic changes in Andean communities engaged in cultivating the coca leaf thousands of miles away from the major centers of cocaine consumption. Indeed, although a great deal of local-level research has yet to be undertaken, it would seem that the cultivation of coca and the processing of its by-products will soon rival—if it has not already—the profound effects that other export commoditites have had on the physical, socioeconomic, and political landscape of the Andean countries. The purpose of this volume is to understand this struggle over the control of coca in contemporary Bolivia—how and why it surfaced— and what it has meant for Bolivian peasants to be producing a valuable, yet "illegal," good for the primary consumption of North Americans.

Aims

This book attempts to achieve four interrelated aims. The first and primary aim is to systematically examine some widespread and rippling social and economic consequences that producing coca for the international cocaine market has had for members of Pampa, a high-altitude Bolivian peasant community in the department of Cochabamba, most of whom were migrating to Bolivia's humid lowlands and growing coca. My objective here is not simply to demonstrate the different ways in which Pampeños were rapidly and inexorably swept away or subsumed by (abstract) "market," or "capitalist," forces or by anonymous and distant capitalists. Rather, I wish to stress their active participation in the cocaine market as a consequence of past and ongoing attempts to defend and enhance their livelihood in the face of recurrent state and international policies that have systematically endangered their living standards. At the same time Pampeños have not only become deeply enmeshed in and have actively contributed to the expansion of the cocaine market. By often successfully resisting state policies, they have also (and unfortunately) ominously set the stage for even harsher, and perhaps far more effective and deadly, state—and international—repressive efforts against them and their livelihood.

The second aim is to account for the emergence of Bolivia's cocaine market and examine the unfolding of the present conflict over coca and its by-products. As will soon become clear, an increasing demand for cocaine by North American consumers during the past decade, the direct and active role that Bolivian state officials played in the drug trade, the ambitions and needs of foreign or domestic capitalists, or other factors in themselves are insufficient to account for the emergence and conflictive nature of this market at any particular moment in time. Rather, it was the result of the progressive concatenation of historically convergent, cumulative, and reinforcing processes taking place in Bolivia and elsewhere that in different ways and periods set the stage for and allowed a segment of Bolivia's peasantry to take an active role in the appearance and creation of this market. These processes included, for example, the development of the mining industry during Bolivia's colonial period and its corollary of forced labor drafts and expansion of early commodity markets, which included coca; the structural limitations of and developmental policies implemented after the agrarian reform and decades of declining living standards in the rural countryside; a downspin in traditional Bolivian exports for world markets in the 1970s; and a growing population and a decreasing land base in heavily populated peasant regions.

These processes were paralleled by and interlocked with structural changes in the North American economy, reflected in the increasing marginalization of the poor during the 1970s and 1980s and the increase in cocaine consumption and distribution. In turn, these social and economic changes intersected with favorable ecological and technical dimensions of coca production—coca's amazing adaptability to the eastern Andes environment and its ability to absorb large amounts of labor. Clearly, then, Bolivian peasants did not suddenly "decide" one day to grow coca for this market simply because it was profitable and timely to do so. Evolving, cumulative, and intertwined national and international contexts not only structured the ways in which options, opportunities, and constraints were perceived by Bolivian peasants but were also deeply embedded in their daily and ongoing decisions and strategies.

The third aim of this study is to examine how and in what specific contexts Bolivian peasants forged links with and contributed to the emergence of this market. As I will attempt to demonstrate, these linkages were the result of sequential (though not necessarily linear) and cumulative choices, many having at the time little or no overt relationship to a cocaine market. These choices were undertaken in response to and largely structured by interlocking and constantly shifting ecological, political, and economic processes, some of which I have mentioned. One objective of this study is to place Bolivian peasant options, choices, and strategies centering on the cultivation of coca within the general contours of these processes and to demonstrate how they both reflected and powerfully shaped them.

The fourth and final aim of this book is to examine critically and adopt a position on current narcotics and economic development policies in Bolivia, largely devised and implemented by foreign policymakers. My linking of development and narcotics policies is not fortuitous, and there are three reasons why I jointly discuss them. The first, as we shall see in greater detail, is that it is important to examine development policies following the agrarian reform inasmuch as these constituted a fundamental underpinning of the emergence of Bolivia's cocaine market. The second reason is that development programs and initiatives currently under way in and near Bolivia's coca-producing regions do not have as their primary and ultimate goal to enhance living standards of the rural peasantry but, instead, are primarily governed by overt (and sometimes not so overt) concerns and efforts to reduce coca cultivation by peasant cultivators and do away with cocaine and coca paste trafficking. These development programs and initiatives—and, in fact, most of the development aid that has recently flooded Bolivia—would today have little reason for being were it not for the existence of a deeply entrenched and widespread market for coca and its by-products, and the effectiveness of these programs is measured largely in terms of how many coca hectares have been taken out of cultivation—or cocaine-processing "laboratories" destroyed—and the like.

My third reason for critically examining the underpinnings and outcomes of these policies has to do with the responsibility that anthropologists have toward the people they study and work and live with. It is not sufficient for anthropologists concerned with development issues to confine themselves to ascertaining whether or how development projects and policies "work" or "do not work" at the local level. Anthropologists are ethically bound to sound the alarm when policies implemented from "above" and in a clear context of the naked use of power will result in massive social and economic dislocations; in short, anthropologists should adopt an advocate role grounded in their knowledge and expertise (cf. Arnould 1989). This is especially necessary in present-day Bolivia, where, in a politically and ideologically charged climate, coca-cultivating peasants are often construed by those wielding economic and political power (including economic assistance policymakers) as villains and criminals to be forcefully repressed and where development and narcotics policies appear to be setting the conditions for levels of conflict, violence, and bloodshed unknown in recent memory. I hope, perhaps naively, that my discussion of development and narcotics policy issues will somehow result in a more peaceful, equitable, and just solution to Bolivia's coca quagmire.

To a large extent this entire study pivots on one particular commodity, coca, and its four aims took shape gradually as I grappled with and attempted to provide satisfactory answers to key questions and concerns centering on the coca leaf.[1] Central among these was why there existed competition and conflict over coca in the first place and what it was about coca that made it especially valuable and worthwhile to struggle over. Other questions inevitably surfaced: Why and how did the control over coca emerge as a central issue during the 1980s in Bolivia? Had analogous attempts to control coca surfaced in the past, and, if so, how were they similar or different, and what could we learn about the present by closely examining these past events? Embedded were issues hinging on production, distribution, and consumption. What was needed to produce and distribute coca? How were labor and other resources mobilized and accessed? What happened to peasants who were devoting substantial resources to producing a commodity that now satisfied an international demand, and why were they willing to do so? My attempts to answer these and other questions inevitably led me to explore issues and connections beyond the confines of a "community" and to examine when and in what ways these intersected.

Subsistence and Accumulation

The well-known fact that large numbers of peasants in Bolivia (and Peru) are not only massively taking up the cultivation of coca—a commodity that quickly enters a capitalist market—but vigorously defending their right to do so, flies directly against the well-entrenched myth of the "subsistence-oriented" peasant. According to this myth, peasants are

> inserted in a non-capitalist mode of production which revolves around the intensive use of family labor, the non-accumulation or investment of capital, and simple reproduction (i.e., the quest for subsistence and replacement). (Cook 1986:83–84)

Peasants, in other words, strive to produce just enough to satisfy their subsistence needs, are generally adverse to producing significant surpluses for the market, and consequently avoid cash or exchange relations. This view of peasants as inherently subsistence oriented and antagonistic to market exchanges has a long history and has been shaped by diverse theoretical traditions.

In American anthropology such an approach was firmly established by Robert Redfield and his students, whose views dominated peasant studies for over 30 years. Redfield conceptualized peasants as rural cultivators with a distinctive set of values, attitudes, and worldview ("culture"), outside the orbit of market exchange, and contrasted their "traditional" way of life to other "modern" societies (Silverman 1979).

Redfield's theoretical position was inscribed within the context of the emergence of "modernization theory," a series of approaches to the study of Third World societies that emerged primarily in the United States after World War II and influenced by eighteenth- and nineteenth-century social evolutionary theory and notions of progress (Tipps 1973:200–201). While proponents of modernization often quarreled over concepts and units of analysis, they agreed that societies fell into two camps—modern, meaning advanced capitalist societies, and its antithesis, traditional societies. Modern institutions and values not only "represented an appropriate model to be emulated by other, less fortunate societies" (Tipps 1973:209), but it was during the course of modernization, or "modernity," that Third World societies shed their traditional (and supposedly backward) values and institutions (all inimical to development) and "caught up" to the modern and "advanced" societies. Moreover, this dichotomy was replicated within traditional societies in the form of "a polar distinction between city and countryside [that corresponds] to developed versus underdeveloped and modern versus traditional" (Kearney 1986:333–34). These polar contrasts were paralleled, in the rural areas of traditional societies, by a deep divide between a dynamic, growth-oriented (capitalist) agriculture and a stagnant, subsistence-oriented (peasant) agricultural sector (Klarén and Bossert 1986:9–10). Although modernization theory has been criticized at length, its portrayal of peasant economic behavior as driven by a logic of subsistence still endures in certain academic and, perhaps more important, policy-making circles.[2]

Another important intellectual tradition that contributed to the image of a subsistence peasant stemmed from Chayanov's *The Theory of Peasant Economy* (1986). Originally published in 1924–25 and first translated into English in 1966, Chayanov's book "made history" as its English translation coincided "with a dramatic 'face to the peasants' realignment of attention which took place in the 1960s" (Shanin 1986:1, 21). In anthroplogy Chayanov's theory was popularized by Sahlins (1972) in the midst of the acrimonious "substantative-formalist" debate in economic anthropology. Chayanov, according to Roseberry (1986:73), "presents a model of a primordial economic past [the] concept of domestic production as an original, non- and anti-capitalist economic form."[3] Although Chayanov did not dismiss the possibility that peasant family farms could accumulate wealth and capital (see, e.g., Chayanov 1986:119; cf. Lehmann 1982:142–43), his conceptual approach consisted of studying peasant "family farms" as divorced from the wider capitalist system and employing only family labor. Within this analytic frame he then argued that levels and intensity of production were primarily a function of the relationship between household size, labor availablity, and a culturally acceptable (or determined) level of needs (see esp. Chayanov 1986:12). Given unchanging needs and a stable household size, the family farm will produce just enough to satisfy its needs and no more. To put it differently, the family farm has no propensity to accumulate surplus above and beyond that determined by its availability of labor and culturally construed needs.

Another line of research that has stressed the inability or unwillingness of peasants to accumulate and solidified the image of peasants struggling to remain outside capitalist exchange and production relations has been the risk and decision-making literature in economic anthropology. In this line of work peasants are by and large conceptualized as "risk averters" who place a high premium on minimizing and avoiding risky, but perhaps more profitable, economic strategies. Peasants, in other words, strive to constantly maximize security and generally shy away from high-risk strategies that will yield them profits or allow them to accumulate surpluses. Much of this work has focused on the adoption of new agricultural techniques or higher-yielding crop varieties and has examined economic and ecological variables—for example, current prices, input costs, expected yields, likelihood of drought or too much rainfall—that seem most immediately relevant to individual decision making (cf. Wharton 1971; A. Johnson 1971; Cancian 1980; Ortiz 1980; Barlett 1980; Chibnik 1990:279–80).

Last, neo-Marxist approaches to the study of peasantries and agrarian change, which emerged as a direct critique of the modernization paradigm and as an attempt to provide quite different explanations for poverty and underdevelopment, have also contributed to the myth of a subsistence-oriented, nonaccumulating peasant.[4] Two slightly different but related views are important here. The first is that persistent poverty and underdevelopment in Third World countries is the result of surplus extraction by industrial capitalist societies. Morever, this "outward" flow of wealth is replicated at different levels (nation-state, rural regions, peasant communities, peasant households). The result is that, at the level of the economic unit, or household, peasants are simply unable to accumulate wealth, for their surpluses are constantly being "drained away" by capitalists (e.g., de Janvry 1981:19–20; C. Smith 1983:309–10, 335; 1984:62–63; Lehmann 1986a:606). The second view, and a corollary of the first, is that peasants, well aware of the fact that their insertion into capitalist exchange and production relationships are ultimately detrimental to their livelihood, manifest a deeply rooted "aversion to" or "logic" against capitalism (cf. Long 1984:3–4; Lehmann 1986a:603). It is at this juncture—one in which peasants strive to remain outside the capitalist market—where, as Cook and Binford (1990:17) and others have noted, neo-Marxists and modernization theorists share common ground.

The Nonaccumulation Fallacy

Modernization theorists view peasants as dominated by traditional values (a priority on subsistence, a reluctance to shed a way of life, and so forth) that essentially maintain them outside the orbit of market exchange, only tangentially integrated to the wider national (capitalist) economy. Scholars influenced by Chayanov stress that household demographic dynamics and culturally prescribed needs set limits to accumulation, result in an inner drive to simply satisfy basic reproductive needs, and to some extent determine the degree to which peasant households engage in market transactions. The risk and decision-making literature portrays peasants as stubbornly resisting high-risk strategies with potential for accumulation and, as a consequence, also a deeply rooted aversion to producing goods for the market. Some neo-Marxist approaches emphasize the inability of the peasantry to retain surplus to any significant degree and likewise underline the propensity of peasants to shy away from capitalist relations of exchange and production. A common thread underlying these different approaches is the homogeneous explanations for poverty, underdevelopment, peasant goals, expectations, and livelihood strategies, and the effects and consequences of capitalist relations of production and exchange. They also share what Cook and Binford (1990:15) have recently called the "nonaccumulation fallacy," a perspective emphasizing the inability and/or unwillingness of peasants to accumulate surplus or wealth.

In recent years an alternate body of literature on petty (or "simple") commodity production has emerged that provides a useful perspective from which to gauge the heterogeneity of peasant goals and livelihood strategies, the ever-shifting conditions under which peasants opt to engage in wider capitalist markets, the different types of relationships that they forge within wider economic circuits, the quite diverse responses by peasants to threats to their livelihood, and the disparate consequences of these strategies and responses.

In these studies peasants and other small-scale, and often rural, cultivators appear heavily engaged in producing commodities for the capitalist market. These market commodities can be agricultural, such as wheat among North American farmers (Friedmann 1980) or coca cultivated by Chapare migrants, or nonagricultural, such as weavings (C. Smith 1984), grinding stones (Cook 1982, 1986), or steel implements (Kahn 1980).

In addition, producers operate in a sociopolitical environment in which the factors of production—land, labor, and capital—can circulate freely (de Janvry 1981:97; Goodman and Redclift 1982:84; K. Moore 1984:13). Furthermore, producers own or control their means of production (de Janvry 1981:97; Goodman and Redclift 1982:81; K. Moore 1984:13; Kahn 1986:59), and the household retains its role as the major productive decision-making unit (Roseberry 1986). An additional distinguishing feature of petty commodity producers (and one that is still the subject of considerable debate) is that by and large they employ little or no wage labor (Cook 1982:10; Lehmann 1982:138; Kahn 1986:54; Stein 1984:279; C. Smith 1984:80; 1986:54; Friedmann 1986:125). Recently, Cook and Binford (1990:10) have put forth a "generic" concept of petty commodity production that has four fundamental features or characteristics: (1) "regular and exclusive" production of markets for market exchange; (2) "small-scale private enterprise" in which the means of production are directly controlled by producers and labor is nonwaged; (3) "mutual independence of production units"; and (4) production is "never to the exclusion of capital accumulation or profit."

This body of work on petty commodity producers suffers from a number of drawbacks. One, for instance, is the profusion of different terms that refer to essentially identical units of analysis.[5] Another, perhaps more serious, difficulty consists of analytically distinguishing between commodity producers and "peasants," particularly when nonagricultural commodities are the principal ones produced and marketed.

Despite these difficulties, from the vantage point of this book the literature on petty commodity production offers distinct advantages over other approaches. First, these studies underline the fact that peasants do not display an intrinsic logic, or "rationality," toward "subsistence," an aversion to the market, to capitalistlike activities, or toward wealth or capital accumulation itself. These studies also stress that, given the appropriate conditions, peasants will intensify production (e.g., Vandergeest 1989) and accumulate surpluses. They also emphasize the different ways in which peasants and other producers creatively confront and grapple with shifting political and economic conditions and contexts—local, regional, and international.

As we shall see, coca-producing migrants in the Chapare have hardly been representative of the nonaccumulating peasant so often portrayed in the "peasantist" literature (Cook 1986:83–84). They responded quickly, decisively and, in many cases, successfully to a range of state policies that threatened their livelihood. Their response centered on vigorously pursuing a strategy of producing a valuable commodity for the market— coca. Well aware of market prices and returns and quite cognizant of the environmental, economic, and political risks involved, they constantly and quite often successfully maneuvered around and undermined state-sponsored attempts to limit the cultivation and marketing of coca. Many engaged in a variety of land and labor relationships that allowed them to expand and intensify coca cultivation. Although they were in large measure responding to state fiscal and agricultural development policies that were progressively undermining their economic livelihood, many went far beyond the goal of simply satisfying their "subsistence needs," striving to and often accumulating wealth and capital. And, in the process, they had a profound impact on the course of peasant-state relationships in Bolivia during the 1980s.

The strategies pursued by coca-cultivating peasants in the Chapare of Bolivia entailed a great deal of risk. They faced, for example, environmental risks such excessive rainfall and crop infestations and diseases. Yet coca cultivation continued to expand even after the disastrous 1982–83 floods, and, despite knowledge that the harvest of immature coca leaves would lead to the appearance of *estalla* (a disease that affects coca plants), Pampeño migrants nevertheless intensified coca harvests during this period. Another risk they faced during this period of runaway inflation was wildly fluctuating prices, although the overall trend was for coca returns to parallel, and sometimes outpace, inflation.

The gravest risk to their livelihood, however, was not ecological or economic but, rather, political. Political risk emerged from a variety of state (Bolivian and United States) repressive policies designed not only to roll back the spread of coca cultivation and cocaine-related activities but also to "regain" control of a territory now perceived to be under the control of drug (cocaine) traffickers. These repressive policies included restrictions to the marketing of coca leaves and/or their outright confiscation and a variety of coercive actions designed to eradicate coca. Political risk, of course, also enhanced economic risk, but, instead of switching to politically less risky but unprofitable alternate crops, Chapare peasants expanded coca cultivation. As I will argue, given an accelerated fall in the terms of exchange of traditional highland crops and steadily deteriorating living standards (a pattern aggravated by runaway inflation in the 1980s), Chapare peasants faced a greater threat to their livelihood if they did not aggressively pursue coca cultivation. These peasant migrants were not merely risk averters but also important actors in a high-stakes gamble, constantly facing head on major risks to their livelihood.

Peasants, Coca, and Capitalism

The expansion of coca production in Bolivia during the past decade also presents an interesting case study from which to gauge the analytic usefulness of different explanations offered for the persistence of peasant socioeconomic forms deeply inserted in capitalist exchange and production relations. Modernization theorists posited that in the process of modernity and development peasants would shed their supposedly anachronistic and backward social institutions and economic organization. A parallel line of thought emerged in the 1960s and 1970s from among some neo-Marxist scholars, who argued that development (i.e., the spread of capitalist relations of production and exchange) in agrarian hinterlands would sweep away and destroy noncapitalist modes of production. Despite their profound differences, then, both assumed the inevitable demise of the peasantry.

Other scholars soon began to question this scenario of inevitable demise, giving rise to the now famous "differentiation debate." In particular, these scholars focused their attention on the fact that the peasantry seemed not to be withering away despite capitalist development. They furthermore believed that explanations of agrarian change that posited a uniform spread of capitalism (and the disappearance of the peasantry) were too mechanical, critiqued the view of a peasantry totally, and easily, overwhelmed by the onslaught of capitalist expansion, and, in particular, dismissed the assumption that the important actors in this process of agrarian change, peasants and capitalists alike, shared similar goals and interests.

As a result, three explanations surfaced that attempted to account for the "survival" of the peasantry, and noncapitalist forms of social and economic organization, in regions clearly dominated by capitalist production and exchange relations (for good reviews of this literature, see, for example, Long and Roberts 1978, 1984:8–10; Guillet 1980; Roseberry 1983:192–208; C. Smith 1983; Caballero 1984:27–30; Long 1984:3–24; M. Painter 1985; Lehmann 1986a, 1986b; J. Collins 1990:3–24).

The first posited that the persistence of the peasantry was a functional requirement of capitalism. By growing their own subsistence crops, peasants who offered their labor to capitalist enterprises assumed part of their own costs of reproduction and therefore lessened production costs of capitalists. (Another way that capitalists minimized costs, the argument went, consisted of encouraging nonwage forms of labor recruitment to attract and retain peasant labor. As we shall see in chapter 7, this is one explanation put forth to explain reciprocal and nonwage labor in the Andes.) It was, then, in the interests of capitalists to see to it that peasants were not transformed into full-time wage laborers: capitalism, or, more precisely, capitalists, "needed" peasants in order to maximize their profits.

The second explanation, largely derived from Chayanov's notion of "drudgery," argued that peasants survived in the marketplace because they enjoyed a competitive advantage over capitalist enterprises in that they could produce "cheaper" goods. By drastically cutting back on consumption and working more, by "overexploiting" their labor, peasant households were capable of producing and marketing goods with a rate of return unacceptably low for capitalist enterprises. The third explanation for the stubborn persistence of peasantries posited that peasants will strive and pursue different strategies to resist being drawn into capitalist circuits of production and exchange; the idea of a peasant logic toward "subsistence" is a corollary of this explanation.

From the perspective of this study the three explanations have definite limitations. We can dismiss the last explanation from the outset: while peasants will no doubt resist attempts to undermine their subsistence base and be transformed into a wage-earning proletariat, it is clear that peasant migrants to the Chapare have not avoided but have vigorously pursued commodity production for the market. The two other explanations for the "survival" of peasant forms of socioeconomic organization are equally problematic: the first assumes that production for the market is dominated by capitalists who control and extract considerable amounts of (subsidized) peasant labor, while the second explanation posits capitalists and peasants competing against each other to deliver to the market commodities with the lowest possible price. Neither scenario, however, is present in the Chapare. There, coca-producing capitalist enterpises are conspicuously absent, and coca cultivation is the almost exclusive domain of tens of thousands of small-scale peasant cultivators who control their means of production and do not offer their labor to capitalist enterprises, although landless peasants will offer their labor to other coca-producing, land-based peasants. Coca-cultivating migrants were, and are, heavily engaged in production that ultimately satisfies an international market, but by and large their major point of intersection with this market has been in the realm of exchange. There is no doubt that peasant-based coca cultivation contributes to accumulation by cocaine elites. The principal means of elite wealth and capital accumulation, however, given the extraordinary price gap between each node in the trafficking circuits, has consisted not in the control of production or the deployment of labor but, instead, in the realm of exchange and distribution (Henman 1985; Tullis 1987; Henkel 1988; E. Morales 1989; Bureau of International Narcotics Matters 1990, 1991; United States House of Representatives 1991:26–27).[6] Trafficking elites do, indeed, "buy cheap and sell dear."

But the proliferation of peasant-based production in the Chapare cannot be explained solely on the basis of its usefulness and/or profitability for the cocaine elites. Such a functionalist explanation would not take us very far. In particular, it would gloss over the different processes (including state policies that undermined the profitability of highland agriculture) that have sparked migration to the Chapare, enabled migrants to access land and labor, and allowed the political and economic conditions necessary for expanded coca cultivation. Moreover, such an interpretation would treat the absence of large-scale, capital-intensive coca enterprises as unproblematic.

In fact, peasant-based coca production was thriving in the Chapare not because it was subsidizing capitalist production or because peasants were overexploiting their labor or competing with and undermining capitalist enterprises. Rather, peasant production was thriving partly because the cocaine trafficking elites had shunned away from the direct control of coca production; given the insignificant cost of coca leaves in the whole pyramid of exchange and capital accumulation, little would be gained by attempting control over the cultivation of coca leaves. Moreover, any attempt to gain control over land and labor in the Chapare would have been met by stiff competition from a multitude of well-organized coca-producing peasants, who no doubt would have successfully thwarted any attempts by cocaine elites to achieve a vertical integration of an essentially underground industry. Such an attempt would have also entailed costly and complex forms of labor control and intense competition for available labor with the thousands of land-based peasants already present in the Chapare. In fact, probably one of the most important reasons why trafficking elites have left coca cultivation in the hands of smallholders is because the productive process is so labor intensive, and the primary tasks involved in coca production—from clearing the forest to harvesting and preparing coca leaves for sale—have remained essentially the same for centuries (see chap. 3).[7]

Large-scale, capital- and labor-intensive enterprises centering on the cultivation of coca and the processing of coca paste and cocaine hydrochloride in the Chapare would have been easy targets for antidrug operations and other repressive efforts by the state (despite the fact that, as we shall see, Bolivia's cocaine industry has resulted in clear and substantial benefits for sectors of the state apparatus). Hence, the absence of capital- and labor-intensive coca estates or plantations can also be explained as a result of a deliberate strategy by cocaine elites of "shifting disproportionate risks" to peasant migrant cultivators, as Leons (1986) and Tullis (1987) have hypothesized. Traffickers, with necessary contacts to avoid police detection and with mobile capital, would not bear the brunt of antidrug campaigns. These same forces, which in different ways resulted in a lack of direct control over coca production by the cocaine trafficking elites, were also responsible for inhibiting differentiation in the Chapare within the peasant migrant class.

Inequality was by no means absent in the Chapare: some migrants had more land than others, were more successful in attracting and retaining labor, and had accumulated far more wealth. Furthermore, the

Chapare was flooded with landless migrants who entered into a variety of labor relationships with other land-based migrants. Nevertheless, a systematic process of socioeconomic differentiation from within the land-based peasant class did not emerge.[8] Intense competition from thousands of other coca producers with relatively similar means of production made it extremely difficult to achieve a truly competitive edge over others. Seasonal migration and wildly fluctuating coca prices also made it difficult and costly to retain a considerable amount of labor for lengthy, uninterrupted periods of time. The ability of many landless migrants to move about and work for other owners or to acquire their own land plots, despite signs of increasing land scarcity (see chap. 4), also contributed to considerable social and economic mobility. The lack of alternate productive investment opportunities in the Chapare and constant and heightening political and economic risks from anti-drug campaigns, especially coca eradication programs, also contributed in different ways to the absence of differentiation.

Finally, we cannot overlook the role of the state in fostering or inhibiting differentiation among coca-producing migrants as well as capitalist development in the Chapare. Contrary to the case of the Department of Santa Cruz, where state development policies were largely responsible for the emergence and spread of capitalist agriculture (see chap. 3), the role of the state in the agricultural and economic development in the Chapare has always been negligible. During the first phases of migration to the Chapare, state efforts were limited primarily to providing land grants to incoming migrants. During the 1980s coca boom the state unsuccessfully tried to interrupt the marketing of coca and by the late 1980s and early 1990s had embarked on a systematic campaign to eradicate coca fields in the Chapare.

"Tradition": Isolation or Deep Engagement?

Silverman (1979:57) has noted that "those who follow Redfield in stressing the importance of 'tradition' among peasants (and among the elite who influence them) tend to see change—but not tradition—as problematic." Those "who follow Redfield" would include proponents of the modernization paradigm, who view tradition as consisting of a constellation of relatively unchanging values, norms, expectations, and patterns of socioeconomic organization almost mechanically transmitted from one generation to another and which hamper development.

For others, however, tradition should not be construed as the "dead weight of the past" (Roseberry 1989a:56) but, rather, as a cultural and social repertoire whose content, form, and function are constantly re-created and deployed to meet changing social, economic, and political exigencies. Some of the earliest works adopting this vantage point emerged from studies on African rural-urban migration where, it was shown, "customs" were constantly reorganized (and recreated) in contexts of ethnic and political conflict (e.g., Cohen 1969). In American anthropology Eric Wolf and Sidney Mintz were possibly the first to dismiss the notion of tradition as a body of unchanging social and cultural forms. Mintz, in particular, stressed that,

> so described, the conceptions of "traditional culture" and of the "small-community way of life" change radically. The social-relational aspect of behavior makes of "the traditional" no longer something "surviving" or "conserved" from the past, but rather a pattern of and for behavior that remains viable, though its symbolic meanings and its actual utility may have become quite different. In peasant societies, "blind custom" is neither blind nor customary, and the differential distribution of power, wealth and status will affect the uses of patterned behavior, as well as its meanings for those who engage in it. (1973:97)

Two recent essays capture the essence of these new approaches to the contextual and historically contingent understanding of tradition. Spiegel (1989) reviews other current work on "tradition as resource" and specifically shows how recourse to South African tribal tradition is used as an ideological tool for perpetuating apartheid in South Africa by the white minority. For his part Hanson (1989) has argued that important features of Maori myth and cultural traditions are really "cultural inventions," inventions that anthropologists, among others, have created and perpetuated.[9]

Other authors have stressed that we cannot assume isolation and an unchanging social, economic, and cultural content, even in the presence of seemingly traditional diacritica. R. R. Wilk (1989:45) has remarked, for example, that his

> historical study of the Kekchi economy found that their households had been mixing various forms of subsistence farming, cash crop

production, and wage labor for at least 400 years. Yet Kekchi villages still seem traditional and unacculturated, and each time a new wave of peripheral-capitalist development washes over them, it appears to be the first time they have emerged from the primeval forest.

One key analytic thread of these perspectives is not merely that a reinterpretation of *tradition* requires a dynamic approach to the study of social and cultural forms but also that these cannot be studied apart from wider contexts within which they acquire relevance.

A reconsideration of traditional forms of nonwage labor in the Andes is an especially appropriate theme to reconsider in the context of migration and coca production (see J. Weil 1980a, 1980b, 1989; M. Painter, 1991). While a great deal of work has appeared in recent years on how nonwage Andean labor patterns are adaptive responses to local environmental, productive, and economic conditions, this book posits that the predominance of nonwage labor in Pampa during Bolivia's coca boom can be primarily explained by the multiple linkages that Pampeños forged with wider market forces. This interpretation implies that it is not the isolation of Pampeños from wider market forces and their reluctance to engage in commodity production that best explains nonwage labor but, rather, quite the opposite: it is *precisely because* so many Pampeños were migrating to the Chapare, cultivating and marketing coca, and responding to wider and constantly fluctuating economic and political conditions that best explains why wage labor was virtually absent in Pampa. In the following pages I posit that the various forms of reciprocal and nonwage labor in Pampa were not merely "transitional" forms—passively awaiting to be swept away by capitalist forces—but patterns that derived their resilience precisely from a wider capitalist market. At the same time, while some Marxist approaches, as we have seen, have been especially adamant in emphasizing the role of capitalist production and exchange relations in "perpetuating" peasant social and economic rganization, including nonwage forms of labor, this book also argues that the overwhelming role of nonwage labor in Pampa, centered on the production of the potato, cannot be explained by the "functions" that nonwage labor provides for capitalism.

Organization of Book

In chapter 2 I present a brief overview of the physical, historical, and social landscape of the region of Cochabamba, including the Chapare, and the peasant community of Pampa. Chapter 3 examines the different yet intersecting and cumulative ecological, socioeconomic, and political processes that set the stage for the blossoming of the cocaine market by the early 1980s. I emphasize in this chapter the historic role of coca in Andean society and culture, interests in and policies concerning migration and settlement to the eastern lowlands, and coca's adaptability to environmental conditions present in eastern Bolivia. An important part of this chapter consists of critically examining how state development policies after the agrarian reform set the stage for the emergence of Bolivia's coca market and its current "coca problem." This chapter concludes with an analysis of the intense migration taking place to the Chapare and the expansion of coca cultivation there in the mid-1980s.

Chapter 4 centers on the intense migration from Pampa to the Chapare, the growing social and economic inequality among Pampeños (and other migrants) in the Chapare, and the different ways in which wealth garnered by an elite group of Pampeño migrants was invested and symbolically displayed in Pampa and some of their ramifications.

In chapter 5 I turn to Pampa's land tenure system. Here I particularly emphasize the interplay of the massive migration to the Chapare and newly emerging patterns of accessing land. An important goal of this chapter is to highlight the different ways in which labor migration, hyperinflation, and the accumulation of wealth by prosperous migrants were undermining patterns of access to land and sparking new forms of differential access to productive resources in Pampa.

The expansion of coca cultivation in the Chapare was closely intertwined with agricultural production strategies in peasant communities expelling labor to the Chapare. Chapter 6 takes up this issue in Pampa by focusing on the cultivation of the potato, Pampa's most important cash and subsistence crop. This chapter has two goals. The first is to document the fact that the expansion of coca cultivation was paralleled by a curtailment of land sown in potatoes and, more generally, a decline in potato production in peasant areas experiencing intense migration to the Chapare. The second goal is to examine the manner in which the differential insertion of Pampeños in the cocaine market structured different potato production strategies undertaken in Pampa by migrants and nonmigrants at the height of the coca boom. I conclude this chapter by claiming that one important reason for the decrease in potato production was a shortfall in labor as a result of the massive flow of Pampeños to the Chapare.

The theme of labor is taken up again in chapter 7. My goal in this chapter, however, is to examine the different patterns of labor mobilization and deployment within a context marked by a curtailment of potato cultivation in Pampa and a flow of labor to and expansion of coca cultivation in the Chapare. The major aim of this chapter is to argue that the overwhelming role of nonwage and reciprocal labor in potato cultivation was precisely one outcome of the emphasis by most Pampeño households on coca commodity production and their close links with wider economic circuits centered on the international drug trade.

In chapter 8 I turn to key political and economic events that took place in Bolivia and Pampa between mid-1985 and the summer of 1992. I begin the chapter by teasing out key repercussions of the neoliberal economic model adopted by the state in the summer of 1985. The thrust of this chapter, however, is to critically examine current state efforts at implementing coca eradication and substitution programs, how repression and efforts at coca eradication are being challenged and resisted by peasant migrants, and the looming potential for massive violence in Bolivia's coca-producing regions. I also briefly examine some important social and economic changes that took place in Pampa between the time I left the field in mid-1985 and my brief return visits in the summers of 1991 and 1992.

Finally, in chapter 9 I note some of the major implications of this book and suggest some strategies for ethnographic fieldwork and analysis concerned with linkages to and in the contexts of broader social, political, and economic processes.

One caveat needs to be raised. Readers of this book may ask themselves why I have devoted so little attention coca paste trafficking and other illegal activities directly related to the drug trade. I have considerable personal knowledge of Pampeños who were involved in these activities. Yet, despite the fact that all personal and place names that appear in subsequent chapters are pseudonyms, I have decided not to discuss the participation of Pampeños in coca paste trafficking or similar activities in order to enhance the anonymity, and personal security, of all who offered me their trust and friendship. I am quite aware that such an omission may vitiate some of my arguments and conclusions. Nevertheless, I am convinced this is a small price to pay to protect my fellow Pampeños from the increasingly repressive environment in which they live.

Chapter 2

The Regional and Local Landscape

Bolivia, as many others have correctly stated, is a land of startling contrasts. The fifth largest country of South America, it is rich in natural resources and also the poorest. Spanish is spoken predominantly in its few large cities and many smaller towns, while the dominant languages throughout most of the rural countryside are Quechua and Aymara. Bolivia is divided into three major geographic regions: the high and cold plateau, or altiplano (4,000 to 4,500 meters elevation), lying between the eastern and western Andean mountain chains (Cordillera Oriental and Cordillera Occidental, respectively); the intermontane valleys in the easternmost part of the Cordillera Oriental (at about 2,600 meters elevation); and the vast tropical and subtropical lowlands (Oriente) beyond the eastern flanks of the Cordillera Oriental (map 1). Spanning these three major regions are ten ecological zones (Wennergren and Whitaker 1975:19–20; 84–85). Eighty percent of Bolivia's population is concentrated in the altiplano and valleys, which jointly constitute just 30 percent of Bolivia's territory.

Cochabamba

Cochabamba, the sixth largest of Bolivia's nine departments (major political units), displays an analogous division of its physical landscape and distribution of its population (maps 2 and 3). The numerous intermontane valleys (cf. Vargas et al. 1979) make up over half of the department, while the remainder is almost equally divided between the highlands and lowlands. Cochabamba is Bolivia's most densely populated department and has the third highest demographic density relative to its cultivated acreage. It is in Cochabamba's highlands and valleys that the bulk of the population resides, demographic density is highest, and the largest percentage of cultivated land is found (Monte de Oca 1982). Two-thirds of Cochabamba's population is rural (Instituto Nacional de Estadística 1982:101), the greater part living in small peasant communities.

21

Map 1. Ecologic zones of Bolivia

Quechua is the language of choice in 64 percent of Cochabamba's house-holds, followed by Spanish (Albó 1981:6).

Cochabamba's agricultural and economic core has historically cen-tered on three major intermontane valleys and their adjacent highlands: the central or lower valley (*valle central* or *bajo*), the drier high valley (*valle alto*) to the south, and the Sacaba Valley, the smallest of the three, to the east (map 4). Cochabamba, a prime agricultural region, accounts

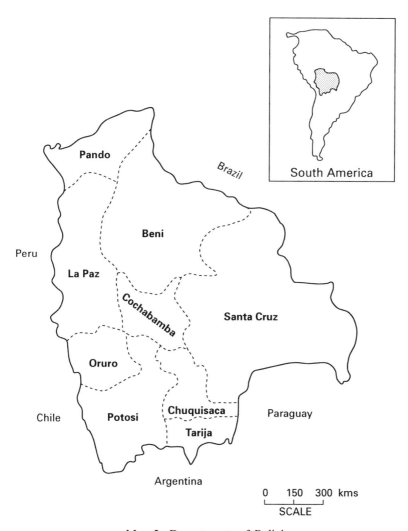

Map 2. Departments of Bolivia

for one-third of Bolivia's agricultural output (Laserna 1984) and, in the Chapare, most of the country's coca.

Cochabamba has played a pivotal role in Bolivian history: during colonial times Cochabamba earned fame as Bolivia's breadbasket when its warm and fertile valleys supplied a large part of grains and other

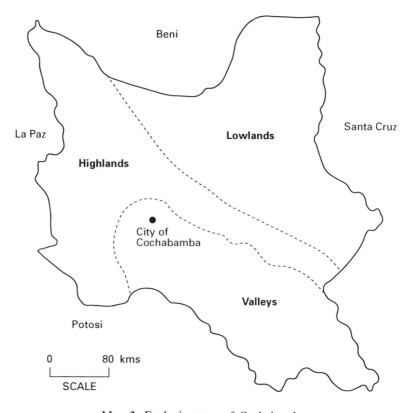

Map 3. Ecologic zones of Cochabamba

agricultural staples for the growing population of the famous mining city of Potosí; it was in Cochabamba's *valle alto* that the agrarian reform law was signed in 1953, and today Bolivia's coca production is concentrated in Cochabamba's eastern Chapare.

Offshoots of Aymara-speaking Andean highland polities were present in Cochabamba's valleys since the Tiwanaku period (ca. A.D. 500–1200) (Mujica 1985), clearly reflecting the deep historical roots of the Andean pattern of access to far-flung resource zones in different ecological tiers (cf. Masuda, Shimada, and Morris 1985). The Quechua-speaking Incas consolidated their control over the Cochabamba Valley region a few decades prior to the Spanish conquest (Wachtel 1982; Larson 1988a:25–31). Incan administrators profoundly altered the human and agricultural landscape of the valleys by replacing some of the original

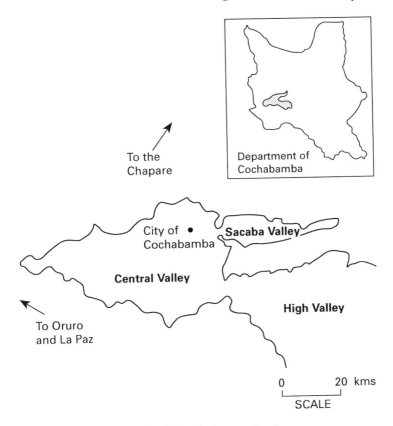

Map 4. Cochabamba's central valleys

inhabitants with ethnic enclaves of highland polities and drafted seasonal colonists loyal to the Incan state and by appropriating tracts of fertile valley lands for maize cultivation and, in the eastern *yungas* of what is now Pocona, coca (Larson 1980; 1988a:25–31).

The collapse of the Incan administration after the Spanish conquest led to a "mass exodus" (Larson 1980:21) of Incan-sponsored seasonal colonists and members of highland ethnic enclaves. Groups of Andeans who remained behind were shortly afterward carved out among prominent Spaniards in *encomiendas*—grants of native communities—and required to pay tribute to the grantees (*encomenderos*) (Larson 1988a:33–43). *Encomiendas* soon gave way to the famous *reducciones,* the systematic concentration of dispersed Andean groups into nucleated settlements, or communities, each with its clearly defined territory. Through the reducciones the colonial state attempted to evangelize Andean peasants, stem the growing power of the *encomenderos,* and insure the survival and relative well-being of the Indian population.

Colonial officials had a vested interest in assuring the well-being of Andean communities. Corporate communities provided tribute in cash, kind, and especially labor, which sustained the colonial bureaucracy. Large amounts of cheap, subsidized labor would increasingly be required to mine silver at Potosí and from which the state extracted a royal tax. A labor draft (mita) was soon imposed on Indian communities, which were forced to annually send a proportion of their adult males to Potosí and other mining centers (Larson 1988a:51–74; Sánchez-Albornoz 1978; Spalding 1982:331–32, 1984:159–67; Stern 1982:80–92).

The *reducciones,* tribute, the growth of silver production at Potosí, the labor *mita,* and the consolidation of landed estates (*haciendas*) in Cochabamba went hand in hand. Soon after the conquest Spaniards appropriated Incan state lands in Cochabamba's valley floors. It was after the Indian population had been "reduced" into settlements, however, that haciendas quickly emerged and expanded, particularly in areas such as the Sacaba Valley that were devoid of Indian communities (Larson 1980, 1988a:74–81).

By the eighteenth century haciendas occupied most of the fertile lands in the valleys and highlands of Cochabamba. Increasingly onerous tribute (including labor) obligations between the seventeenth and nineteenth centuries, and periodic droughts and famine, resulted in a massive flight from and the virtual depopulation of Cochabamba's corporate Indian communities, and a massive migration throughout all of Alto Perú (e.g., Sánchez-Albornoz 1978, 1982, 1983a, 1983b; Zulawski 1987, 1990; Canedo-Arguelles 1988; Evans 1990). Many fleeing community members swelled the labor ranks of the emerging Cochabamba haciendas. Hacienda owners, short on labor and eager to expand agricultural, especially grain, production for the Potosí market, shielded former community Indians from state officials (Larson 1988a:79–101). Service tenantry emerged on Cochabamba haciendas as incoming migrants acquired subsistence plots in return for labor on desmesne land. In time a variety of land and labor relationships emerged between tenants and hacienda owners. In addition to providing labor on desmesne lands, tenants sharecropped and rented hacienda land and provided an assortment of payments in cash or kind. These mechanisms, bolstered by shared norms of reciprocity, enabled peasant tenants to achieve de facto control over the greater part of land in many (if not most) haciendas (Larson 1988a:188–201; cf. Langer 1985).

The fate of estate agriculture in Cochabamba was always intimately tied to production for external markets. During Potosí's boom periods estate agriculture flourished, while it languished during the downturns of silver exports. By the late 1770s the economic position of hacienda landowners had seriously deteriorated. Markets for hacienda products— especially the Potosí market as well as the interregional trade with Argentina and Southern Peru—had dwindled. Haciendas were burdened with debt, and landowners faced increasing competition in the marketplace from their own tenants and from peasant cultivators in the highland provinces near Potosí (Jackson 1988:70–77; Larson 1988a:210–41). Increasing taxes and recurrent ecological crises compounded the state of decay of Cochabamba haciendas by the late nineteenth century. A vigorous land market appeared in Cochabamba as debt-burdened hacienda owners progressively sold fragments of their land to their peasant tenants. Coupled with attempts by liberal regimes to undermine the economic base of Indian corporate communities, this ushered in a process of land fragmentation and the appearance of independent freeholder peasant communities (*piquerías*) (Jackson 1988:192–209; Larson 1982:26–28; 1988a:210–41, 298–316). By the onset of the twentieth century *piquerías* and haciendas emerged as the two most important forms of rural organization in Cochabamba's highlands and valleys. Rising population and increasing land fragmentation has led to widespread small-to-tiny landholdings, or *minifundios*, particularly in peasant communities nearest to local and regional markets (Centro de Investigación y Promoción del Campesinado 1979; Dandler, Anderson, León, Sage, and Torrico 1982; Laserna and Valdivieso 1979).

In the Sacaba Valley floor rich soils, excellent irrigation from the surrounding highlands, and the absence of corporate Indian communities facilitated the early appearance and rapid proliferation of haciendas. The typical land use pattern in the early years of estate development in Sacaba consisted of intensive cereal cultivation on the valley floor and grazing and tuber production in the surrounding highlands (Larson 1988a:180).

As early as the 1570s haciendas or portions of haciendas were already sold in the valley of Sacaba (J. M. Urquidi 1949:189). By the late seventeenth century there were at least 26 estates in the ecclesiastical jurisdiction of Sacaba.[1] The process of hacienda fragmentation (including land purchases by peasants) described for Cochabamba as a whole was replicated in the Sacaba Valley. In the last decades of the eighteenth century a handful of landowners controlled a substantial part of the Sacaba Valley.[2] But by the early twentieth century there were over 4,500 properties in Sacaba, almost 75 percent of which had less than one hectare of land (Jackson 1989:267).[3] As was the case throughout Cochabamba, most hacienda fragmentation in Sacaba occurred in the valley floor, while highland *estancias* remained mostly intact.

The Chapare

The Chapare, occupying 40 percent of Cochabamba's land area, is currently Bolivia's most important coca-producing region (map 5). Lying east of the Cordillera Oriental, the Chapare is a vast tropical and subtropical rain forest of over 24,000 square kilometers (Tolisano 1989; Henkel 1971). Annual rainfall ranges from 2,500 to more than 7,000 milimeters. Most of the precipitation falls from October to March. Chapare's soils are generally of poor quality: only 10 percent of the Chapare is apt for unrestricted crop production, while over half is unsuited for agriculture (Figueras 1978:36; Henkel 1971:27; Bostwick 1990:18, 64; Tolisano 1989:1-2, 17-20).

Three types of landforms predominate in the Chapare. The first, made up of subtropical forest on higher-altitude hills on the easternmost slopes of the Cordillera Oriental, makes up about 15 percent of the Chapare's land area. Twenty percent of the Chapare is formed by alluvial plains covered by tropical forests. The remaining part of the Chapare is covered by floodplains subject to flooding throughout most of the year. The greater part of agriculture in the Chapare is centered on the alluvial plains (Henkel 1971:17-21; Tolisano 1989: 2, 17). This vast tropical and subtropical region displays a rich diversity in terms of climate, soil types, flora, and fauna. At least nine Holdridge life zones have been identified in the Chapare (cf. Tosi 1983; Tolisano 1989:17).

Historically, the Chapare had been populated by numerous ethnic groups that never succumbed to Incan domination (Henkel 1971:107-36; Larson 1988a:246-48; for other parts of the Andes, see Saignés 1985; see also Gade 1979). Never truly "isolated," the sparsely populated Chapare was nevertheless effectively disengaged from major political and economic concerns of the central governments throughout most of Bolivia's colonial and republican periods. Although official interest in expanding the agricultural frontier in the Chapare emerged as early as the

Map 5. The Chapare

mid-nineteenth century, concerted state-sponsored colonization efforts, including the granting of huge land concessions in Bolivia's eastern lowlands, would not take place until the beginning of the twentieth century (see chap. 3).

Pampa

For about the first 200 years what would later become the hacienda and peasant community of Pampa remained an *estancia* (high-altitude grazing area) of a Sacaba Valley floor hacienda. Pampa surfaces in the documentary record as a distinct hacienda in the mid- to late eighteenth century.[4] According to a 1881 agricultural census, Pampa was one of the largest and most productive haciendas in the Sacaba valley area by the turn of the nineteenth century.[5] Contrary to many neighboring haciendas and *estancias* during the eighteenth and nineteenth centuries, Pampa remained an intact hacienda up to the 1953 agrarian reform.[6]

Pampa lies in a high, rugged, and frigid zone (3,050 to 3,850 meters elevation) 35 kilometers east of the city of Cochabamba, Bolivia's third largest city and the capital of the department).[7] It nests in the small mountain chain (*serranía*) of Tuty, which separates it, the valley of Sacaba, and the province of the Chapare, from the *valle alto* to the south. The *serranía* of the Tunari, north of the Sacaba Valley and the *valle central,* faces Pampa to the northwest. The high plateau of Colomi and, beyond, the eastern foothills of the Cordillera Oriental, lies to the northeast. The town of Sacaba, capital of the Chapare province and 15 kilometers from the city of Cochabamba, is the valley's most important settlement. On a clear and bright day most of the Sacaba Valley floor to the west, as well as the eastern fringe of the city of Cochabamba and the *valle central,* can easily be glimpsed from Pampa's northwestern sector (fig. 1).

At the eve of the agrarian reform Pampa, like other haciendas, was sharply stratified. An administrator supervised six loyal peasants (*kurakas*)—one from each of Pampa's six neighborhoods, or *lugares*— who mobilized peasant labor on desmesne lands, enforced work discipline, and collected numerous tax and tribute payments for the landowner (*hacendado*). In a pattern reminiscent of pre- and post-colonial Andean societies (e.g., Spalding 1984:34; cf. Stern 1982), Pampa's *kurakas* were also entitled to a supply of labor from the hacienda's land-based peasants. Pampa's most prominent *kurakas* would decades later spearhead migration to and settlement in the Chapare.

Peasant households were stratified into two principal categories: *pefaleros,* who enjoyed relatively secure usufruct rights to land, and peasants lacking desmesne land and dependent on the *pefaleros* for their subsistence. Social and economic relations between *pefaleros* and non-*pefaleros* mirrored those existing between themselves and the *hacendado*. Landless peasants could be evicted by their *pefaleros* without prior approval from the administrator and were subservient to them. Since labor available to a *pefalero* would often be drawn from dependent and impoverished households, access to more land could be translated into a larger labor force, which in turn would be used to secure additional desmesne land. Some *pefaleros* and *kurakas,* the *q''apaq runas* (wealthy people), amassed considerable wealth by mobilizing dependent labor.

Fig. 1. The Sacaba Valley

According to agrarian reform records, by the early 1950s 79 percent of Pampa's cultivated land (551 hectares of a total of 804) was under peasant control. This land, divided into at least 600 plots of land (*lotes*), was later reduced (*reducido*) by agrarian reform personnel into larger, contiguous plots of land (*fajas de continuidad*). The amount of land under peasant and not hacienda control was almost certainly an outcome of the progressive institutionalization of land tenure rules (chap. 5), which included tenant rights to inherit land and the distribution of additional land to offspring by the *hacendado*.

The absence of a commoditized land market in Pampa and the lack of *piqueros* with secure and legally sanctioned access to land in Pampa profoundly shaped its land tenure system after the agrarian reform. It ushered in norms against the widespread buying and selling of land. Furthermore, it reinforced a sense of solidarity among Pampeños that later crystallized into institutional barriers against access to land by "outsiders" (*ajenos*). As we shall see in chapter 7, this would in turn generate formidable obstacles for land accumulation within Pampa's boundaries by present-day wealthy migrants not classed as community members.

Pampa, transversed in its northeastern tip by the paved Cochabamba-Chapare road, is easily accessible from the city of Cochabamba or town of Sacaba, where one can board a bus, truck, or taxi traveling to the Chapare. Relatively flat stretches of farmland at an average altitude of 2,600 meters elevation soon give way to mountainous terrain several hundred meters above the Sacaba Valley floor. As a driver approaches Pampa, the abandoned and decaying hacienda house appears on the left of the road, followed by an old chapel on the right. Seconds later one is at the entrance of the pueblo, a dense urbanlike settlement with almost 100 dwellings in the lowest crop zone (see chap. 5). It is a neatly planned settlement, with crisscrossing paths forming hexagonal units, each with a common patio and latrine.

An air of affluence pervades the pueblo. Absent here are thatch-roofed dwellings common in other rural communities. All have red tile roofs instead. Most houses are one-story units built of simple adobe mud bricks, but others are elegant, white-washed, two-story buildings, some with glass windows, cement and/or tile floors and iron gates. Several one- and two-story houses are completely built of cement blocks. Trucks, pick-ups, and cars are easily visible as are numerous television antennas. In 1985 the pueblo boasted seven taverns (*chichería, aqa huasi*), where bottled beer, corn beer (*chicha, aqa*), and cane alcohol (*trago*) could be purchased. Kiosks sell much needed items such as matches, soap, and bread. The affluence in the pueblo is a direct result of coca wealth.

All dwellings in the pueblo have running water (installed with funds from the United States Agency for International Development [USAID]), and all but a few of Pampa's dwellings have electricity. In the southeastern corner of the pueblo there is a rarely used technical shop (*taller*), manned by a full-time artisan (*maestro*) and stocked with carpentry and welding tools. The pueblo also has a large red-brick building that houses a dozen, rarely used public showers, also financed by USAID.

Bordering the pueblo to the northeast is a school with five one-story white-washed buildings, a small amphitheater, and a large open field. To the northwest, on a small hill across the paved Cochabamba-Chapare road, a massive, six-meter-high stone church, the site of the town of Sacaba's new vice-parish, was under construction. Plans at the time were for the church, which was completed in 1990 (see chap. 8), to house half a dozen priests and nuns, display Italian-imported stained-glass windows, and be surrounded by well-kept gardens.

Social activities of significant importance to the entire community take place in and around the pueblo. The peasant union's (*sindicato*) monthly meetings are often held at the steps of the new church, where participants have an ample view of the pueblo and of the Sacaba Valley to the west. Mother's Day festivities, ceremonies celebrating the anniversary of the agrarian reform (*Día del Indio*), and the annual fiesta commemorating the appearance of the Virgin Mary in 1879 center around the school amphitheater, the new church, and the pueblo.

Beyond the pueblo dwellings are scattered throughout the six neighborhoods, or *lugares* (Colpana, Chaupi Pampa, Chimpa Pampa, Loma, Condor, and Tuty), where much of the daily social interaction between neighbors and close kin takes place. Clusters of politically powerful patrilineally related males reside in each *lugar*. While leading patrilineally related kin groups in each *lugar* command a great deal of authority, the *lugares* themselves do not display any formal internal organization. (Nor are these localized kin groups indicative in any way of patrilineal descent groups.)

It is to kin and neighbors in each *lugar* Pampeños first turn when in need and from whom reciprocal labor work groups are recruited (see chap. 6). The *lugares* reflect and convey local knowledge of significant features of the social and physical landscape. For instance, Chaupi Pampa simultaneously indicates the place where the Balderrama have historically resided, an intermediate crop zone, and a denser population than the *lugar* lying just above it (but less so than the lower one of Colpana). In each *lugar* toponyms allow Pampeños to pinpoint and differentiate finer characteristics of the local terrain (such as differences in slope, soil conditions, and irrigation needs) as well as the location of land plots. Idiosyncratic local histories are associated with each *lugar* as well.[8]

Pampa is an autonomous peasant union or *sindicato*. The term *sindicato* has several meanings. In its first and broadest sense it refers to those living within Pampa's boundaries and who describe themselves (and are described by others) as "Pampeños." It is in this sense that the term *sindicato* is synonymous with community. In a narrower sense *sindicato* refers to the political entity that emerged after the agrarian reform and mediates between Pampa as a collective unit and outside institutions and which is the ultimate authority in intracommunity affairs. It is in this latter, narrower political meaning that the term *sindicato* is discussed here.

An annually elected executive committee represents the *sindicato*.

Its most important members (nominated for one-year terms) are the general secretary (*secretario general*), the secretary of relations (*secretario de relaciones*), and the justice secretary (*corregidor*). The first is the maximum political authority within the *sindicato*. The second takes over leadership of the *sindicato* in the absence of the general secretary. The *corregidor* settles disputes, usually over land, and plays an important role in the final validation of inheritance rights. Each of Pampa's neighborhoods elects a representative (*vocal*) to serve on the committee with the responsibility of looking after the interests of their respective *lugares*. The *sindicato's* membership meets monthly to discuss and decide upon matters pertaining to the community. Each *afiliado* (household head with permanent usufruct rights to land) is required to attend. Attendance, particularly by younger migrant members, is, however, often sparse, and sometimes meetings are canceled for lack of quorum. By the late 1980s and early 1990s, when most of Pampa's adult males were migrating to and cultivating coca in the Chapare, few Pampeños were attending these monthly meetings.

Quechua is always spoken within the household. Pampeños address each other in Spanish only in the presence of government officials, non-Quechua speakers, and/or important guests. Spanish is highly esteemed however, and its knowledge is an important criterion for leadership positions. In fact, serious disputes with schoolteachers invariably revolve around claims that students are not learning Spanish well or quickly enough. Most women, elders, and children are monolingual Quechua speakers.

The majority of Pampeños were classed as non-Indian (mestizo) by colonial and republican tax records, despite the fact that only a handful knew some Spanish and that they were culturally classed as Indian (*Indio*) by urban dwellers and the landowning elite. *Indio*, a disparaging term, is heard only in confrontations. Pampeños prefer to call themselves *campesinos* (peasants) or *runakuna* (people), and vehemently contrast themselves with altiplano dwellers whom they call *laris*. (*Lari* is a disdainful term that, for Pampeños, connotes ignorance, poverty, and primitiveness.)[9]

Households

In recent years communities have been replaced by households as significant units of analysis of social and economic change at the local level, despite the array of theoretical and methodological difficulties in determining their content and boundaries (Netting, Wilk, and Arnould 1984).

A widespread conceptualization of the household is that offered by Orlove and Custred for the Andes. "An individual household," Orlove and Custred (1980:37) write, "is defined by the common residence of its members and by the pooling of their resources to form a single unit of production and consumption." Four assumptions underlie this definition: (1) a household is composed of a stable group of interacting individuals; (2) members cannot simultaneously belong to more than one household; (3) the household head exercises sufficient authority over the allocation and deployment of labor and other resources; and (4) household members share identical interests or goals.

All four assumptions can be questioned. The first two, residential propinquity and single household membership, suffer from what might be called "sedentary bias" in that they overlook the fact that population mobility continuously recreates patterns of household membership across space and time and redistributes resources and economic activities between and among seemingly discrete and independent households (Wilk and McNetting 1984:19; Yanagisako 1979:164–66; Guyer 1981:98; Schmink 1984:93–94).[10] Furthermore, conflicting demands on labor stemming from migration and the cultivation of cash crops (J. Collins 1986a:665–67; Guyer 1981:99–101; Schmink 1984:95) reveal that the last two assumptions—that household heads exercise sufficient control over resources, including labor, within the household and that all members share identical goals—are also, as we shall see, fraught with difficulties. The nature and organization of households may not be an outcome of an orderly developmental cycle (Goody 1958) but, rather, of sudden, unexpected outside opportunities and/or demands, such as availability of land in frontier regions or the possibility of growing lucrative cash crops. In contexts of intense mobility, as in Pampa, some households may function as not much more than residential units with little coordination of productive activities between their members, while others may not stray far from the ideal definition proposed above by Orlove and Custred (see also Wilk 1989).

Yet, despite the shortcomings of delimiting households based on residence, this was precisely the criterion I used for my household census. In order to do otherwise I would have had to undertake a detailed analysis of production and distribution within and between hundreds of households, a daunting task that seemed to fall outside the scope of my research objectives. I considered individuals as members of a household if they were unambiguously associated with a discreet dwelling (*casa, huasi*) and lived part or most, although not necessarily all, of their time in Pampa.[11] I made no assumptions regarding the stability of household membership or the extent to which household members coordinated, or did not co-ordinate, their productive activities. Indeed, I was quite aware that many Pampeños formed part of other households in the Chapare. A total of 253 households, 70 percent of them nuclear-type households, were present in Pampa in 1983. Sixty households with 319 persons, or almost 20 percent of Pampa's population, were located in the pueblo. Fourteen households were headed by non-Pampeños, 13 of them in the pueblo. The mean number of household members was 5.6. Pampa's population totaled 1,427 persons, 739 males and 688 females (table 2.1). Over 45 percent of Pampeños were under 15 years old, a percentage virtually identical to that of other Andean rural peasant communities (e.g., Mitchell 1991:34). Pampa's age-dependency ratio—the relationship between the number of dependents for each 100 persons in their productive years— was 97.7.[12]

TABLE 2.1   Household and Population Distribution, Pampa, 1983–84

Lugares	Number of Households	Percentage All Households	Population	Percentage of Total Population
Colpana	106	42.0	577	40.4
Chaupi Pampa	67	26.5	393	27.6
Chimpa Pampa	16	6.3	93	6.5
Loma	42	16.6	217	15.2
Condor	16	6.3	111	7.8
Tuty	6	2.3	36	2.5
Total	253	100.0	1,427	100.0

Source: Field data, 1983-84.

Chapter 3

Coca and the Politics of Development

Migration to the Chapare and the spread of coca commodity production there has not taken place independently of systematic agrarian policies enacted by successive Bolivian governments, most of which are harmful to peasant livelihood and some of which show remarkable continuity through time. In order to understand how the cultivation and marketing of coca has so quickly assumed such a central position in Bolivia's economic and political structure it is important to first grasp the central role of coca in Andean society, the adaptability of coca to the eastern lowlands, and the technical requirements of coca production. I first briefly examine the historically different contexts of the production of and competition for coca in Andean societies. This is followed by a detailed analysis of the productive requirements of coca cultivation. I then turn my attention to agrarian and economic policies implemented by successive Bolivian governments and emphasize how they had led, by the early 1980s, to a serious economic crisis that severely affected the majority of Bolivia's population. Last, I account for the consolidation of the Bolivian cocaine market and examine the implications it has had for coca cultivation and regional migration in the Chapare.

Coca and the "Tropical Frontier"

Coca, a gloss of an Aymara word meaning "tree" or "shrub" (Rost-woroski 1973), is a perennial plant domesticated in lowland Amazonia and at least one variety (Huánuco, or "Bolivian," coca) in eastern Peru thousands of years ago. The ecological habitats of its two domesticated species and four varieties range from the desert, thorn scrub environment of northern Peru and Ecuador to the wet Amazonian rain forest (Plowman 1984a:134–35, 132). Huánuco coca is the most common variety cultivated in the Peruvian and Bolivian lowlands, northwestern Argentina, and Ecuador's Pacific rim (Plowman 1984a:133–34, 1984b:62–64, 1986).

The leaves of the coca shrub contain an impressive array of vitamins and minerals (Plowman 1984b:94; Duke, Aulik, and Plowman 1983 [1975]; Carter and Mamani 1986:435–68), an especially important fact given the generally poor diet of Andean peasants. Coca dampens hunger and thirst (for a recent overview, see Burchard 1992) and relieves sensations of weariness and pain. Coca chewing may also be an efficient response to specific high-altitude stressors such as cold (Hanna 1983 [1974]) and low oxygen levels (Fuchs 1978; but see Bray and Dollery 1983).[1]

Coca, often used in ways other than chewing, is also used for a wide range of medicinal purposes. Coca leaves can be boiled, ground, toasted, or used dry; they can be used alone or mixed with other substances; and they can be drunk as a tea or used as an ointment, bathing solution, or in massages, to cure dozens of folk illnesses (Carter, Morales, and Mamani 1981; Carter and Mamani 1986:293–370; Hulshof 1978).

Coca also serves important economic roles. In many parts of the Andes coca functions as money, that is, as "a medium of exchange, a standard of value, a means of deferred payment and a way to accumulate wealth" (Mayer 1988:5). Coca leaves are also necessary for mobilizing labor, either in agriculture or mining (Nash 1979). In addition, many social relationships and situations call for the consumption and exchange of coca leaves. Marriage rituals, which solidify relationships between different kin groupings, invariably require gifts of coca (Carter 1977; Isbell 1978). The offering and use of coca also cements other social obligations, functions as an index of cultural identity, and serves as a medium of communication between humans and supernatural beings (Carter and Mamani 1986:241–92, 371–434; Allen 1988; Harris 1983; Mayer 1988; E. Morales 1989:1–24).

Coca has always been highly valued product in the Andes and, as such, the object of considerable interest and competition. In pre-Incan times many highland Andean polities cultivated and harvested coca by sending seasonal migrants to and/or establishing migrant enclaves (*mitmaq*) in lower-level and warmer ecological zones (*yungas*). Coca leaves, and many other goods, were traded through far-reaching networks that spanned the ecologically diverse Andean landscape (Salomon 1986:105–9; Rostworowski 1970, 1973; Masuda, Shimada, and Morris 1985). Control over the production and distribution of coca was a marker of status, wealth, and power (Salomon 1986:90).

As the Incas overran the Andes, they wrested control of many coca fields from conquered non-Incan polities. The Incas extended and consolidated their control and hegemony over the Andes partly by building on preexisting social and cultural patterns, especially in the realm of reciprocity and the redistribution of status-laden goods (e.g., Murra 1975:23–44, 1980; Stern 1982; Spalding 1984; Salomon 1986). Coca quickly became part of the political and economic repertoire through which the Incas consolidated their grip on the Andes. For instance, the Incas distributed coca leaves and awarded usufruct rights to coca fields in an attempt to gain the allegiance of ethnic lords and polities, seized coca fields from rebellious subjects, and imposed a variety of tribute levies on local polities, which often included coca (e.g., Stern 1982:20–2; Spalding 1984:81; Netherley 1988:262–75). After the demise of the Incan state rival ethnic groups fiercely competed for land and other resources, a struggle often expressed in feuds and lengthy court litigations over coca fields (Stern 1982:31–33; Rostworowski 1988).[2]

The production and consumption of coca rapidly increased after the Spanish conquest, especially after the discovery of silver in Potosí in the mid-1500s. Silver mining was the economic foundation of the early colonial state and the means through which Spain fueled its mercantile expansion. The production, distribution, and consumption of coca was soon also contested between the Spanish conquerors and their Andean subjects in this new context of colonial political economy. The early colonial period witnessed a long and bitter debate over the prohibition of coca production in the Andes, not unlike the contemporary controversy over coca. Some, but not all, church officials called for the eradication of coca, arguing that, because it was deeply embedded in the Andean cosmology and worldview, coca was an intractable barrier to Christianization of the "pagans." And, indeed, coca was a crucial underpinning of rituals and beliefs that Andeans vigorously defended when confronted by the intense anti-idolatry campaigns waged against them by the colonial church and state (see, e.g., Hernández Príncipe 1923 [1622]; Arriaga 1967 [1621]; Duviols 1977 [1971]; Mannarelli 1985). In present-day Bolivia coca still plays a prominent role in a constellation of rituals that express and generate solidarity and resistance (Nash 1979; Platt 1983).

The most vocal opponents to coca eradication were, not surprisingly, the mine owners (and allied vested interests), who feared that silver production would drastically decline and the entire basis of the early colonial economy would collapse if miners were not supplied with adequate supplies of coca. Juan Matienzo, a jurist and mine owner, eloquently articulated these concerns in a letter to the viceroy of Peru in the sixteenth century:

> If coca were abolished the Indians would not go to Potosí. Neither would they work nor mine. And lacking coca, it is evident that all would be lacking if coca is wanting, there will be no Perú, the land will become depopulated, and the Indians will return to their pagan ways. (Cited in Gagliano 1963:52)

The early colonial debate on Andean coca chewing, which had a long-lasting imprint on the Andes, was therefore inscribed in a matrix of competing, and to some extent convergent, interests: some, but not all, church officials intent on ridding the Andes of pagan beliefs and, by extension, coca chewing; mine owners and colonial officials (both with a strong interest in expanding silver production), who feared that without coca labor would be lacking and silver stop flowing from the mines; and, as we shall see, Spaniards and mestizos who controlled the highly lucrative distribution networks in Potosí's economic space and members of Andean communities fortunate enough to have access still to prized coca fields. In the end powerful vested interests won out over the abolitionists (Gagliano 1963; cf. 1978). In Ecuador, far removed from the principal centers of mine production, coca was soon afterward outlawed.

   The surge in silver mining and the presence of thousands of drafted peasant laborers in Potosí spurred vast commercial and trading networks throughout the Andes through which a wide range of essential goods not available in the high and cold altiplano mine environment were supplied—such as coca, which dampened harsh working conditions and was an important part of Andean rituals carried out in the deep and dangerous mine shafts (Glave 1983, 1985; Santamaría 1987; Saignés 1988). Spaniards and mestizos quickly dominated the distribution of coca leaves to the mines, "the most lucrative commercial activity" (Larson 1980:7) in the 1550s and 1560s. The coca trade, taxed by colonial officials, also proved to be a significant source of revenue for the Crown.[3] Spaniards also established plantations worked by Andeans in former Incan coca fields (Stern 1982:36; Wightman 1990:114–16), and they obtained coca leaves through tribute levies (Stern 1982:38; Romano and Tranchand 1983; Larson 1988a:47). The *yungas* to the east of Cuzco was the most important center of coca production during Incan times and Potosí's early boom period. Soon, however, coca produced in the steep subtropical valleys east of La Paz in Upper Peru (present-day Bolivia) virtually replaced coca from Cuzco in the silver mines (Klein 1982:56).

Spaniards and mestizos may have dominated the lucrative coca trade to Potosí, but Andean peasants were also quick to enter this lucrative trade (Stern 1982:38, 161). Many highland-based, Aymara-speaking *ayllus* (kin-based corporate communities) that retained preconquest claims to coca fields in the *yungas* east of La Paz increased their cultivation of coca, aggressively marketed their harvests, accumulated surpluses, and prospered (Klein 1982:55; Santamaría 1987). By the mid- to late eighteenth century the total amount of coca produced from the *yungas* of La Paz surpassed that of the Cuzco region (Klein 1986:57; but see Parkerson 1989:273). Aymara *ayllus* retained control of their coca fields in the eastern *yungas* until the late 1700s, after which many lost their fields to encroaching Spaniards, who set up large-scale coca plantations (Klein 1986:55–58; Santamaría 1987). Coca estate owners soon organized themselves into an important political and economic lobbying group, the Sociedad de Propietarios de Yungas (Carter and Mamani 1986:91–95).

Until the recent coca boom the *yungas* east of La Paz had constituted Bolivia's most important coca-producing region. Before the Spanish conquest coca had been grown in the Chapare (Larson 1980:2; 1988a:47; Klein 1982:56), but production was insignificant when compared to that of La Paz *yungas*. By the late eighteenth century small estates specializing in coca production for the market at Potosí had emerged in the Chapare (Larson 1988a:188, 254–55). A law passed in 1850 awarded land concessions in the Chapare, and some Cochabamba Valley landowners established coca plantations worked by laborers drawn from their valley haciendas (J. Weil 1980a:91–92; Henkel 1971:57). Coca production in the Chapare would not surpass that of the La Paz *yungas* until the late 1960s, and until the advent of Bolivia's recent coca boom the region and Department of Cochabamba imported from La Paz most of the coca consumed by its population. As recently as the 1930s, the Chapare produced a mere one-half of 1 percent of Bolivia's coca (Henman 1985:148; for other estimates, see Parkerson 1989:272). By 1950 the Chapare's production was estimated at one-third of the national output (Klein 1986:58). Yet by 1985, at the height of Bolivia's economic crisis and demand for coca leaves, the Chapare was producing 90 to 95 percent of Bolivia's coca (Henman 1985:148).

Bolivia's sparsely populated, undeveloped, and resource-rich eastern lowlands have long been viewed as a panacea for economic and social ills in the highlands and valleys. In the mid-eighteenth century the Intendant Viedma hoped to address the economic stagnation of highland and valley haciendas and curb demographic pressures in heavily populated peasant areas by constructing roads, especially to the nearby Chapare, linking the lowlands and highlands, establishing agricultural enterprises that would cultivate sugar, coca, and other export crops, and recruiting highland peasant labor to work in these enterprises (Larson 1988a:245–56). Viedma's aspirations would be achieved many years later: "with remarkable foresight, Viedma's scheme anticipated, by almost two centuries, the opening of the Chapare jungle to small-scale colonizers who cultivated coca and other crops for the markets of Cochabamba" (Larson 1988a:255).[4]

The first official effort to lay the groundwork for migration to and agricultural expansion of the eastern lowlands can be traced to a "colonization" law of 1886. This law reiterated state domain over Bolivia's vast tropical and subtropical "unused lands" (*tierras baldías*) and stipulated that these could be legally transferred by the state to individuals willing to settle in, or "colonize," the lowlands (Hiraoka 1974:129). In the following decades military reconnaissance expeditions were sent into the Chapare and nearby lowland areas to delimit areas suitable for colonization. Forest populations, such as the Yuracaree, were viewed as an obstacle to colonization and the establishment of "large industries" (*grandes industrias*). As a result, they were "ordered" to cluster in small villages and placed under the supervision of the military (G. Urquidi 1954:49, 250–52; see also Centro de Investigación y Desarrollo Regional 1990:69–70).

Bolivia's 1886 colonization law also led to the creation of a ministry of colonization (Blanes and Flores 1982:27), which soon began enticing European migrants to settle in the lowlands with offers of vast amounts of land (see esp. Oficina Nacional de Inmigración, Estadística, y Propaganda Geográfica 1903). Between 1903 and 1915 over 17 million hectares of land were allotted to settlers in the lowlands, primarily in the Department of Santa Cruz, most of them Europeans (Hiraoka 1974:133). These land concessions would be the direct antecedents to the agro-industrial enterprises that postagrarian reform economic policies would encourage decades later.

The early 1920s witnessed the first state-sponsored attempts (carried out by the army) at relocating highland-based peasants to the *yungas* of La Paz. A decade later, after the disastrous Chaco war with Paraguay, the Bolivian army also organized migrant settlements in Santa Cruz. It was also during the Chaco war, and in the context of security concerns, that a narrow gravel road was built linking the city of Cochabamba with Villa Tunari in the Chapare.

Colonization and agricultural development efforts focused on the eastern lowlands would reach a new stage during World War II. As early as 1941, United States development planners stressed the need for adequate communications and transportation links to the eastern lowlands and determined that "the highest priority" should be given to a highway linking the city Cochabamba with Santa Cruz (qtd. by Heilman 1982:58). One year later the United States offered Bolivia economic assistance to pursue its plans for the agricultural development of the eastern lowlands in return for secure access to tin. A $25-million grant to Bolivia stressed the need for import substitution of agricultural goods, which would be primarily achieved by capitalist agricultural enterprises in Santa Cruz. The Bolivian Development Corporation was soon organized: its first project was to finance the construction of the highway linking the cities of Cochabamba and Santa Cruz (Thorn 1971:165–66; W. Moore 1990: 33–34).

For its part the Bolivian government, also eager to "develop" its lowlands, tapped into its greatest resource: huge amounts of state-claimed lands. By 1945 tens of millions of hectares were awarded to commercial enterprises and offered (to a great extent unsuccessfully) as enticements to potential lowland settlers, including many foreign nationals (Hiraoka 1974). The United States, assuming that Bolivia's "Indian" population would "not go beyond the subsistence stage," soon urged the Bolivian government to encourage large-scale European immigration to Bolivia's lowlands (Heilman 1982:125–29). Only after the 1952 agrarian reform, however, would a systematic, energetic, and well-funded policy of encouraging peasant migration to the eastern lowlands—the *yungas* east of La Paz, the Chapare, and the area of Yapacaní in Santa Cruz—take off (see Wessel 1968; Zeballos-Hurtado 1975; Stearman 1976, 1985). As we shall see, these renewed efforts at resettling peasants to the eastern lowlands occurred as part of an economic development model geared toward elite capital accumulation to the detriment of the highland and valley peasantry.

Coca Cultivation

Coca shrubs thrive in the ecological conditions of eastern Bolivia, and especially in the Chapare, where they grow well in all its soils and ecological zones (Bostwick 1990:108). According to C. Weil (1980:203), "The optimal growing conditions for coca include an altitude between 300 and 1800 meters above sea level, a mean annual temperature between 18 and 26° C, and an average annual precipitation of about 100 mm, conditions which generally are met in the Chapare." Coca shrubs, the seedlings of which can be harvested after only one year, can survive for up to 40 years with little or no fertilizers and, with proper weeding, can maintain relatively good production levels even in highly leached soils (Plowman 1984b:81). Coca also tolerates extreme fluctuations in temperature (Eastwood and Pollard 1987:260). Huánuco coca, the predominant variety in the Chapare, yields four harvests annually, while other varieties yield two or three (Henkel 1986:5). The use of pesticides and enhanced management techniques can, however, raise the number of harvests to six (Plowman 1984b:81).

Coca is also less susceptible to disease and insects than other lowland cash crops such as coffee and rice (Henkel 1986:5–6). In addition, "coca has the advantage over crops such as bananas and citrus of low perishability" (J. Weil 1980b:17). Coca's major limiting factor is poor soil drainage (Duke 1976:331). Although coca shrubs are extraordinarily adapted to the lowland tropics, it is important to note that intense and continuous harvests of their leaves are maladaptive in the long run (J. Weil 1980b:17). Since most nutrients are stored in the leaves, continuous cropping steadily erodes soil fertility, and coca fields taken out of production must lay fallow for many years before other crops can be planted.

The cultivation of coca is an elaborate and labor-intensive undertaking. A first step is to have an adequate supply of seedlings or seed at the time of planting. Seedlings can be purchased just before planting or grown in seed beds prepared about a year before planting. The forest cover is cut down and quickly burned, usually during the winter months (June to August). Furrows or holes are then dug into the ground, and the seedlings (or at times just seeds), mixed with ash and other organic matter, are placed in them. Transplanting seedlings into a hectare of land can absorb about 24 person-days of labor (Brooner 1981:1:10; C. Weil 1980:207; Subsecretaría de Desarollo Alternativo y Sustitución de Cultivos de Coca [SUBDESAL] 1988:6–7; E. Morales 1989:52–53). Rarely is an entire hectare of land planted in coca all at once. Chapare migrants have traditionally planted rice and corn as consumption and cash crops during the first year (with coca entering the planting cycle during the second year) and often intercropped coca with other crops such as cassava (Henkel 1971; Blanes and Flores 1982; J. Weil 1980a:94). This planting strategy, as we shall see, was undergoing rapid changes during the mid-1980s coca boom.

The coca fields (*cocales*) are weeded once or twice before the harvest, and shrubs are sometimes pruned to prevent them from growing too tall. Each weeding requires about 18 person-days for one hectare of coca (C. Weil 1980:208-9; Brooner 1981:1:9-10). Harvest of the newly planted *cocales* can take place less than a year later and after just six months if seeds were directly planted into the soil (E. Morales 1989:53-54). The harvest is always undertaken manually. Shrub leaves mature all at once and must be quickly harvested before they begin to fall onto the ground. During the first harvest of a *cocal* the leaves are carefully picked one at a time to insure that the stem is not damaged. In subsequent harvests entire stems are stripped with one swing of the hand and arm (SUB-DESAL 1988:11; E. Morales 1989:54).

Once harvested the leaves must be dried within two or three days to prevent mildew (C. Weil 1980:209; Carter and Mamani 1986:84; SUB-DESAL 1988:12-13). Although Pampeños,whenever possible, usually sun-dried their leaves in the Chapare, unexpected weather sometimes forced them to transport their leaves to and dry them in Pampa (see chap. 4). Once dried the leaves are then carefully pressed into bales (*tambores*). Two *tambores* make up one *carga* of about 125 pounds, the standard unit of sale (C. Weil 1980:209-10; Brooner 1981:1:11).[5]

Yield estimates of Chapare's *cocales* have ranged from 2,551 to 7,600 kilos per hectare (see, e.g., Brooner 1981:1:11; C. Weil 1980:210; Henkel 1971:232; SUBDESAL 1988:19). The reasons underlying these wildly divergent estimates are many and include the presence of coca plants of varying ages (and hence different yields) within the same field, the degree of intercropping of coca with other crops, the fact that coca is sown in different types of soils, assumptions regarding the number of times a *cocal* is harvested, the fact that yields vary according to seasons (e.g., higher during the rainy season), and a lack of distinction between ideal yields and amounts actually harvested by migrants. As expected, estimates of total coca production in the Chapare, and of the profitability of *cocales,* are likewise contradictory. Recent reports (e.g., *Bureau of International Narcotics Matters* 1991:87; SUBDESAL 1988:19-21) agree, however, that a *cocal* in the Chapare with most of its plants in their most productive years (2 to 15 years old) and harvested four times a year will yield around 2.7 metric tons of dried coca leaves.[6]

Estimates of the profitability of coca fields—the net income that a migrant can obtain from one hectare of coca—have also varied considerably. To a large extent conflicting claims of the profitability of *cocales* are also the result of the problems already outlined; but they also have to do with differing assumptions regarding production costs. Nevertheless, some of the most detailed studies undertaken to date on coca cultivation agree that production costs average between 30 and 35 percent of the market value of the four harvests from a hectare of mature coca plants (Carter and Mamani 1986:103; Henkel 1971:232). Let us for the moment assume that coca production costs on May 18, 1985, averaged 35 percent. On that day one *carga* of coca in the city of Cochabamba was worth U.S. $185 (see table 3.1). If we also assume for the moment that the value of the *carga* was identical to the farm gate price in the Chapare and that each of the four harvests yielded 15 cargas of dried coca leaves, then a coca migrant *could have,* under ideal conditions, netted U.S. $7,215 from one hectare of coca. Other researchers have correctly stressed that rarely do migrants harvest the entirety of the potential yield of their coca plots. In addition, my hypothetical "profit potential," to quote Henkel (1971:232), assumes that migrants sell the entirety of their harvest—an assumption difficult to defend. Furthermore, coca prices fluctuated considerably in the mid-1980s, and we

TABLE 3.1   Potato and Coca Prices, in U.S. Dollars and Thousands of Pesos Bolivianos at Comparable Dates, 1983–85

	Potatoes			Coca	
Date	$b	US$	Date	$b	US$
3/18/1983	8	18	3/18/1983	100	250
8/17/1983	25	33	8/17/1983	125	163
2/7/1984	29	15	2/17/1984	270	135
5/30/1984	55	17	6/28/1984	800	200
10/15/1984	350	25	10/13/1984	3,600	257
11/14/1984	600	35	11/18/1984	6,000	353
2/8/1985	500	5	2/8/1985	18,000	163
5/1/1985	2,000	8	5/1/1985	22,000	88
5/18/1985	2,500	9	5/18/1985	55,000	185

Note: The U.S. dollar equivalent is based on the parallel (black market) rate. Potato prices reflect the price of one sack (*carga*) of 225 pounds in the town of Sacaba and the city of Cochabamba. Coca prices are those of 125 pounds in Cochabamba and Sacaba.

cannot realistically assume that farm gate prices were identical to those in Cochabamba. Nevertheless, even if a migrant obtained *one-fourth* of the hypothetical profit potential (or just over U.S. $1,800), this amount would have still been far higher than that he or she could have obtained by selling the entirety of his or her harvest from one hectare of potatoes on the same day (chap. 6).

Coca was a labor-intensive crop well suited to absorb the massive labor migration that was taking place to the Chapare (see chap. 3). E. Morales (1989:54) calculates that in eastern Peru 225 person-days are needed from the time one hectare of forest land is cleared and planted in coca until its first harvest. Henkel (1971:210) provides a slightly higher estimate (260 person-days) for the Chapare. Coca cultivation requires over three times as much labor as other labor intensive lowland crops such as coffee and rice (table 3.2), and a large proportion of this labor was devoted to harvesting leaves, followed by weeding.[7] Indeed, by the late 1970s coca cultivation was already absorbing 75 percent of the labor time allotted to agricultural tasks in a Chapare settlement (C. Weil 1980:190; J. Weil 1980a:52) and generating a full two-thirds of the average income of colonist households (J. Weil 1989:303). Labor needs after the first harvest of a *cocal* are not as high for the amount of time needed, and labor originally expended in clearing land is no longer necessary. In addition, labor needs decline as coca plants lose productivity in subsequent years (cf. Figueras 1978:159). It is important to stress here that, despite coca's high labor costs, these are only marginally higher

TABLE 3.2   Annual Labor Needs of Major Chapare Crops, (in Person-Days per Hectare)

Crop	C-P	%	P	%	W	%	H-P	%	Total
Coca	42	16	8	3	120	46	90	35	260
Coffee	24	27	8	9	20	23	36	41	88
Rice	40	48	4	4	16	19	24	29	84
Bananas	20	26	4	5	24	32	28	37	76
Peanuts	30	43	4	6	16	23	20	28	70
Yucca	30	50	2	3	12	20	16	27	60
Maize	30	63	2	4	12	25	4	8	48

Source: Adapted from Henkel 1971:210. More recent estimates of labor requirements for one hectare of coca are strikingly similar (e.g., Brooner 1981:3:20). Annual labor requirements of coca, and of other perennial crops such as coffee, decline after the first planting, since little or no labor is expended on land clearing in subsequent years.

Note: C-P = Clearing/Planting   P = Planting   W = Weeding   H-P = Harvesting/Processing
% = Percentage of Total Person-Days

than those needed to cultivate potatoes, the principal highland and valley staple and cash crop (see chap. 6).

Coca can also absorb this labor input during most of the year. Henkel (1971) has schematized the peak monthly activities of coca production in the Chapare (fig. 2; see also J. Weil 1989:314). Yet coca labor requirements are not necessarily constrained by a rigid seasonal schedule, as figure 2 might suggest. Migrants may have *preferred* to plant coca seedlings in September and October (see fig.2) but sowing can actually take place during or prior to the rainy season (December to March) (Henkel 1971:190; Blanes and Flores 1982:216–17). Chapare migrants enjoyed considerable flexibility in allocating their time and labor when planting, harvesting, and weeding coca (J. Weil 1980a:141). Hence, one of coca's key advantages is that coca-cultivating migrants can spread out their labor requirements throughout most of the year (see esp. J. Weil 1989:318–19, 321; also C. Weil 1980:294) and, therefore, interdigitate their labor needs and risks between their highland and lowland crop fields.

Agrarian Reform, Development, and Accumulation

On April 11, 1952, a broad-based and ideologically diverse coalition (Movimiento Nacionalista Revolucionario [MNR]) seized power in Bolivia after three days of fighting. The purpose of the MNR was to transform Bolivia from an underdeveloped and dependent country, whose oligarchic political and economic structure had evolved around tin production and absentee landownership, to an independent, modern, capitalist country. Although the revolution first surfaced in Bolivia's mining centers and urban areas, soon thereafter a wave of peasant uprisings swept through the departments of Cochabamba and La Paz. Initially reluctant to consider the issue of agrarian reform—many top MNR leaders and some cabinet ministers were medium-sized landowners themselves—the MNR was soon forced to bow to peasant unrest and the specter of massive violence in the countryside. On August 2, 1953, well after the MNR assumed power, a far-reaching agrarian reform law was enacted in Ucureña in Cochabamba's *valle alto*. The major goal of the agrarian reform in the altiplano and *valles* was to overhaul an agrarian structure characterized by absentee landownership, impoverished peasants with tenuous access to land, onerous labor and tribute obligations to landowners, and low productivity. This goal would be attained by expropriating estate (hacienda) lands and awarding them to their peasant

December	January	February	March	April	May	June	July	August	September	October	November
H	H	W		H	W	L	L-W	L-H	P	P-H	W

Source: Adapted from Henkel 1971:207.
Note: L = land preparation P = planting W= weeding H = harvesting

Fig. 2. Seasonal labor requirements of coca

tenants, stimulating agricultural investment, productivity and commercialization, enhancing political participation by the large peasant population, and stimulating peasant migration to the eastern lowlands (Dandler 1983 [1971]; Malloy 1970:156–205; Thorn 1971:160–62; Dunkerley 1984:65–74).

In Cochabamba the breakup of large estates took place primarily in the valley floors, while in the highland areas of the department many landowners, including Pampa's owner, retained partial or total control over their haciendas (Turovsky 1980; Dandler, Anderson, León, Sage, and Torrico 1982). Furthermore, the agrarian reform failed to restructure Bolivia's land tenure system totally and to abolish labor and other rent obligations to estate owners completely (Graeff 1974; Turovsky 1980). In the southern provinces of Cochabamba, Chuquisaca for example, far removed from the centers of revolutionary upheaval, rural elites not only successfully circumvented agrarian reform policies but, in fact, consolidated their economic and political control over the rural countryside (Healy 1979; Havet 1985). An equally serious limitation of the agrarian reform was that it failed to significantly improve the productivity of labor and thwart the fragmentation of land through inheritance and land sales (Rasnake and Painter 1989:6).

Post–agrarian reform Bolivian governments followed an economic development model that translated into the direct management of key economic sectors (e.g., by nationalizing key mining enterprises) and the infusion of large amounts of capital into other export-oriented industries. The agricultural component of this model was predicated on two related premises. The first was that highland and valley agriculture was backward and incapable of satisfying the needs of an expanding internal market and of producing a surplus of export commodities. These goals, therefore, could only be attained through large-scale, capital-intensive agribusiness enterprises in the eastern lowlands, primarily in Santa Cruz. There the goal of state development efforts was not to break up large landed estates (which were partly the result of previous colonization efforts), but, rather, to quickly tranform them into export-producing capitalist enterprises. The second premise was the apparent presence in the highland and valley regions of a massive surplus of (supposedly unproductive) labor (Gill 1987; Eckstein 1983; W. Moore 1990; Zeballos-Hurtado 1975).[8]

Agricultural development therefore centered on two related strategies, both envisioned by Viedma almost two centuries earlier and grounded on development efforts that had begun to emerge in the early 1940s. The first consisted of vigorous efforts at resettling tens of thousands of highland and valley-based peasants to the sparsely populated lowlands of the Chapare and Santa Cruz and the steep subtropical valleys east of La Paz (map 6). An underlying rationale for this colonization policy, in Bolivia and elsewhere in Latin America, has been that of avoiding coming to terms with serious inequities, such as growing landlessness and poverty (Lassen 1980) in heavily populated and politically volatile peasant regions (Thiesenhusen 1971, 1984, 1987). In 1963 the National Colonization Plan (Plan Nacional de Colonización) "designated the Chapare as a priority settlement area." Two years later the National Institute of Colonization (Instituto Nacional de Colonización)—which has since spearheaded migration to and settlement of the Chapare and other lowland regions—was organized (Rasnake and Painter 1989:1–2). And in 1972 the major paved highway linking the city of Cochabamba with Villa Tunari in the Chapare was completed.

The second and most important agricultural strategy centered on promoting (especially during the 1970s) the production of export crops and accelerating private capital accumulation by lowland agribusiness enterprises, especially in Santa Cruz. This strategy rested on awarding large land concessions—totaling almost 10 million hectares in the department of Santa Cruz alone (Dandler 1984:110)—and funneling of tens of millions of dollars in technical assistance, loans, credits, and subsidies. The result was the emergence and consolidation of huge agro-industrial concerns controlled by increasingly powerful economic and political elites in the departments of Santa Cruz, Pando, and the Beni (Grupo de Estudios Andrés Ibañez 1983; Gill 1987:51–57; Eckstein 1983; Stearman 1985; Heilman 1982:97–106; Henman 1985; Malloy and Gamarra 1988:96–113; Dunkerley 1984:220–24; W. Moore 1990).[9] It is precisely these elites, who capitalized from development and foreign assistance programs and contributed to Bolivia's onerous foreign debt by the early 1980s, who later played an important role in the consolidation of the country's cocaine market.

Bolivian and foreign development planners not only favored through a preferential outlay of scarce fiscal resources lowland colonization over traditional highland agriculture, but their policies were also heavily biased toward agribusiness enterprises to the detriment of small-scale agriculturalists. Lowland agribusinesses consumed the bulk of fiscal resources (e.g., loans) allocated by the state to agriculture, funds that could have

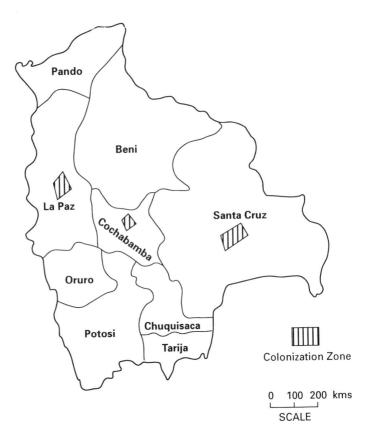

Map 6. Bolivia's major colonization zones

been used to increase the productivity of highland peasant agriculture. In addition, many agribusiness enterprises defaulted on their multimillion dollar loans, losses that were subsequently absorbed by Bolivia's Agricultural Bank (Malloy and Gamarra 1988:102; Heilman 1982:97–113; Gill 1987:185; Dunkerley 1984:222; World Bank 1984; Eckstein 1983:110–15, 123–24; W. Moore 1990:36–44).

These agricultural policies were deceptively successful: while Bolivia gained self-sufficiency in many, primarily urban, consumer staples (such as cotton, rice, sugar, cooking oil, and beef) and exported considerable surpluses of these and other products by the late 1960s, the social and economic costs were high.

In the highland and valley regions this developmental export strategy failed to significantly and structurally improve the agricultural infrastructure and potential of the countryside as well as the nutritional and health standards of the rural population as a whole. Indeed, by the early 1980s the overall living standards of the highland and valley peasantry, deplorable for the majority of the population, had plunged to the level prevalent a decade earlier. Heilman (1982:262) cites a USAID study that concluded that "there was more malnutrition in these two areas [i.e., the altiplano and valleys] in the early seventies than in the early sixties" (see also Eckstein 1983:119), and by 1982 real per capita income had regressed to the levels prevalent 10 years earlier (OAS 1984:1).[10]

A consistent decline in the terms of trade of major crops (Dandler 1984:126–27; Maletta 1988:101–2) was one important factor contributing to the erosion of living standards of the peasantry. Between 1963 and 1975 the value of all principal highland peasant crops dropped by 13 percent, and the decline of tubers was almost 40 percent (Naciones Unidas 1982:145). While potato production increased 3.3 percent annually between 1963 and 1972, primarily due to more land pressed into cultivation and the growing use of chemical fertilizers, the value of tubers (including potatoes) declined at an annual rate of 4.6 percent in the same period (Naciones Unidas 1982:143). This decline was especially pronounced in the case of the potato: its purchasing power, relative to some key staples consumed but not produced by peasants, declined by well over 50.0 percent between 1963 and 1975. By late 1975 peasants had to produce and market over twice as many potatoes to buy, for instance, the same amount of lard as in 1963 (Naciones Unidas 1982:156–57).

There is, in fact, evidence that suggests that, had it not been for increased production and additional land cultivated, overall peasant income would have declined in absolute terms between 1950 and 1973 (Naciones Unidas 1982:159). This decline accelerated in the late 1970s and early 1980s, precisely during the period in which agricultural enterprises benefited the most from state and foreign technical and capital inflows (W. Moore 1990:41–45). Between 1976 and 1982 the costs of agricultural inputs outpaced prices that peasants obtained for their crops by a margin of at least four to one (Urioste 1987:73, cited in Rasnake and Painter 1989:39). For example, potato prices rose by 67 percent, while inputs rose 223 percent, and transport costs increased by 235 percent (Dandler, Anderson, León, Sage, and Torrico 1982:90). This gulf widened as a result of economic measures passed by the government in

August of 1985, particularly after the halt of gasoline and fertilizer subsidies (see chap. 8). The declining terms of trade had, not unexpectedly, a negative impact on peasant production and income. While potato production increased after the agrarian reform, overall agricultural production measured in terms of its contribution to the gross domestic product dropped from 26 to 18 percent between 1960 and 1980 (Munck 1984:36, cited in Browman 1987:181).

Development policies in the early 1980s showed striking similarities with prior patterns and were clearly inconsistent with programs designed to stem the production of narcotics (a fact that peasants are certainly aware of). As in previous decades, agricultural investment was generally bypassing most of the highland and valley regions. For instance, Bolivia's 1982–84 agricultural investment program called for channeling almost one-fourth of all resources to the livestock sector (which no doubt continued to benefit and enrich powerful lowland cattle ranchers) and 18 percent for state-supported colonization efforts. A more telling example of the favoritism displayed toward agro-industrial entrepreneurs is that the departments of Santa Cruz and Beni were destined to absorb more resources than the four departments (La Paz, Cochabamba, Potosí, and Oruro) with the highest concentration of peasant cultivators combined (World Bank 1984:84–85, 94–95). Overall, between 1980 and 1987 (with the exception of the drought-stricken 1982–83 agricultural season), there was an absolute decline in fiscal resources geared toward improving the productivity of highland peasant agriculture (J. Morales 1990). A not-so-new policy of "export-led growth in the lowlands" (Pattie 1988:147–48) was fully underway in the late 1980s, and USAID-paid "development experts" were, once again, strongly encouraging support of migration of highland and valley peasants to the lowlands and emphasizing agricultural export commodities—a policy that, incidentally, contradicted USAID development–funded efforts aimed at stemming migration to the Chapare (see chap. 8):[11]

> With the recent steep drop of international prices for tin and hydrocarbon products, aggressive production of agricultural exports is no longer a luxury but rather, is a necessity, and is recognized as such by the Paz administration. Given its overrriding concern to restore growth, the Bolivian government will naturally be inclined to tilt its scarce resources toward the commodities with the greatest potential for short-run gains. This implies an emphasis on several

commodities in the lowlands that are produced, processed, and exported by large commercial enterprises. For its part, USAID should be prepared to support this thrust. However, to the extent that its support could have a direct impact on small- and medium-sized producers and on laborers, USAID would come closer to accomplishing its objective of equitable economic growth. Therefore, opportunities to promote export products produced by small- and medium-sized firms should receive attention. Products in which Bolivia has a comparative advantage (such as coffee, flowers, and alpaca) should continue to receive support in the valleys and highlands, even though the short-term growth rate is lower than that of soybean, lumber, and beef. Another way to attain the goal of equitable growth is to facilitate the entry of small- and medium-sized firms into commercial export activities. *Migration of the highland populations to the tropical areas* where agricultural expansion is taking place is a necessary, although insufficient, step in this direction. (Pattie 1988:149)

It is worthwhile to stress that, to the dismay of public officials in Washington and leading development organizations, peasants themselves appear to have "found," as it were, the ideal crop and economic strategy that development experts have long been searching for. In fact, coca cultivation satisfied 7 of Thiesenhusen's (1987) 10 requisites for rural development: (1) it was admirably adapted to and therefore, within limits of intensity, did not lead to environmental degradation; (2) technological requirements were simple and within easy grasp of peasant cultivators; (3) the infrastructure and marketing arrangements were adequate; (4) returns and demand were sufficiently high (and constant) to encourage continued production; (5) idle land was pressed into cultivation; (6) its high labor requirements mean that it had the capacity to make a significant inroad on unemployment and subemployment; and (7) it encouraged grass roots participation by rural cultivators.

Economic Crisis

The economic development model that was implemented after the agrarian reform and vigorously pursued especially after 1964 (Malloy and Gamarra 1988:71–116; W. Moore 1990:36–38) faltered almost from the outset. Its structural flaws clearly surfaced by the early 1980s with the emergence of an acute economic crisis that gripped Bolivia. This was a crisis that coincided with and was worsened by the deep global recession and debt crisis.

The nationalization of mines after the agrarian reform occurred precisely when the mineral content of mine ores had reached a low ebb. This problem was exacerbated by widespread corruption, increasing production costs, and a systematic state policy of decapitalizing the state mining corporation (and transferring its small surpluses to other state-owned sectors). As a result, for decades enormous deficits plagued COMIBOL, the state-owned mining corporation. The collapse of international tin prices in 1985 aggravated these conditions (*Europa Yearbook* 1986:510; Bailey and Knutsen 1987:47–48; Dunkerley and Morales 1986:92; Crabtree, Duffy, and Pearce 1987; Fox 1986). Oil production and hard currency earnings also fell, a result of depletion of easily available reserves, lack of capital for further explorations, and mismanagement (Bailey and Knutsen 1987:47; *Europa Yearbook* 1986:510). A steady decline in the mid- to late 1970s of international prices of agricultural export commodities produced by agribusinesses in Santa Cruz (such as sugar, cotton, and soya) led to a steep drop in production (Stearman 1985:35–38; Gill 1987; Economist Intelligence Unit 1986:23). In addition, foreign loans and other capital inflows to these enterprises began drying up.

This overall drop in export earnings coincided with the mushrooming of Bolivia's external debt. As a consequence of the "debt-led growth" period of the 1970s (Jameson 1989:88; cf. W. Moore 1990; Malloy and Gamarra 1988:96–113), when transnational banks and other international lending agencies were eager to hand out billions of dollars to spur investment and capital accumulation, Bolivia's foreign debt rose from U.S. $670 million in 1970 to over U.S. $5 billion in 1986. Between 1983 and 1984, 57 to 73 percent of Bolivia's export earnings were earmarked toward servicing its debt (Bailey and Knutsen 1987:48; Dunkerley and Morales 1986; Pattie 1988:2). Other Latin American countries fared no better during these years of economic "growth," despite accumulating massive debts. By the mid-1970s, for example, the bottom 60 percent of Latin America's population was worse off than during the previous two decades (Thiesenhusen 1977). Landlessness and unemployment were also on the rise (Lassen 1980). By the mid-1980s economic prospects were even gloomier. Production and income had drastically plunged throughout Latin America, and tens of billions of dollars in net transfers to service an enormous and growing debt flowed out of Latin American countries to financial centers in the core industrialized countries (see Canak 1989; Frank 1988:13–15), a hemorrhage in large measure achieved by the implementation of crushing austerity measures that, in Bolivia and elsewhere in Latin America, fell disproportionately on the poor.

By the early 1980s Bolivia's deteriorating economy was compounded by political uncertainty, a surge in inflationary trends, a host of contradictory fiscal policies, massive capital flight (see esp. Conaghan 1991:2), an inability by the state to obtain additional international credits, and the ruinous 1982–83 drought. The ensuing fiscal bankruptcy and runaway inflation—by mid-1985 inflation had reached an astounding 20,000 to 50,000 percent (Economist Intelligence Unit 1986:22; Sachs 1987; Cole 1987)—led to an overall drop in the gross domestic product of about 25 percent between 1981 and 1986 (Jameson 1989:81; Pattie 1988:2).

Hyperinflation rapidly eroded the purchasing power of wages, which by 1984 "had fallen (in real terms) to 56 percent of their 1979 level" (Jameson 1989:86). Between 1983 and December of 1985 alone the parallel dollar equivalent of the monthly minimum urban wage fell from U.S. $42.80 to a mere U.S. $16, a drop of almost 70 percent (Economist Intelligence Unit 1986–87:8). Inflation also had a devastating impact on peasant crops. Despite rising prices, the principal highland crops produced by peasant cultivators failed to keep pace with runaway costs (Prudencio and Velasco 1987:71–77), simply accentuating the declining terms of trade that had been occurring for decades. While some authors suggest that rising potato prices outstripped production costs (Prudencio and Velazco 1987:80–81), it may very well be that intermediaries and not peasants reaped the most from rising prices (J. Morales 1990).[12] The fall in real income during this period led to an absolute and accelerated decline in the living standards of the urban working class and the peasantry.

Although definitive studies are lacking, the coca leaf was perhaps the only major peasant agricultural commodity that generally managed to retain, and at times even increase, its real value during the economic crisis that engulfed Bolivia in the 1980s (cf. de Franco and Godoy 1990:12). Furthermore, coca prices far outstripped those of potatoes, the major highland peasant crop. On February 8, 1985, for instance, 100 pounds of coca leaves were worth 30 times as much cash as 225 pounds of potatoes (table 3.1; see also chap. 6).

Migration and the Cocaine Market

Migration to the Chapare and the emergence of Bolivia's cocaine market cannot be explained by "the culture of the Chapare farmers and the physical and social structure of the area itself" (Delaine 1979:202), individual attributes (such as psychological or personality traits) of migrants, or of deliberate actions or decisions undertaken by capitalists intent on accumulating capital—although the latter has no doubt occurred.[13]

Rather, these processes are best interpreted as the result of the convergence of three conditions: (1) economic development policies fostered and funded by foreign development agencies, which, as we saw in the previous section, led to the emergence of a powerful lowland agribusiness capitalist class, ushered in a severe decline in living standards, and fostered the migration of peasants to (and awarded many of them land in) the Chapare; (2) an optimal environment for coca growing in the Chapare; and (3) the rise in the international demand for cocaine.

Lowland agribusiness capitalists who greatly profited from economic development programs played the crucial role in consolidating the Bolivian cocaine industry. As the economic recession deepened in the late 1970s, lowland agro-industrial capitalists turned to processing coca paste and cocaine. By then these elites had mustered the political and economic power, and the necessary networks and protection from sectors of the state (especially military) apparatus, to undertake, with considerable success, the complex tasks of financing, organizing, and consolidating coca paste and cocaine processing and smuggling operations in eastern Bolivia (Henman 1985; Henkel 1988; Dunkerley 1984:292–344; Bascopé 1982; Malloy and Gamarra 1988:144–46; Healy 1986; Stearman 1985:36–39; Gill 1987:185–86; Latin American Bureau 1982; Canelas and Canelas 1983).

At about this same time the international (primarily United States) demand for cocaine rose sharply, and street prices tumbled. From a costly commodity consumed by the privileged wealthy, cocaine consumption in the United States spread quickly—like sugar during the early stages of British industrialization—"downward" among many more members of other social classes (Mintz 1985:95). Cocaine consumption in the United States spiraled out of control beginning in late 1984 and mid-1985, when relatively inexpensive (and far more powerful) rock cocaine, or crack, appeared in the United States—precisely at the height of Bolivia's coca boom (cf. Johnson, Williams, Dei, and Sanabria 1990; Johnson, Hamid, and Sanabria 1992). Underpinning this seemingly uncontrollable spiral was a process of deepening poverty and sociocultural and economic marginalization of many United States inner-city neighborhoods and an increasing rigidity of ethnic and class cleavages (see, e.g., Bourgois 1989; Wacquant and Wilson 1989; Zinn 1989; Sanabria 1991). It was during this period as well that concerns about the burgeoning "underclass" (and the underclass debate) surfaced in North American political spheres, academic circles, and centers of public policy-making (cf. Wilson 1989; Tienda 1989; Jencks and Peterson 1991).

In Bolivia during this period eastern lowland capitalists were successful in organizing the production and distribution of coca paste and cocaine, and there was a systematic decline in peasant and urban living standards. These factors, coupled with the increase in the global consumption of cocaine and the consolidation of major trafficking organizations, led to an increase in the demand for and cultivation of coca leaves and spurred a massive flow of labor to the Chapare.

By the late 1970s about 15,000 hectares of coca were cultivated in the Chapare; in 1983 this number had risen to over 58,000 (Brooner 1981:1:19–20; Healy 1986:112). The tonnage of leaves harvested also increased exponentially. Some 19,000 metric tons of coca leaves were harvested in 1977 (Bascopé 1982:81), between 44 and 58,000 tons in 1980 (Brooner 1981:1:21), and perhaps as many as 152,000 tons in 1984 (Healy 1986:112).[14] Between 1980 and 1988 the percentage of land sown in virtually every important Chapare crop (such as rice, corn, bananas, and citrus) declined relative to coca. With the exception of yucca, often intercropped with coca, the rate of new land sown in coca was unmatched by any other crop in the Chapare (Tolisano 1989:2, 25). By 1988 almost half of the Chapare's cultivated area was reportedly sown in coca (SUBDESAL 1988:103; Tolisano 1989:24).

The rapid expansion of land sown in coca was also accompanied in some settlements by an intensification in coca cultivation, an increase in the number of harvests before the full maturation of coca leaves. Some Pampeños claimed to be harvesting immature leaves because of the high price of coca, incessant rumors of impending forced coca eradication programs, and generalized political and economic uncertainty. Intensification was also documented in the Chapare by Blanes and Flores (1982:172) and E. Morales (1989:64) in eastern Peru.

Migration to the Chapare and the demand for coca was also ushering in crop specialization. Migrants would traditionally plant rice during their first year in the Chapare and coca in the second. This planting strategy, the advantage of which was to provide a crop that could satisfy both consumption and cash needs, was being replaced by one in which coca entered the farming cycle in the very first year. Another long-standing and related strategy—the intercropping of coca with other crops—was being abandoned by some migrants who were cultivating monocrop coca fields (Eastwood and Pollard 1987:260; Brooner 1981:3:22; SUBDESAL 1988:29, 88, 103–4). Pampeño migrants specializing in coca were almost always young sharecroppers or wealthy migrants with a large percentage of their land under cultivation, oftentimes in more than one colony (see chap. 4).

This trend toward an incipient intensification and specialization of coca cultivation contrasted with the historically documented strategy of productive diversification by Andean peasants (e.g., Dandler 1982; Larson 1988a:208–9; cf. Long and Roberts 1984). While intensification and specialization was increasing the ability of land-based peasants in the Chapare to absorb more migrant labor and accumulate wealth (see chaps. 3 and 4), both processes also raised the vulnerability of migrant household economies to fluctuations in coca prices and generated considerable resistance to coca eradication efforts.[15] As we shall see in chapter 8, the premature harvests of coca leaves would later lead to the appearance of *estalla,* a disease that afflicts coca shrubs (Henkel 1971:61–63; Parkerson 1989:279), which would in turn contribute to the decision of many Pampeño migrants to voluntarily destroy their coca plants.

Migration to the Chapare had slowly increased during the late 1950s and early 1960s, with most migrants engaged primarily in seasonal migration. By the late 1970s and early 1980s migration to the Chapare dramatically increased (Blanes and Flores 1982:6; Healy 1986). Migration to the Chapare was facilitated by two factors. The first was that peak labor demands of highland and lowland crops, in Bolivia as well as in Peru and Ecuador, only partially overlap (Henkel 1971; C. Weil 1980; J. Weil 1980a, 1980b, 1989; J. Collins 1984, 1988; M. Painter 1984; Ekstrom 1979). Highland-lowland production complementarity and seasonal migration was further enhanced by the paved road to the Chapare (financed by development assistance and completed in 1972). The early to mid-1980s witnessed a frenzied flow of migrants to the Chapare. On any given day hundreds of vehicles, each loaded with passengers, household goods, and supplies, could be seen traveling on the paved road en route to the Chapare. It is no exaggeration to say that the Chapare was attracting a massive floating population eager to participate in what appeared to be the riches of the cocaine market.[16] The crushing economic stabilization program of late 1985, in which tens of thousands of miners and other government workers lost their jobs and many others saw their already low living standards decline even further overnight, accelerated the flow of migrants to the Chapare (see chap. 8). Some of the unemployed miners were later relocated and given land in Ibabo, one of the settlements colonized by Pampeños.

Coca plantings and the sporadic, almost imperceptible, manufacture and distribution of coca paste and cocaine of the mid-1960s (Henkel 1971) gave way 20 years later to a large, increasingly complex, and extremely profitable cocaine market. By the first half of the 1980s coca leaf cultivation and the processing of coca paste and cocaine was generating between U.S. $1 billion to U.S. $4 billion in Bolivia, many times the total value of combined official exports (Eastwood and Pollard 1987:267; Henkel 1988:64; Tullis 1987:252; Economist Intelligence Unit 1986:24).[17] Between 250,000 and 500,000 persons were directly or indirectly making a living from coca (Tullis 1987; Blanes and Flores 1982; Eastwood and Pollard 1987:265). The greater part of the coca produced in Bolivia was, and still is, destined for the illegal market and not legal consumption (Henkel 1988; Bureau of International Narcotics Matters 1990, 1991). By late 1989 and early 1990 coca leaf production amounted "almost to 30% of the gross national agricultural product and more than 60% that of Cochabamba" (Bostwick 1990:31).

Chapter 4

Mobility, Inequality, and Wealth

In the preceding chapter I stressed the manifold ways that economic development policies structured and generated intense migration to the Chapare and contributed to the appearance of the cocaine market and the spread of coca cultivation. But how intense was migration to the Chapare from peasant communities tightly drawn into the cocaine market? What role did the massive flow of migrants to the Chapare and the spread of commodity production there have on emerging patterns of land and labor control in the lowlands? Which peasant migrants reaped the greatest rewards during these boom years, and how did they do so? How was wealth accumulated, invested, and displayed by prosperous migrants?

Peasants on the Move

Migration in Pampa is as old as the community itself, and an image of an immobile peasantry inexorably tied down to the hacienda through labor obligations to the landowner, or to rich and powerful peasants, before the agrarian reform would be misleading. The early to late colonial period was one of intense migratory flows throughout Cochabamba (see chap. 2), and the hacienda of Pampa was certainly no exception to this general pattern. As late as the turn of the twentieth century, death certificates of Pampeños in the local parish archive (in the town of Sacaba) still alluded to characteristically early colonial terms as *forastero* (stranger) and *caminante* (drifter).

Published data with which to analyze in detail Pampa's demographic history, and particularly to compare and contrast past and recent migratory patterns, are unfortunately not available.[1] Nevertheless, there is little doubt that, as a result of unequal access to resources, the period preceding the agrarian reform was one of intense demographic instability. My genealogical census, for example, revealed dozens of individuals and entire domestic units abandoning Pampa just prior to the agrarian reform and being replaced by others. Some peasant households that were unable or unwilling to continue providing labor and other tribute payments to the landowner or other rich peasants, or that incurred in serious breaches of discipline, were forced to abandon Pampa, their shabby dwellings razed and their land plots reassigned to others. Other households abandoned Pampa voluntarily in search of better prospects elsewhere.

The majority of those who left voluntarily appear to have settled in nearby *piquerías* (particularly in the Sacaba Valley and the *valle alto*), where, presumably, they bought land. Some moved into other haciendas. A few others migrated to the Chapare, where decades later they encountered other Pampeños migrating there as a result of government colonization efforts, and at least one Pampeño even settled in Chile. Many settled in La Paz and in the southern province of Mizque. In turn, peasants arriving in Pampa came mainly from the nearby valleys and surrounding highlands.[2]

After the agrarian reform the lowlands of Santa Cruz were singled out by the government as a major colonization zone (see chap. 3). Pampeños learned of the availability of land there through radio broadcasts and from personnel from the Instituto Nacional de Colonización (INC) who traveled throughout the surrounding countryside extolling the virtues of settling in Santa Cruz—especially the fact that each migrant would receive free 50 hectares of land, an immense amount compared to that available in Pampa.

In general, Pampeños were not very enthusiastic about settling in Santa Cruz. None had ever lived there, they were unfamiliar with tropical agriculture, and many were deeply skeptical of government promises. Moreover, the journey was long, difficult, and potentially dangerous. The time and difficulty involved in traveling to Santa Cruz also implied that maintaining social and productive ties and obligations in Pampa would be arduous. Nevertheless, Pampeños did leave. Most settled in Yapacaní, one of the first settlements organized (in 1958) northwest of the city of Santa Cruz (see Stearman 1985). The first Pampeño left en route to Yapacaní in late 1959, in the midst of a period of high inflation and an economic stabilization program (Thorn 1971:167–68) strikingly similar to that implemented in mid-1985 (see chap. 8).

There were two major migratory streams from Pampa to Santa Cruz. The first, from about 1959 to 1968, coincided with the formal division of land plots and the funneling of financial and technical support to

Yapacaní and neighboring colonies. The second stream, which lasted from about 1969 to 1979, overlapped with the expansion and increasing labor needs of agribusiness enterprises in Santa Cruz (see chap. 3).

At least 116 adult Pampeños (mostly males) obtained land or otherwise lived and worked in Santa Cruz between 1959 and 1979.[3] Most remained in Yapacaní from one to three years. The majority of these migrants were young males who had not acquired a land grant in Pampa after the agrarian reform. Others had yet to inherit land. Yet not all who left for Yapacaní did so out of lack of land: all members of 20 land grant households also moved to and obtained land in Santa Cruz in this period, three of which never returned to Pampa.

With few exceptions, most Pampeños arriving in Santa Cruz between 1959 and 1968 settled in Yapacaní. They either obtained a state land grant there or worked with a relative who received one. At least 19 Pampeños were granted land plots in Yapacaní between 1959 and 1971. Most Pampeños who arrived between 1969 and 1974 were single males who worked as seasonal laborers in the numerous agricultural enterprises in the area, particularly in the cutting of sugarcane and the harvesting of cotton.

Land abandonment was high in Yapacaní. Most migrants sold their land, sometimes to other Pampeños. Others passed their land grants on to close kin who later arrived in Yapacaní. (This occurred, e.g., with my field assistant who took over a plot of land from an elder brother who had acquired the land just two years earlier.) Of 19 original land grants awarded to Pampeños in Yapacaní only 7 were reported still in their hands by 1983. Of the 116 Pampeños who lived in Santa Cruz between 1959 and 1979 only 36 remained in Santa Cruz by 1984, all in Yapacaní. Several have become successful cattle ranchers. Most Pampeños who relinquished their land in Yapacaní later acquired land grants in the Chapare.

Shortly after some Pampeños began migrating to Yapacaní, others were focusing their attention on the Chapare, which was slowly being "opened up" to agricultural colonization by government officials.

Migration to the Chapare differed in important ways from that of Yapacaní. Although the journey to the Chapare over the old and narrow gravel road was long and difficult, it was perceived as less so than travel to Yapacaní. Since this road passed near Pampa and travel to and from the Chapare could be accomplished in less than two days, migrants could easily interdigitate their labor between lowland and highland agricultural pursuits and maintain social ties with Pampa. Pampeños who had migrated to Yapacaní were not as fortunate.

Migration to the Chapare was also better organized. Government officials recruited a Pampeño (a former hacienda *kuraka*) to travel to and familiarize himself with the future settlements. He soon encountered and received assistance from several former Pampeño tenants who had moved to the Chapare before the agrarian reform. He was instrumental in subsequently organizing two settlements, both consisting largely of Pampeños and members of nearby communities. Pampeños achieved top leadership positions in these two settlements, a trend that continues up to the present. Finally, the Chapare has attracted, even before the coca boom, a far greater number of migrants than to Santa Cruz. Many hundreds of Pampeños have traveled to the Chapare, and many have remained there. Few Pampeño households, as we shall see, have not had at least one member living or working in the Chapare. Although many, if not most, of the early migrants to the Chapare did not obtain land in Pampa after the agrarian reform, or obtained only meager plots of land compared to their better-off counterparts, others, particularly former *pefaleros* and *kurakas*—bilingual, in positions of authority, with well-established contacts with national officials and extensive landholdings in Pampa, and able to mobilize community labor on their crops fields—also migrated. They were the ones who spearheaded early migration to the Chapare and assumed top leadership positions in the first colonies established in the Chapare.

By the mid-1980s most of Pampa's migrants had land in five major Chapare settlements, or colonies (*colonias*)—Ichoa, Isiboro, Chimoré, Ichilo, and Ibabo. All but the last were located east of the town and river of Chimoré (map 7). The core area, including Ichoa, Isiboro, and Chimoré, settled in the early 1960s and 1970s and referred to by Pampeños as the "colony of Pampa" (Colonia Pampa), is where the overwhelming number of Pampa's migrants actively engaged in coca production were concentrated.

The Cochabamba-Chapare road transverses Ichoa and Isiboro on their southern fringes. The strategic position of Ichoa and Isiboro cannot be emphasized enough, as Pampeños arriving from Pampa needed only to walk a short distance to arrive at their land plots. By the 1970s Pampeños constituted the majority of *afiliados* in these colonies (table

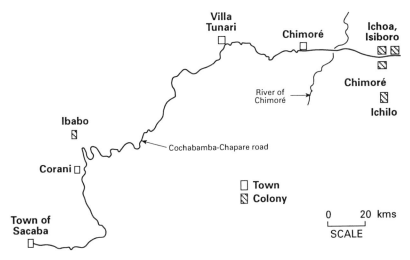

Map 7. The Chapare colonies

4.1) and may have represented one-third of all household heads in Pampa at the time.

Ichilo, about twenty kilometers southeast of Chimoré, boasted the greatest number of migrants from Pampa. Sixty-five percent of Ichilo's *afiliados*, each entitled to 20 hectares of land, were Pampeños (table 4.1). Moreover, top leadership positions of the *sindicato* were invariably held by Pampeños, and the *sindicato*'s monthly meetings often took place in Pampa itself. Other migrants originally from communities bordering Pampa were related to Pampeños through affinal kinship ties.

TABLE 4.1   Number of Pampeños as Afiliados in the Colonies of Ichoa, Isiboro, Chimoré, and Ichilo, 1970s

Colony	Date	No. of Afiliados	No. of Pampeños	Percentage of Pampeños
Ichoa	1972	43	19	44
Isiboro	1972	36	26	72
Chimoré	1977	70	23	33
Ichilo	1979	185	113	61
Total		334	181	54

Source: Unpublished materials at the Instituto Nacional de Colonización (INC), La Paz.

Although the distance from Chimoré was not great, it was not easy to arrive at Ichilo. Until quite recently there was no major road leading to this colony but, rather, narrow footpaths. The area is heavily forested, and several streams and two major rivers first had to be crossed. Pampeño migrants often recalled how extremely difficult and dangerous it was to reach Ichilo during the rainy season, when constant downpours would turn narrow footpaths into knee-deep mud trails, and swollen rivers could only be crossed with canoes or by grasping onto a rope that had been flung to the other side of the river by a particularly good swimmer. During the rainy season the walk from Chimoré to Ichilo might take as long as two days, and often the swelling of the rivers (due to heavy rainfall) discouraged Pampeños from attempting to reach it. These difficulties are now a thing of the past, for the newly constructed road linking the city of Cochabamba with Santa Cruz via the Chapare has made it quite easy for Pampeños to reach Ichilo (see chap. 8). It is significant to bear in mind, however, that these stories stressing the difficulties and dangers of colonizing the Chapare settlements invariably surface when, faced with increasing repression and eradication efforts, Pampeños adamantly cling to their claim that they have the right to their land in the Chapare and the right to continue to cultivate coca.

Ibabo, the last major settlement colonized by Pampeños, was located northeast of the town of Corani in the "Yungas de Corani." Ibabo's landscape differed from that of the other settlements. It was rugged as opposed to flat, and the colony was at a higher elevation (the *yungas* range from 800 to 2,000 meters elevation), with subtropical vegetation prevailing. Eleven Pampeños were affiliated with Ibabo, each of whom had received 25 hectares of land.

The pace of outmigration to the Chapare colonies heightened since 1972. In that year the paved all-weather road linking the city of Cochabamba with the Chapare was completed, allowing Pampeños quick and easy access to the Chapare. The completion of this road was financed by development funds and coincided with the slow but soon dramatic increase in the demand for coca leaves.

By late 1984 more than 200 adult Pampeños were affiliated with a lowland colony. Many were permanently residing in the Chapare, while others claimed permanent residence in Pampa. Some were affiliated with more than one colony, that is, had jural control over land in more than one settlement, a pattern that can be traced to at least the early 1970s (see J. Weil 1989:302). Other Pampeños claimed to "have" land in the

Chapare but had not yet been awarded land grants (e.g., sharecroppers). Finally, some claimed to "just work" in the Chapare. The number of Pampeño households that by late 1984 had at least one member migrating to or otherwise with access to land in the Chapare totaled 204 (table 4.2). These 204 households represented over 80 percent of Pampa's 253 households. Well over half had permanent access to land there.

Migrants with land grants rarely traveled alone to the Chapare but were often accompanied by spouses, elder offspring, siblings, and other kin. Single migrants could rarely go it alone, as most of the food to be consumed (e.g., potatoes) had to be carried along (as well as other necessities such as salt and kerosene), and extra labor was required for the clearing of high-forest vegetation. This was particularly true of migrants traveling to Ichilo—with only small patches of land planted in cassava, plantains, and, occasionally, coca.

When the general assembly of Ichilo, with 113 Pampeño members, overlapped with the harvest of coca (or of other crops) in Ichoa, Isiboro, and/or Chimoré, groups of Pampeños could be seen at any given moment slowly making their way down from Pampa's *lugares* to the pueblo. There, on the side of the road leading to the Chapare, dozens of Pampeños, all burdened with sacks of food and other supplies, awaited the trucks and other vehicles that endlessly passed by Pampa en route to the Chapare. The festive scene, which sometimes lasted for several days, was one of mass exodus. After a few days, when they had all departed, Pampa resembled a ghost town, with virtually only the old and the very young left behind.

Intense migration to the Chapare was an understandable response to a socioeconomic context marked by an accelerated deterioration of the national economy in the 1980s, the strong demand and high prices of coca, political instability and risk resulting in a maze of often contradictory fiscal policies (and inevitably deleterious to peasant livelihood), and an agricultural development policy designed to benefit agro-industrial concerns and not the bulk of small-scale peasant producers.

Yet migration to the Chapare was also a response to environmental risk. The ever-present possibility of harvest failures due to frosts, crop infestations, or drought are, of course, risks that peasants and other agriculturalists worldwide must confront. In Pampa and elsewhere in the Andes peasants have attempted to cope with these environmental risks and uncertainties by spreading out crop activities over a range of vertically arranged crop zones and gaining access to far-flung resource zones (see chap. 6). The most important way that Pampeños coped with the 1982–83 drought was by having gained access to land and crops in the Chapare.

The drought that afflicted the altiplano and *valles* and the accompanying floods in the eastern lowlands were catastrophic.[4] Livestock herds were decimated and agricultural production dropped an average of 50 to 80 percent. Damage to the agricultural sector alone reached U.S. $700 million, and hundreds of millions of dollars in food imports were required to offset crop deficits (Naciones Unidas 1983:35; *Presencia* 1983a). The severe drought had particularly disastrous consequences in the highland department of Potosí (*Los Tiempos* 1983a; 1983b; Prudencio 1984), where it led to a mass migration to La Paz and Cochabamba and even to nearby Chile (*Presencia* 1983b; *Los Tiempos* 1983c, 1983d, 1983e). The drought also led to comparable damage to highland agriculture in neighboring Peru (Browman 1987:175–76).

Although the drought did not lead to the degree of human suffering in Pampa as in the altiplano, it did cause much damage. Many Pampeños reported a drop from 50 to 85 percent in harvest levels when compared to the 1981 season. Although this drop was partly the result of frost and/or crop infestations, most of it was undoubtedly due to the drought. Pampeños (especially those with access to ample irrigation water) who salvaged and sold part of their harvests were able to capitalize on the severe shortage and high prices of potatoes in nearby marketplaces. About 15 Pampeños whose potato plantings were insured by the Aseguradora Boliviana Agropecuaria, a private agricultural insurance firm sponsored by USAID, were able to recover part of their losses (see also *Los Tiempos* 1983f.).

One critical factor that mitigated the drought's impact was the varied sources of irrigation water that Pampa enjoyed. Although the water

TABLE 4.2   Households with at Least One Member Working or with Land in the Chapare, Late 1984

Category	Number	Percentage
Afiliados	138	68
"Having" Land	37	18
"Working"	29	14
Total	204	100

Source: Field data, 1984.

volume of all streams dropped markedly, they proved amazingly resilient in supplying Pampa with water. (The intensity of the drought can be gauged by the fact that the lake of Parina, larger than the irrigation lake of Kuyuq Qocha, had by March of 1983 completely dried up.) Pampeños also successfully diverted water from Pampa's streams that neighboring communities had rights of access to, despite the watchful eyes of the "water observers" (*yacu q''awas*) from these communities.

Pampeños with access to potable water were in a decidedly advantageous position vis-à-vis others. The stream of Sapanani, the source of Pampa's potable water, provided an uninterrupted supply of water throughout the drought. Pampeños with access to this water were able, through the use of buckets and some with even a few hoses, to irrigate nearby plots of land. Some Pampeños were also able to avail themselves of water from migrants who had cut back on production (see chap. 6).

Yet by far the most effective means by which many Pampeños staved off the disastrous drought was by having access to land in the Chapare. In effect, for Pampeños the drought reaffirmed the critical importance of access to land and crop production in the Chapare colonies as a hedge against unforeseen and unpredictable shifts in their natural (and political) environment. In a similar vein, during the 1992 drought, which according to Pampeños was as severe as the one in 1982–83, a great number of Pampeños had almost literally fled to the Chapare.

Despite the heavy rainfall during 1982–83 in the Chapare, which ruined many crops, many Pampeños did harvest rice, cassava, and other crops and hauled them back to Pampa to supplement the shortfall of potatoes. Some migrants with sufficient cash simply bought potatoes elsewhere, usually in Colomi, while others with coca bartered it for potatoes. Pampeños without access to land in the Chapare traveled and worked there in exchange for lowland crops. Others worked in the Chapare during the coca harvests. Despite floods in the Chapare, coca was harvested, and Pampeños rapidly took advantage of the dry conditions in Pampa and the ease with which it can be reached from the Chapare in order to dry their coca leaves there (fig. 3).

Not unexpectedly, Pampeños with coca in the Chapare fared much better than others during the drought. Wealthy Pampeño migrants had little in common with altiplano peasants, who faced grim prospects of malnutrition and near starvation. At least half a dozen peasants from Potosí appeared in Pampa during the drought, and it was through them that Pampeños acquired firsthand knowledge of the critical conditions

Fig. 3. The drying of coca leaves in Pampa

in the altiplano. All found some work in Pampa, either in the potato harvests or as laborers in house building or construction activities; some women found work as weavers.

An important feature of migration to the Chapare, and a logical outcome of highland-lowland production complementarity, has been its seasonal nature. Historically, Pampeños have migrated to the Chapare to sow and harvest lowland crops, returning to Pampa during the sowing and harvest of their highland crops. While the majority of Pampeño migrants continued migrating seasonally to the Chapare and retained their land in Pampa, the 1980s economic crisis and the high returns on coca cultivation were giving way to a trend to spend considerably more time in the Chapare and, in some cases, to outright permanent migration. Pampeños constantly told me of household members, other kin, and neighbors, who were in the Chapare (or, as many often stated, "inside" [*uk"upi*]) for quite some time and whose date of return to Pampa was unknown. A substantial number of Pampeños were spending more time in the lowlands than in Pampa itself. For example, during the household census 75 household heads reported at least one member spending more time in the Chapare than in Pampa. This represented almost 33 percent of all households and almost 40 percent of those with at least one member either working or with access to land in the Chapare.

Some young and highly mobile migrant household heads would spend four or five straight months in the Chapare. The case of Juan was representative of this trend to spend increasingly more time in the Chapare. I used to come across Juan quite often during the early stages of my fieldwork. I often visited Juan, as his house was directly across from the nurses' station, where I slept, and I had included him in my survey of potato production. In time, however, it became ever more difficult to encounter Juan in Pampa. An entry in my journal dated June 18, 1984, indicated that I had not seen Juan for three months and that he was not expected back in Pampa until September.

The slow demise of seasonal migration was but a step away from permanent migration. Whereas few Pampeños permanently settled in Santa Cruz, at least 110 (and perhaps many more) Pampeños were permanently residing in a Chapare settlement by late 1983, almost all in the colonies of Ichoa, Isiboro, and Chimoré. Most of them had left Pampa in the late 1970s and early 1980s. While many migrants occasionally returned to Pampa to visit friends or relatives, others had not done so for several years. As we shall see, the prolonged absence of Pampeños had important ramifications for patterns of access to land, crop production strategies, and the deployment of agricultural labor in Pampa.

Migration to the Chapare presents an interesting contrast with seasonal migratory patterns to the eastern Tambopata Valley in Peru studied by J. Collins (1988). Migrants to the Tambopata Valley cultivated coffee, the major cash crop, but a variety of intersecting processes mitigated against permanent or semipermanent migration: insecurity of land titles and fluctuating coffee prices, both of which enhanced economic risk (1988:20–22); the inability of neither coffee cultivation nor highland agriculture to generate enough income to satisfy basic household needs (1988:160–61; cf. M. Painter 1986:230–31); and small land plots, lack of additional available land, and declining yields, all expressed in an intense "competition for land" (J. Collins 1988:82–83, 159–60).[5] The context of coca cultivation in the Chapare was far different. Most land-based migrants had secure access to land as long as they were officially registered as *afiliados* of a lowland settlement (and irrespective of whether they had secured land titles). Moreover, coca cultivation during the 1980s provided far higher returns to Pampeño migrants than coffee for Tambopata migrants. Last, land plots in the Chapare settlements were far larger than in Tambopata, many Pampeño migrants had access to land in more than one settlement, and, despite some evidence of land conflicts and competition for available land, migrants were still able to enter unclaimed lands and plant coca.

Inequality

A recurrent and well-studied process in lowland frontier regions has been the emergence of inequality and social differentiation. This process has been generated by an interplay of factors such as declining soil fertility, low prices that migrants obtain for their crops, poor marketing mechanisms, lack of official credit, debt bondage, and the presence of expansive plantationlike enterprises absorbing land and labor (see, e.g., Roberts 1975; Foweraker 1981; Schmink 1981; Shoemaker 1981; Brass 1983; Bunker 1985; J. Collins 1986b; J. Collins and Painter 1986:17–19; Gill 1987; Hecht 1989).

Inequality was also evident in the Chapare in the mid-1980s, although its roots can be traced to two decades earlier. This was a process largely structured on coca production and rising coca prices and deteriorating living standards in the altiplano and valley regions. It was grounded on differential access to land and labor by an emergent class of wealthy migrants who consolidated multiple landholdings and garnished large amounts of labor from impoverished landless migrants and other land-poor peasants. Interestingly enough, it would be members of this elite peasant class who, as we shall see in chapter 8, were mainly responsible for the proclaimed "success" of coca eradication efforts in the Chapare in the late 1980s and early 1990s.

Almost 25 years ago Henkel (1971) strongly suggested the emergence of inequality and differentiation among peasant settlers in the Chapare. Henkel distinguished three land-use stages—pioneer fringe, commercial core, and zone of decay—each marked by different proportions of cash and subsistence crops; land under cultivation, fallow, and virgin forest; and types and amount of labor employed. The pioneer fringe, the stage of initial settlement, was characterized by the predominance of high forest growth, subsistence over commercial crops, and an almost total absence of wage labor. In the commercial core cash crops, rice and coca, loomed important, cultivated land surpassed high forest, and the use of wage laborers and/or sharecroppers increased dramatically. Finally, in the zone of decay land fragmentation was widespread, yields decreased, and the predominant type of labor employed reverted to that of the pioneer fringe—that is, primarily household labor.

Henkel's model rested on several assumptions difficult to defend during the 1980s, such as a slow transition from subsistence to cash crops and a relative absence of agricultural commodities with both high prices and inelastic demand. Nevertheless, the important point is the emergence of inequality in the mid-1960s—less than a decade after large-scale peasant migration to the Chapare—and the role of coca in this process of growing inequality. For example, among the 162 household heads interviewed by Henkel in the commercial core, where wage labor and sharecropping were widespread, coca accounted for over 75.0 percent of the value of all products sold (Henkel 1971:211). Eight of these had an income of over U.S. $2,000, twice as much as 79.6 percent of their counterparts. These eight household heads, Henkel wrote, "were large scale coca farmers who have managed to work out satisfactory labor arrangements with sharecroppers and peons for the cultivation of coca on an extensive scale" (1971:212). Ten years later J. Weil (1980a:406) suggested that the "emergence of a rural proletariat is perhaps the most probable scenario [in the Chapare]," and C. Weil (1980:427) noted that some households in the same Chapare settlement were "expand[ing] economically." Inequality was clearly on the rise in the mid- to late 1960s and clearly intensified in the following decade, despite the presence of an egalitarian ideology in Chapare colonist settlements in the early 1970s (J. Weil 1980a:360, 1989:300).

Other research undertaken in the early 1980s also confirmed how coca cultivation was contributing to increasing inequality in the Chapare. Blanes and Flores (1982) distinguished four types of colonies—from "highly specialized" to those with little or no coca—based on the average amount of land in coca, household size, and the type and amount of labor deployed by migrant households. "Specialized" colonies had far more land under coca, their households were larger and with a greater proportion of nonresident kin, employed a higher proportion of wage (and or contract) laborers and sharecroppers, and had wealthier households (Blanes and Flores 1982:86–107). The spread of wage labor (cf. Rasnake and Painter 1989:34)—the presence of landless migrants laboring for others with usufruct rights to land—was paralleled by the emergence in the Chapare of what E. Morales, referring to eastern Peru, has called "planters-entrepreneurs" (1989:72) In Pampa, by contrast, migration and coca cultivation were bolstering, and not undermining, nonwage labor arrangements (see chap. 7). Some enterprising Pampeño migrants in the Chapare, capitalizing on access to labor and expanding coca production, had accumulated significant wealth and were disengaging themselves from crop production in Pampa (see chap. 6).

Migration to and the expansion and intensification of coca cultivation in the Chapare hinged on access to land and complex modes of securing and retaining labor. Pampeños with land in the Chapare were able to meet their increasing labor requirements as a result of three factors. The first was the trend toward the withdrawal of land under cultivation in Pampa (see chap. 6). This was both a consequence of and an important factor in the expansion and intensification of coca cultivation as it absorbed labor normally deployed in highland agricultural pursuits. The second was the slow erosion of seasonal migratory patterns as more Pampeños remained on a semipermanent or permanent basis in the Chapare. The last factor that enabled Pampeños to gain access to sufficient labor was the influx of peasants from Bolivia's highlands (some from as far away as Potosí) without secure access to land in the Chapare.

In Ichoa, Isiboro, and Ichilo three partly overlapping migrant categories had emerged based on the type and amount of land they held and their structural position within local labor arrangements: (1) those who maintained their state land grants relatively intact or (to a lesser extent) the few migrants who purchased entire land grants; (2) migrants who acquired small plots of land via inheritance, purchase, or sharecropping; and (3) wage and/or contractual laborers (peones).

Members of the first category (i.e., those with relatively intact land grants) made up the minority of afiliados in Ichoa, Isiboro, and Ichilo. They had the most coca under cultivation, usually from one to three hectares. (Other migrants admitted having more hectares of land in coca.) The amount of coca cultivated by these migrants, probably higher than they admitted, was primarily a function of access to labor: those successful in mobilizing plentiful labor invariably had more coca under cultivation. These migrant households were the wealthiest and most influential, had access to the largest labor force, and employed the most complex means of accessing labor.

Miguelino was a good example of members of this first category of wealthy, land-based migrants with access to considerable coca land and labor. He had 20 hectares of land in Ichoa, of which, by his own account, some two to three (and probably more) were planted in coca. Miguelino, who had no children of his own, actively recruited the services of numerous sharecroppers, some with whom he maintained fictive kin ties (*compadrazgo*). The number of sharecroppers he had varied from year to year but usually ranged from 9 to 12. Some had been sharecropping his land for several years, and most lived with, and relied on the labor from, their spouses and children. The most important, and sometimes the only, crop that his sharecroppers planted was coca. The sharecroppers retained one-half of their harvests. As sharecroppers elsewhere (see, e.g., Lehmann 1986b) they provided an invaluable pool of labor that permitted owners of the land for which they worked to expand production and accumulate wealth and capital (see Henkel 1971:203–5, for the importance of sharecroppers in generating additional wealth and profits). For example, in addition to their own household labor, Miguelino's sharecroppers also recruited extra-household labor, mainly from their home communities, particularly during the coca harvests. Miguelino also directly hired wage and contractual laborers, especially for the clearing of land, weeding, and harvests.

Other migrants were in a less enviable position than Miguelino. For instance, Ponce had only one hectare of land under coca but relied on his two teenage sons to help him during the weeding and harvesting of coca. His wife, who usually remained in Pampa with their younger children, rarely traveled to the Chapare. Ponce, like Miguelino, also employed the services of sharecroppers. Each of his sharecroppers had access to about 3,200 square meters (two *catos*) of coca, and all had their own *peones*.[6] Ponce also counted on additional help from his brother, who had a land grant in nearby Isiboro, and his sharecroppers. An elder *criado* (literally "servant") was permanently attached to Ponce's household and looked after Ponce's coca fields when he was away.

Some land-based migrants hired during the harvests 20 or 30 *peones* for a few weeks at most, but many were hired for longer periods of time. One Pampeño, for instance, reported employing ten laborers during 1983, five of whom remained for one month on his land and the others for over three and a half months. *Peones* were also shared, or "loaned" out, between land-grant household heads and their sharecroppers in the Chapare to satisfy reciprocal *ayni* labor obligations. (Reciprocal labor exchanges, as we shall see in chapter 7, also took place between Pampa and the Chapare colonies.)

Prominent migrant household heads with large (and sometimes several) land grants capitalized on extended kinship networks, sharecropping arrangements, and payment in coca or in cash to amass considerable labor and further expand their land under cultivation. An excellent example of a wealthy and prominent migrant who secured a considerable amount of labor through a variety of intertwined mechanisms was Luis, one of the most powerful and wealthiest household heads in Pampa and the Chapare. Luis, his teenage and unmarried son, and his father and four brothers, constituted five separate households in Pampa, each in control of a land grant in Ichilo. Luis also had an additional land grant in Isiboro. Jointly they controlled a total of 140 hectares of land. An excellent example of what Long and Roberts (1984:217) have called a "confederation of households," Luis, his father, and four brothers went out of their way, perhaps more than other kin-linked households, to coordinate their productive activities in Pampa and the Chapare. For instance, they commonly traveled together in Luis's truck en route to Ichilo, where they shared their labor in clearing the forest cover on each other's land. Members of his extended family were sometimes accompanied by contractual and/or wage laborer, some who were shared between Luis and his brothers.

In addition to payment in coca Luis also employed the tactic of promising a sharecropping arrangement in order to attract and retain additional labor, thereby permitting him to expand his scale of operations. Luis was able to secure not only the labor of his sharecroppers but also to draw upon labor from his household and others, including wage laborers, who he was able to recruit. These included many of his approximately 50 godchildren. As a potential source of land and wealth and with a large labor force within their orbit, wealthy and increasingly powerful migrants such as Luis attained a remarkable degree of prominence. These heads of family, or peasant "enterprises" (Friedmann 1986:125; Lehmann 1982a:133–135; cf. Cook 1982, 1986; Cook and Binford 1990), were sometimes referred to by other Pampeño migrants as *patrones* (landowners).

Other migrants were not as fortunate as Luis in securing labor in the Chapare. Elariano was one of the largest landholding peasants in Pampa but was unable to mobilize sufficient labor to rapidly expand coca cultivation on his and his wife's land grants in Ichilo. Part of the reason for this stemmed from Elariano's small household: his wife usually remained behind to take care of their two small children. Furthermore Elariano, unlike Luis, had considerably more difficulties in securing labor from his close kin. Elariano and his brothers, for instance, rarely exchanged *ayni,* or reciprocal labor, in Pampa or otherwise supported each other in productive tasks. Last, his income derived solely from potato production in Pampa, and he was therefore unable to compete with others in the Chapare who offered higher wages either in cash or in coca to attract labor. Elariano attempted to make up for his relative lack of labor by using a gasoline-powered chain saw for the felling of trees. Yet he readily admitted that this strategy was not sufficient to offset his lack of labor power, especially given the amount of weeding that his future coca plants required.

Sharecroppers and other migrants who inherited small portions of land in the Chapare were the second most important category of land-based migrants. They had far less coca under cultivation and were less wealthy than their counterparts described above. Their land plots, almost always totally under coca, ranged from just one to three *catos.* That is, although they had less coca than their wealthier land-grant counterparts, they were more specialized migrants and normally did not divide their time between subsistence and cash crops. Some sharecroppers had tiny house gardens that provided them with consumption crops, but by and large they were fed by the owner of the land (usually kin), bought their subsistence staples from others, or brought them down from Pampa. They furthermore had access to only minute plots of land in Pampa.

Leopoldo was one of these young, specialized colonists often without secure access to land (or land titles) in the Chapare. Eighteen years old, he sharecropped from his godfather just one *cato* of coca in Isiboro. He usually left his wife and his one-year old son behind in Pampa when he traveled to the Chapare. Leopoldo had inherited 2,000 square meters of irrigated land and slightly over 2,600 square meters of rain-fed land in Pampa. Marcialino was in an identical situation. Twenty-six years old and with three children all under five, he sharecropped one-half hectare of land in Chimoré, of which two *catos* (or about 60 percent of his land) were in coca. Marcialino had inherited from his father 1,530 square meters of irrigated crop land and 2,000 square meters of rain-fed land in Pampa.

Wage, contractual, and other laborers paid in kind constituted the third, and perhaps numerically most important, migrant category in the Chapare. During the coca harvests sharecroppers relied heavily on laborers paid in kind or cash. Some of these laborers were simultaneously sharecroppers on someone else's land. For instance, Leopoldo regularly relied on four or five laborers who also sharecropped his godfather's land. Since he paid them in cash or in kind, Ponce referred to them as *peones*. Many *peones* were drawn from the large and mobile population migrating to the Chapare who did not have secure access to land.

Most *peones* employed by Pampeños during the coca harvests were not from Pampa. Yet Pampeños from households in Pampa who did not have secure access to land in any of the Chapare colonies also formed part of this labor pool. A common strategy of many migrants had been to travel to the Chapare to work in different colonies with the hope of securing a sharecropping arrangement or acquiring enough knowledge of the area to obtain a state land grant subsequently. The former was the case particularly during early stages of settlement, when *afiliados* heavily relied on labor provided by kin without lowland land in the initial stages of forest clearance and crop production. Many of the latter in fact lived and worked in different colonies for some years before obtaining their own land. Ponce was a case in point. He was single and only 16 years old when he first arrived in the Chapare in 1956. In the following three years he worked as a laborer in four different colonies, always on land belonging to kin, before securing his own land grant in Ichoa.

Inequality, predicated on differential access to large amounts of coca land and labor and driven by high coca prices and returns on coca cultivation, was accentuated by a relative shortage of land. The demand for coca paste and cocaine hydrochloride, and the concomitant spread of coca cultivation, had generated an influx of migrants to the Chapare. Yet a large part of the Chapare was not readily accessible to newly arriving migrants. Hundreds of thousands of hectares had been allotted to cooperative and other ventures carved out of state land grants (Blanes and Flores 1982; USAID 1981:9; Multinational Agribusiness Systems 1979:6) as well as to earlier settled migrants. Moreover, the Isidoro-Securé National Park takes up 39 percent of the territory. Last, large areas were unsuited for crop production (see chap. 2).

As a result, and despite the fact that only 6 percent of the Chapare was occupied by migrants in the early 1980s (Blanes and Flores 1982:1), intense migration and relative land scarcity led to increasing competition for available and strategically located land. (This competition was exacerbated by the 1982–83 drought.) During 1983 and 1984 numerous disputes over land boundaries, outright land invasions, and other violent conflicts took place in the Chapare.[7] Pampeños were also drawn into these conflicts. In 1983 they began a year-round armed presence in the colony of Ichilo, after driving off peasants encroaching upon their lands. Land in Ichilo was very valuable (which is why it attracted other peasants) because the road under construction at the time that would link the cities of Santa Cruz and Cochabamba via the town of Villa Tunari would cut across this colony. (This road was completed in 1988.) Land in this colony would have provided migrants easy access to Bolivia's two major cities and centers of coca paste processing and distribution, an especially important advantage to those with coca fields.

Growing inequality and competition for land did not, however, appear to be resulting in a process in which peasants were slowly deprived of their means of production, as has occurred elsewhere in the Latin American lowlands. The absence of capital-intensive expansive agri-businesses in the Chapare (cf. chap. 3), the relative stability of land use that coca cultivation promoted, and the high prices peasants obtained from selling their coca harvests (which may have allowed many to sidestep moneylenders and other sources of debt bondage) all worked against an undermining of peasant-based forms of production in the Chapare. This was in stark contrast to the fate of peasant production in the department of Santa Cruz, where agro-industrial elites successfully appropriated land and labor from peasant settlements (cf. Gill 1987; see also the especially moving account of peasant laborers in Riester, Riester, Simón, and Schuchard 1979).

The Illegal Market

Virtually none of the coca harvested by Pampeños entered the legal market. The particular mechanisms through which coca entered the "black market" were various, the one chosen at any given time depending primarily on the location and intensity of police antidrug operations. Well-established ties existed between many Pampeños and intermediaries, who supplied the bulk of coca leaves to the black market. Some Pampeños with their own vehicles directly transported their coca to these intermediaries, but the general pattern consisted of arranging a place and time for the intermediaries to pick up the coca harvests. Other Pampeños with vehicles directly furnished nearby coca paste operations with coca or, eluding police controls, drove to the *valle alto,* where coca paste was also being processed. (Sometimes coca was hidden in Pampa for short periods and later secretly transported to the *valle alto*.) The coca that entered the black market was processed into coca paste, much of it smuggled to Colombia, where it was converted into cocaine hydrochloride. Increasingly, however, coca paste was also being processed into cocaine hydrochloride in various laboratories that sprung up throughout the lowlands and the *valle alto* (Henkel 1988; Henman 1985; Healy 1986). Coca paste processing in the Chapare and the *yungas* of La Paz, as well as in eastern Peru, was primarily a small-scale venture in the hands of peasants (Healy 1986; Leons 1986; E. Morales 1989). The entry of coca-producing peasants into the processing of coca paste was limited by availability of capital, necessary networks to obtain the indispensable supply of materials, level of expertise, competition from other peasants, and the risks that they were willing to undertake to avoid capture and confiscation of their goods by the police.

By late 1984 the narcotics police had carried out numerous raids in the Chapare. One consequence of these raids was a shift of coca paste operations from the Chapare to communities in the *valle alto,* especially those in the vicinity of the towns of Cliza and Punata (southeast of Pampa). At that time strict road controls had been set up by the police between the town of Sacaba and the city of Cochabamba and between the latter and Cliza and Punata, with the objective of intercepting the flow of coca leaves from the Chapare to the *valle alto.*

Truckers and others involved in the illegal coca leaf trade quickly found other routes to deliver their product to Cliza and Punata. A favorite strategy that emerged in late December of 1984 was the nightly use of a dirt road that cut across Pampa on a southeast axis and which ultimately led to the *valle alto. Sindicato* authorities lost little time in availing themselves of this flow of traffic through Pampa. Spurred on by the *sindicato*'s general secretary, himself a wealthy Chapare migrant, and under the pretext of exercising communal authority over the flow of *ajenos* through Pampa and of procuring much needed funds for public works (*obras sociales*), the *sindicato* erected in January 1985 a round-the-clock roadblock (*tranca*) to take advantage of the flow of coca leaves to the nearby *valle alto*. A fee (*tasa*) was collected from every truck attempting to cross the roadblock to deliver its shipment of coca leaves to the *valle alto*. Initial resistance on the part of some truckers to the payment of the *tasa,* which led to a few bloody confrontations, quickly dissipated, as they encountered dozens of Pampeños armed with sticks and rocks (and a few with shotguns) determined to collect the required fee. Pampeños collected from the *tranca* between 60 and 100 million *pesos bolivianos,* or about U.S. $6,000 to U.S. $10,000 at the prevalent exchange rate. (A massive monetary devaluation in late January reduced the purchasing power of this amount by one-third.) By the end of January rumors that the Leopardos, who by that time had established their head-quarters just outside of the town of Sacaba, had learned about the roadblock and were preparing to raid Pampa itself led to the final lifting of the roadblock.

The Investment and Display of Wealth

Migrants from Pampa no doubt profited by cultivating coca and/or engaging in coca paste activities. The harvest of coca, which was the major peasant crop that maintained its value in a period of hyperinfla-tion, generated considerable income. Even wage laborers without access to land earned considerably more than in Pampa: coca stompers, for instance, often obtained a wage three to five times greater than the one prevalent in Pampa.

It would be a mistake to assume, however, that all migrants were equally capable of accumulating wealth. The Chapare, where large sums of dollars were reported to be circulating and where "rags to riches" tales were common, was one of the most expensive areas of Bolivia. In January 1985, for instance, coca stompers in the Chapare earned 7 million *pesos bolivianos* for a 10-hour shift (6 P.M.–4 A.M.). A bowl of soup and a bottle of beer, however, cost 3 million *pesos bolivianos* (Lagos 1988:143–44). In addition, coca leaves would rot if not kept dried, and cash, goods, and other personal belongings would often (and continue to) be confiscated by narcotics police. These and other circumstances limited the ability of most migrants to accumulate significant wealth. A small group of perhaps no more than 40 Pampeño migrant households with access to large amounts of coca land and labor, and or in control of their own coca paste ventures, nevertheless managed to amass great wealth.[8] It was impossible for me to gather reliable quantitative data on the amount of monetary wealth held by these successful migrants.[9] Never-theless, I was able to indirectly gauge the extent of their wealth by closely examining different ways in which wealth was invested, the public display of which served to validate prestige and success.

One means of investing and displaying wealth was by purchasing television sets. By mid-1985 41 households (or 16 percent of all house-holds in Pampa) owned a television set. The majority of these households were located in the pueblo, all were migrant households, and in all at least one member was, at least minimally, functionally bilingual in Spanish.

Pampeños living in the pueblo also channeled time and resources into upgrading and remodeling their dwellings. The rising cost of construction materials as a result of high inflation did not seem to deter the flurry of house construction and improvements since all of the wealthiest migrant household heads had access to sufficient cash. These activities included interior and exterior whitewashing (the latter often over a layer of cement), construction of cement floors and second-story additions (some with balconies), floor tiles, cement walls with iron gates, and so forth. One Pampeño planned to convert his house bordering the paved highway to Cochabamba into a restaurant to take advantage of the heavy road traffic. Activities related to house construction and remodeling supported three full-time masons (two of whom were Pampeños) who earned five to six times the average monthly wage. Employment of masons did not replace cooperative work parties, or *minkas*.

The culmination of work on a dwelling was invariably followed by a one- or two-day celebration (*ch'alla*). The *ch'alla* was a public event in which the owner of the remodeled house provided food and drink, and often music, to a large number of guests. The greater the number of people attending and the more lavish the celebration, the greater the prestige of the sponsor and the more visible his demonstration of wealth. A wealthy and generous sponsor invariably distributed large quantities of bottled and corn beer and an ample supply of meat. The presence of the parish priest to bless the dwelling or of other prominent individuals, such as political officials, was highly prized.

Yet the most important, conspicuous, and prestigious strategy undertaken by prosperous migrants for investing their wealth was the purchase of vehicles, particularly trucks. By mid-1985 members of 34 (including four non-Pampeño) households, or over 13 percent of all households in Pampa, owned 37 vehicles (15 pickups, 12 trucks, 8 cars, 1 motorcycle, and 1 jeep). One wealthy migrant owned a truck, a car, and a pickup. In another household both father and son were separate owners of pickups. This migrant's father even had a permanently employed personal driver residing with him in Pampa. Most of the vehicles in Pampa were purchased between 1983 and mid-1985 (i.e., at the height of the coca boom), and all but one had been bought since 1979.

At least 10 other Pampeño household heads permanently living in the Chapare (and, hence, not included in the household census) owned another 9 trucks and 3 cars. Other Pampeños at the time were either interested in or in the actual process of buying a vehicle. Since vehicles would invariably be purchased with U.S. dollars, many Pampeños were keenly interested in and aware of the dollar's black market rate. During fieldwork I was often approached by Pampeños asking advice on when and where to buy dollars. The sums of money invested in vehicles were enormous given local living standards: for example, one pickup was bought for U.S. $4,500, the jeep mentioned above for U.S. $2,500, and a car for U.S. $3,500. A used truck was easily worth well over U.S. $15,000. A new large truck during 1984–85 cost between U.S. $70,000 and U.S. $120,000 (Lagos 1988:194).

The presence of vehicles, specifically trucks, in Pampa predated the mid-1980s coca boom. Between 1962 and the early 1970s eight trucks were purchased in Pampa, but all were later sold. All but one seem to have been bought with cash obtained from the sale of potatoes: land was not as fragmented then, potato fields were more intensely cropped, and yields and prices were probably much higher. Vehicles purchased since then were undoubtedly due to coca wealth.

The investment of wealth in vehicles was no doubt an ideal economic strategy in an economic and politically risky environment. In an economic context marked by hyperinflation and lack of other investment opportunities the strategy of investing liquid wealth into vehicles functioned as a shield against the accelerated erosion of the purchasing power of local currency. There were, of course, other options to avoid this continual erosion. Some Pampeños would buy dollars in the black market (a common practice by wealthy migrants). At other times Pampeño migrants simply postponed the sale of coca leaves with the expectation that prices would continue to rise. On February 8, 1985, for instance, one of my godchildren managed to elude police controls and conceal in his house in Pampa about 250 pounds of coca leaves valued at about U.S. $600. His plans were to sell them in the nearby *valle alto*, where small-scale, cottage-level coca paste operations had proliferated. (The value of his coca leaves drastically dropped a few days later due to police antidrug operations in the *valle alto*.)[10] Another option occasionally pursued by a few Pampeños was to invest part of their wealth in cattle: since the price of beef was tagged to the black market rate of the dollar, the price of cattle kept up with inflationary trends.

Compared to other options, however, vehicles had the added advantage of security against theft or confiscation by narcotics police. (Police would invariably confiscate dollars, coca, and large amounts of local currency during their raids. Because of this Pampeños often accused police of being *suwas* [thieves].) But, more important, investing in trucks was an especially attractive option for wealthy peasants because it was a sure means of generating and accumulating additional wealth. Pampeño truckers were especially visible during harvest time in Pampa, where they hauled the recent harvests from one crop zone to another, and on the Cochabamba-Chapare road, where they transported passengers and agricultural products (including coca) to and from Cochabamba, Sacaba, and the Chapare. Other authors have stressed the different ways in which control over transportation enables surplus extraction from the peasantry, accentuates the accumulation of wealth and capital by truckers, and fosters inequality and domination within peasant communities (cf. Loyola 1988; Long and Roberts 1978; 1984; Lagos 1988). Even in a context of drastically low coca prices and little or no inflation, Pampeños continued to invest in vehicles in the late 1980s and early 1990s (see chap. 8). Vehicles, especially trucks and buses, could also easily generate a quick profit if they were later sold. For instance, one Pampeño who bought a jeep for U.S. $2,500 was selling it for U.S. $3,500 just one month later.

Vehicles were also symbolically the most potent way of proclaiming wealth and attaining prestige. As was the case during the upgrading of a dwelling, the purchase of a vehicle (but particularly a truck or bus) was also followed by a *ch'alla*—but one far more elaborate. Preparations for the *ch'alla* required careful planning. Invitations to attend the ceremony were extended to kin in Pampa and neighboring communities. In the meantime other kin would be busily at work for the sponsor garnering food and drink. These ceremonies, some of which lasted two days, also featured musical bands brought in from the city of Cochabamba or the town of Sacaba. In one *ch'alla* a band played for two days and nights, reportedly for a fee of 3 million *pesos bolivianos* (U.S. $15) per hour. In addition to demonstrating wealth, the *ch'alla* also served to establish additional kin ties, such as in *compadrazgo,* and consolidate old ones.

One significant feature of a *ch'alla* for a vehicle was the prominent role that a mass played in it. The mass took place on the first day of the *ch'alla,* usually in the late morning. (The sponsor and many of his guests gathered since early morning to chat and drink.) After mass the statue of the "Virgin of Pampa" was brought out of the chapel. A procession then followed, in which the vehicle, the owner and his dwelling, and the guests were blessed (fig. 4).

According to the parish priest and Pampeños, the rationale of the mass and blessing was to insure the safety of the vehicle and of its riders on the road. Yet the public display of the Virgin's statue and the active role of the parish priest not only surrounded the *ch'alla* with a ritualized atmosphere but also served (and certainly contrary to the wishes of the priests) to publicly legitimize the attainment of wealth and its sumptuous display. Local parish priests often crusaded, especially in weddings and baptisms, against the cultivation of the coca leaf, the manufacture of coca paste and cocaine, and, in their view, the unproductive investment of wealth in trucks and other commodities. Yet, paradoxically, their participation in a *ch'alla* only served to confirm and validate—through the aura of holiness that permeated the ceremony—wealth and the means through which it was attained.

A final example of the display of wealth and validation of prestige, and one with close structural affinities to the *ch'alla,* was the sponsorship of a fiesta "in honor of" (or "in devotion to") the Virgin of Pampa. This fiesta, which predated the coca boom, was different than but had the same origins as the annual community wide Fiesta of Pampa, which celebrated the appearance of the Virgin in Pampa in 1879 and attracted thousands of participants from neighboring communities, the town of Sacaba, and the city of Cochabamba.

Each household head was expected eventually to sponsor a fiesta in honor of the Virgin. By sponsoring such a fiesta, and therefore unequivocally demonstrating devotion to her, Pampeños believed that she would then bestow good fortune, in the form of good health and better and larger harvests, upon the sponsor (*pasante*) and members of his or her immediate household. Some Pampeños emphasized that the Virgin bequeathed prosperity and health equally upon any sponsor regardless of his or her generosity to her (i.e., the lavishness of the fiesta). Others claimed that the Virgin looked favorably upon those who sponsored large and very extravagant fiestas. The sponsorship of fiestas to the Virgin throughout Cochabamba, a theme as yet poorly researched, no doubt is of considerable antiquity.[11] During the coca boom these fiestas were taking on new meanings.

One especially noteworthy fiesta in honor of the Virgin, which I attended, was sponsored by Adriano, one of Pampa's most prominent

Fig. 4. Ch'alla for a vehicle

migrants. Not one but two parish priests appeared at his fiesta and carried out the obligatory mass and blessing. Other prominent guests present during this elaborate ceremony included the mayor and former mayor of the town of Sacaba, other town officials, and even the sub-prefect (the maximal political authority) of the province of the Chapare. Many of Adriano's *compadres* from Sacaba, the Chapare, and surrounding communities also were present. Food, drink, and music (Adriano had hired a musical band from the city of Cochabamba) were ample. Large quantities of bottled beer, corn beer, potatoes and other tubers, and vegetables were lavishly distributed to all those present. In addition, one cow, several sheep, and at least one dozen chickens were slaughtered specifically for this occasion. I estimated that Adriano invested the equivalent of over U.S. $1,100 on the first day of the fiesta (it lasted for two and a half days); this amount represented over 30 times the average monthly salary at the time. The sums of money invested in these celebrations were quite large. Yet, relative to the wealth that enterprising migrants like Adriano had amassed, the amount of money they invested in these celebrations were small indeed and did not necessarily lead to economic hardships; these fiestas were not "leveling mechanisms" that somehow redistributed wealth.[12] It is noteworthy, for instance, that Adriano told me of his interest in traveling to Brazil to purchase a new truck *after* sponsoring his fiesta.

Individually sponsored fiestas, which, at least during the coca boom, clearly functioned as a medium for competitive displays of wealth, the attainment of status, and the expansion and consolidation of social relationships by wealthy migrants, were also impacting upon the traditional organization of other ceremonies. For example, while in the town of Sacaba's parish archive one afternoon I met a woman who had been sent by a migrant relative to arrange for the presence of a parish priest at their community's fiesta. Her relative had planned to sponsor his own fiesta for the Virgin on the same day that his community's fiesta had been scheduled. According to the woman, her relative did not want to partake of the latter but wanted instead to have the parish priest attend the one he was planning "only for himself," where he could invite his own guests and his musical band. He was willing, the woman said, to pay any amount the priest would request to attend. The priest angrily refused.

The lavish displays of wealth by prosperous migrants in surrounding communities were having other aftermaths indicative of and generated by deepening disparities in wealth and status between migrants and nonmigrants. For example, while also undertaking archival research in the town of Sacaba's parish, I came across several couples from communities located in the *serranías* north of the town of Sacaba who wanted to get married secretly in the middle of the night. The reason for these seemingly anomalous requests, they told the priests, was that they (and their immediate kin) were unable to pay for expensive marriage rituals comparable to those undertaken by their more wealthy migrant counterparts. In fact, requests for these "secret marriages" had become so common by early 1985 that the parish priests decided to set aside two nights a week (beginning at three in the morning) to perform them.

It is important to stress that the different ways of investing wealth were invariably undertaken only by wealthy migrants, who made up a minority of Pampa's migrants. It is also worthwhile to note that there were no mechanisms in Pampa capable of siphoning off part of the wealth that these enterprising and successful migrants had accumulated and funneling it toward much needed communal works. While wealth was notably displayed in Pampa, the community treasury, its major source of funds, which in the past stemmed from fines imposed on those

Pampeños who failed to participate in communal works, was always penniless. Much needed public works (e.g., water pumps during the 1982–83 drought or materials for the installation of potable water in the many households that lacked it) did not therefore materialize.

Migration to the Chapare and the cultivation and marketing of coca has had a remarkable impact on the fortunes and life careers of some Pampeños. The following two case studies well illustrate these remarkable changes.

Ramón and Julia. In the late nineteenth century Ramón, a monolingual Quechua-speaking tenant, abandoned Pampa, as had many others before him (see chap. 2). Ramón was fortunate to have had enough wealth to purchase land in a *piquería* near the town of Sacaba. Leaving behind his common-law wife and a son, he was accompanied at the time by various kin, including his sister Felicidad. Decades later Julio, one of Felicidad's sons, acquired a land plot in the Chapare from the Instituto Nacional de Colonización. Like other colonists, Julio planted coca, along with other crops. Julia, his wife, soon afterward began buying and transporting coca and other crops from the Chapare lowlands to the regional markets in and around the city of Cochabamba. By the late 1970s Julia (by then a widow) was in a position to reap the advantage of rising coca prices. She relied on kin to expand her *cocales* in the Chapare. Yet it was in the marketing of coca leaves that Julia's success lay. Soon she had become a prosperous wholesale merchant (*rescatista*) in coca, and her commercial activities and wealth had mushroomed. By 1983 Julia had purchased a large plot of land only a few blocks from the Sacaba town square and had constructed on it an enormous two-story balcony ringed dwelling. She had invested the bulk of her wealth not in land but in a small fleet of trucks and buses deployed in the transport of passengers, coca leaves, and other goods to and from the town of Sacaba, the city of Cochabamba, and the Chapare. By then she was said to be one of the wealthiest *rescatistas* in Sacaba.

Trinidad and Pedro. Trinidad, like his father, a *colono* in Pampa, was Ramón's contemporary. But Trinidad, unlike Ramón, was the head of a large and poor household and remained in Pampa. Shortly after the agrarian reform Pedro, Trinidad's grandson, also acquired land in the Chapare. As almost all colonists, Pedro grew coca and other crops in the Chapare and continued cultivating crops in Pampa. In the mid-1970s, however, as the demand for coca increased and its price outpaced that of other crops, Pedro and his children moved permanently to the

Chapare, where his first grandchildren were born, and devoted increasing time to coca cultivation. During the next nine years Pedro sporadically returned to Pampa. Rarely was he interested in participating in communal works, attending the monthly communitywide gatherings, or cooperating with kin in reciprocal labor obligations. While in the Chapare Pedro did not relinquish his land in Pampa, first sharecropping it but later deciding to simply let it "rest." Pedro's coca fields, and probably some involvement in coca paste processing and marketing, had earned him and his family handsome rewards. In 1984 Pedro and his grown sons and daughters, now reputed to be wealthy persons (*q"apaq runas*), had moved back to Pampa. They continued, however, to travel back and forth to the Chapare. In Pampa Pedro spurned the opportunity to plant enough land in potatoes—Pampa's consumption staple—for his household's needs, preferring instead to purchase potatoes from neighbors or buy them in nearby communities. Pampa's communal gatherings (*asambleas*), a symbol of community cohesion and identity, were disdained by Pedro's sons. They also expressed little interest in inheriting Pedro's land in Pampa. Pedro and his family had rebuilt their home in Pampa and by 1984 were the owners of two trucks and one small Datsun car. By mid-1985 Pedro's eldest son, like Adriano, had plans to travel to Brazil to buy another truck.

Chapter 5

Mobility and Access to Land

In peasant communities economic livelihood generally anchors on access to land, water, and labor. The different ways in which Pampeños access and mobilize labor is explored in chapter 7. This chapter focuses on Pampa's land tenure system, especially the reallocation of usufruct rights to land and water in Pampa sparked by the absence of large numbers of community members, whose major mode of livelihood was centered in the Chapare. In the first section I describe the structure of landholdings in Pampa in the mid-1980s and the different mechanisms through which these landholdings were acquired. I then examine the major norms structuring access to land and water and the various categories of land that intersected with different modes of transmitting property rights and provide a brief historical backdrop of the contexts within which these probably emerged. I turn then to the intersection of access to land and outmigration. The third section focuses on the different ways that outmigration has enabled some Pampeños to accumulate significant amounts of land and, in particular, the ways in which individuals maneuvered around norms and expectations in order to gain access to this land. Finally, I emphasize how intense outmigration, Pampa's strategic position on the Cochabamba-Chapare road, and the presence of wealthy Chapare migrants were beginning to undermine traditional modes of accessing land. We shall see in chapter 8 that these pressures toward an incipient land market, only embryonic in the mid-1980s, had greatly intensified by 1991.

The Structure of Landholdings

After the agrarian reform Pampa's landowner retained ownership of virtually all her desmesne land. Her tenant households were awarded 561 hectares of cultivable crop land (the landowner lost 10 hectares of sharecropped land), or an average of 3.5 hectares for each household. All but two households were assured of both irrigated and rain-fed croplands. In the 1970s Pampa's former landowner sold off part of her land to Pampeños and all of her remaining cultivated land by late 1991 (see chap. 8).

By 1984, 142 households with 830 members, representing 56 percent of all households in Pampa, had access to 360 hectares of land, 225 (63 percent) of which were cultivable. Each household, then, had an average of 2.5 hectares but only 1.6 hectares of cultivable land, or less than one-half that of the average household 30 years earlier. On the average each Pampeño had access to less than one-third of a hectare of cultivable land (table 5.1).

By the mid-1980s land obtained through agrarian reform land grants was still the predominant mode of access to land in Pampa, followed by inheritance (table 5.2). State land grants accounted for just over 56 percent of all land held by the sample households. Almost one-third of the land held was obtained through inheritance, while land purchases accounted for only 8 percent. Permanent sharecropping rights, such as that over land still owned by the former landlord or jurally held by permanent migrants, constituted just over ten hectares (almost 3 percent of all land).

There was also in Pampa a marked inequality in the distribution of

TABLE 5.1   Access to Land by 142 Households and 830 Household Members, in Hectares

	Average Amount of Land	Average Amount of Cultivable Land
Household	2.50	1.60
Household Member	0.43	0.27

Source: Field data, 1984. The amount of land totaled 360 hectares. Cultivable land amounted to 225.4 hectares.

TABLE 5.2   Landholdings of 142 Households by Type of Access, in Hectares

Type of Access	Cultivable	Noncultivable	Total	Percentage of Total
State Grant	119.5	82.8	202.3	56.2
Inheritance	75.5	42.2	117.7	32.7
Purchase	21.6	8.1	29.7	8.3
Sharecropping	8.8	1.5	10.3	2.8
Total	225.4	134.6	360.0	100.0
Percentage of Total	62.6	37.4	100.0	100.0

Source: Field data, 1984.

land (see table 5.3). Forty households (28.2 percent of the sample) with 1.0 hectare or less of land controlled 19.2 hectares, or just over 5 percent of the total land area. At the other extreme 29 households (slightly over one-fifth of the sample) with 4.0 or more hectares controlled 152.1 hectares, or over 42 percent of total land. Furthermore, the members of households with 4.0 or more hectares of land had, on the average, access to nine times as much land as household members with 1.0 hectare or less of land. The Gini coefficient of inequality measured 0.37, indicating substantial but not extreme inequality in access to land (C. L. Smith 1991).

The marked disparity in access to land can also be underscored by comparing the household head with access to the least land with the one controlling the most land: the former had a mere 667 square meters, while the largest landholding household head controlled 16 hectares—or over 200 times as much land. As we shall see, the household head with these 16 hectares managed to accumulate this much land in large measure as a result of the migration of other Pampeños to the Chapare. I mentioned earlier (chap. 4) that most early migrants to the Chapare were unable to acquire state land grants in Pampa after the agrarian reform. Many others, however, were former *pefaleros* and hacienda *kurakas* who has amassed considerable land after the agrarian reform and who spearheaded the colonization efforts and also obtained prized plots of land in the Chapare. This, coupled with the fact that by the 1980s most households in Pampa had migrant members in Chapare, most of them with land there, and the absence of excessive fragmentation of state land grants, belies a neat view of migrants as a class of landless Pampeños and of nonmigrants as consisting primarily of those with large landholdings in Pampa.

In fact, the differences in landholdings between migrant and nonmigrant households were not strikingly significant. For example, on the average migrant households had 2.31 hectares of land in Pampa compared to 3.0 hectares held by nonmigrant households. And, like their nonmigrant counterparts, a substantial amount of the land held by migrant households consisted of virtually intact agrarian reform state land grants (table 5.4).

Average household landholdings, however, conceal important differences. For example, migrant households were often larger and younger, and their per capita access to land in Pampa was far less than that of nonmigrants. On the average a migrant household member had about a third of a hectare of land in Pampa compared with over half a hectare by nonmigrants. By and large, most younger and larger migrant households had far less land than older (migrant and nonmigrant) households (table 5.5).

Furthermore, a significant number of these young migrant households with the least land in Pampa had obtained most of it through small shares of inheritance and had purchased little or no land. Moreover, the amount of land passed on to many young household heads via anticipatory inheritance varied considerably but was often quite small: often from 667 to 2,000 square meters of irrigated land and 1,334 to 3,335 square meters of rain-fed fields. In general, it is these younger migrants with access to a scant amount of land in Pampa who oftentimes also had tenuous access to land in Chapare and who were specializing in coca cultivation (see chap. 4). Interestingly enough, all migrant households, regardless of the stage in their developmental cycle and whether or not they held secure access to land in the Chapare, had on the average

TABLE 5.3   Land Distribution among 142 Households by Landholding Categories, in Hectares

Landholding Range	No. of Households	Average Household Landholding	Per-Capita Land	Total Land	Percentage of Total Land
< = 1	40	0.48	.09	19.2	5.3
+ 1 – 2	19	1.50	.26	28.7	8.0
+ 2 – 3	23	2.40	.39	55.6	15.4
+ 3 – 4	31	3.30	.62	100.8	28.0
+ 4	29	5.40	.81	155.7	43.3
Total	142			360.0	100.0

Source: Field data, 1984.

TABLE 5.4   Landholdings of 142 Households by Migrant Status and Type of Access

Type of Access	Migrant (n=94)		Nonmigrant (n=48)		Total Hectares
	Hectares	Average	Hectares	Average	
State grant	116.1	1.20	86	1.80	202.0
Inheritance	78.7	0.84	39	0.81	117.5
Purchase	17.7	0.19	12	0.25	30.0
Sharecropping	4.5	0.05	6	0.13	10.5
Total	217.0	2.31	143	3.00	360.0

Source: Field data, 1983.

TABLE 5.5 Landholdings, Household Size, and Average Age of 142 Migrant (n=94) and Nonmigrant (n=48) Households

Land-holding Range	Migrants				Nonmigrants			
	No. of Households	Percentage of Households	Average Household Size	Average Age of Household Members	No. of Households	Percentage of Households	Average Household Size	Average Age of Household Members
< = 1	31	33	5.5	16.6	9	19	5.4	23.7
+1 – 2	15	16	6.4	20.3	4	8	4.1	49.1
+2 – 3	15	16	7.5	21.6	8	17	4.1	40.4
+3 – 4	17	18	6.4	28.1	14	29	5.1	31.7
+4	16	17	6.7	23.5	13	27	7.0	31.1

Source: Field data, 1984.

access to about the same amount of land in Pampa. Migrants with land in the Chapare had acquired less of their land in Pampa through inheritance but had purchased more of it than migrant households lacking Chapare land plots (table 5.6).

Elder migrant households with far more land in Pampa—invariably agrarian reform land grant households that had obtained plots of land in the Chapare during the early stages of migration—were, on the average, purchasing more land in Pampa. Moreover, their patterns of access to land in Pampa bore more resemblance to their nonmigrant counterparts with similar amounts of land: the greater part of the land held through state land grants and a higher percentage of land purchased.

Land Tenure and Migration

Pampa's land tenure system, the complex array of (unwritten) rules, expectations, and obligations that structure access to and transmission of usufruct rights to crucial resources, especially land and irrigation water, did not emerge after the agrarian reform but, rather, long preceded it. How and in what contexts this "grid of customs and controls" (Thompson 1976:337) structuring access to land and water emerged in Bolivian (and other Andean) hacienda communities is as yet poorly understood. Nevertheless, recent social historical and anthropological research points to the fact that hacienda owners were not all-powerful and omnipotent and that their peasants not only had access to land but

TABLE 5.6   Landholdings in Pampa by Migrant Households (N=94) with and without Land in the Chapare

Type of Access	With Land in Chapare (N=66)		Without Land in Chapare (N=28)		Total Hectares
	Hectares	Average	Hectares	Average	
State Grant	82.9	1.30	33.2	1.20	116.1
Inheritance	47.8	0.72	30.9	1.10	78.7
Purchase	16.9	0.26	0.8	0.03	17.7
Sharecropping	4.5	0.07	0	0	4.5
Total	152.1	2.30	64.9	2.32	217.0

Source: Field data, 1984.

also exerted considerable control over the land they cultivated. Under-lying and bolstering this control over land were shared understandings, established norms of reciprocity, and mutual rights and obligations guar-anteeing peasants (landed peasants such as Pampa's *pefaleros*) a means of livelihood and sense of economic security. Hacienda owners who attempted to undermine these agreed upon norms faced the prospects of mass uprisings, court suits, and a serious threat to hacienda production (Langer 1985, 1990; for Peru, see Webster 1981; Orlove 1977b:90-91; Deere 1990:87-91). Property rights and their specific modes of trans-mission within the peasant class in Pampa and other Cochabamba ha-ciendas probably emerged long before the agrarian reform in this context of structural limitations to landowner control and, as we shall see, in-corporated typically Andean and non-Andean cultural elements.[1]

In a path-breaking paper titled "Closed Corporate Peasant Com-munities [CCPC] in Mesoamerica and Central Java," Eric Wolf (1957) pointed to the presence of analogous socioeconomic and cultural forms in peasant communities widely separated in space and time:

> They are similar in that they maintain a body of rights to possessions, such as land. They are similar because both put pressures on members to redistribute surpluses at their command, preferably in the oper-ation of a religious system, and induce them to content themselves with the rewards of a "shared poverty." They are similar in that they strive to prevent outsiders from becoming members of the com-munity, and in placing limits on the ability of members to com-municate with the larger society. That is to say, in both areas they are corporate organizations, maintaining a perpetuity of rights and membership; and they are closed corporations, because they limit these privileges to insiders, and discourage close participation of members in the social relations of the larger society. (Wolf 1957:2)

Two intersecting rules defining community membership and delimiting the transfer of usufruct rights to land and water to community members crystallized in Pampa after the agrarian reform; both paralleled key dimensions of Wolf's CCPC model.[2] The first was that former tenants who acquired state land grants (*dotados*) were classed, along with their spouses, as community members (Pampeños), regardless of their place of birth. (The rationale underlying this rule seems to have been to reward those who had "served" the landowner, participated in communal works, and eked out a living in Pampa.) At this point consanguinity surfaced as a necessary condition of community membership as *dotados* transmitted membership rights to their descendants living at the time in Pampa, who in turn would transmit them to future offspring born in Pampa. Although all Pampeños who enjoyed usufruct rights to land during my fieldwork period could trace genealogical linkages to at least one former tenant, or *colono*, patrifiliation and not descent (cf. Scheffler 1985, 1986) has structured the transmission of land tenure rights within the peasant class since at least the agrarian reform.

The second rule established that peasants who abandoned Pampa prior to the agrarian reform of 1952, regardless of their consanguineal or affinal affiliations with present-day Pampeños, were not and could not become community members (i.e., Pampeños). Hence, neither they nor their future offspring were entitled to claim access to community resources and could not become voting members of the *sindicato*.[3] This was the most crucial land tenure rule in Pampa and one that lent the community its "corporate" character. Yet, as we shall see, this powerful communal ideology against the transfer of usufruct rights to land and water to noncommunity members (non-Pampeños) was not sufficient to block land purchases by noncommunity members by the mid- to late 1980s.

Within the broad parameters of the above two rules, there were six specific ways of obtaining access to usufruct rights in Pampa in the mid-1980s: inheritance, sharecropping, purchase, exchange or permutation (*canje*), rental, and an exchange of labor for the right to harvest a furrow of land (*tarpuja*).[4] The first three were the principal means of gaining access to land in Pampa (and, in the case of irrigated crop lands, irrigation water as well).[5]

Several norms structured inheritance in Pampa. The most important, yet perhaps the least followed, rule stressed the bilateral inheritance of land. A closely related rule stressed that only legitimate offspring could inherit land from their father and both *naturales* and legitimate children from their mother.[6] That is, while all legitimate sons and daughters were entitled to an equal share of cultivable land from both father and mother, illegitimate children could only inherit land from their mothers, who, in a typically Andean fashion (Silverblatt 1987:119–24, 219; Spalding 1984:27; Zulawski 1990; J. Collins 1986a:658; Isbell 1978:78–79; Mallon 1983:28), independently maintained and transmitted usufruct rights to land they had inherited (from either mother or father), purchased, or otherwise acquired.[7]

In reality bilateral inheritance was an ideal often not achieved. Sons and not daughters were usually the first to inherit cultivable land, and often the latter did not inherit land at all or received just a token inheritance. More important, inheritance norms were rooted in the pre-agrarian reform period, in an economic and social matrix in which access to and cultivation of land in Pampa insured and was an absolute requirement for a minimum of economic security. Hence, inheritance rights were jealously defended, for they impinged on survival itself, and disputes over usufruct rights to land (and irrigation water) were an almost everyday occurrence.

To a greater or lesser extent this context remained constant up to and during the state-sponsored colonization efforts in the late 1950s: for instance, until recently most Pampeños had engaged in seasonal and not permanent migration and maintained usufruct rights to and continued cultivating land in Pampa.

In the mid-1980s coca boom this context no longer held true. The decline of crop production in Pampa (see chap. 6), land fragmentation, the progressive replacement of seasonal by permanent migration, and the possibilities of accumulation of wealth outside of Pampa's boundaries were intimately related to newly evolving inheritance patterns.

For many young and successful Pampeño migrants deeply engaged in cultivating coca and (some) in the processing of its by-products in the Chapare, tilling land in Pampa was no longer crucial for their economic survival. As a result, some were not pressing claims for their share of inheritance. Their lack of interest in anticipatory inheritance occurred mainly with rain-fed, high-altitude crop lands, which were said to be "too far away" or "not worth the trouble [to plant]." A good example of one of these young migrants who did not press for his inheritance is Federico. Federico, two of his brothers, and his father controlled 120 hectares of land in the Chapare colonies of Chimoré, Ichilo, and Isiboro, and they were quite wealthy. In 1984 he set up his own household and bought himself a small car. In that same year his two brothers, both with coca land in the Chapare, were each owners of a truck. Neither Federico nor his two brothers claimed their share of anticipatory inheritance from their father. I once asked Federico why he had not asked his father to "give him" land once he set up his own household, as had been the case with some other young household heads.

Laughing, he responded, "What for?" quickly adding that he "worked very little" in Pampa. He did, however, "help" his elderly father, who rarely traveled to the Chapare, to plant a "few potatoes." Federico claimed to assist his father by sometimes providing him with cash to buy fertilizers and dung and supplying him with rice and other lowland crops (such as cassava) for consumption.

Migrants also ran the risk of losing their inheritance rights. Although most Pampeños stated that prolonged absence from Pampa would not necessarily result in the loss of inheritance, returning migrants could not always be assured of quick and easy access to their land, especially if they had been away from Pampa for prolonged periods of time. For example, a migrant's siblings might have worked his land in his absence. The investment of their labor could effectively force the returnee to petition (*reclamar*) the *sindicato* to allow him to regain control of his share of inheritance. Migrants could confront other difficulties in securing access to property rights. Pampeños wishing to inherit land were obligated to bury (*p'ampay*) the person from whom the land was to be inherited—usually a son or brother of the deceased—and pay part of the funeral expenses.[8]

Prolonged absence from Pampa and the failure to participate in the required funeral rituals and obligations could result in a loss of inheritance rights. For example, one young Pampeño living in Santa Cruz in the 1970s when his father (a *dotado*) died in Pampa was unable to help bury his father and therefore claim his share of inheritance. He did not attend his father's funeral and participate in the obligatory funerary rituals, as he received the news of his father's death four weeks after the fact. (He claimed that his brothers maliciously withheld news of his father's death so he would not be able to participate in these rituals.) His mother and brothers refused to allot him his share of the inheritance, claiming that he had not fulfilled his "obligations" to his father. By 1985 he had yet to receive his share of inheritance.

In addition, migrants with land in the Chapare and/or land plots in Pampa and attempting to lay claim to their shares of inheritance could face strong resistance from less wealthy brothers or half-brothers. For example, Julián had three sons, two who received land grants after the agrarian reform and were therefore ineligible to inherit land from him (his third son died in La Paz before the agrarian reform). When Julián passed away his entire *dotación* was inherited by Rosenda, a daughter. Rosenda had four children, one of them with Andrógenes, her husband.

Two of Rosenda's illegitimate sons had permanently settled in the Chapare in the early 1970s, while the child she bore with Andrógenes later died. When Rosenda died her land grant, inherited from Julián, passed on to Samuel, her only living (and "illegitimate") son in Pampa. Samuel was not recognized by Andrógenes, his stepfather, but by Isidro, his "natural" father. By this time Samuel had married, inherited his mother's land, purchased land from the *propietaria,* and was sharecropping several plots of coca land in the Chapare. His half-brothers (offspring of Isidro) consequently argued that Samuel did not "need" any more land and pressured Isidro to refuse Samuel's claim to the inheritance of his land.

Sharecropping was widespread and occured primarily on prized irrigated fields in the lower crop zones. Typically, one party provided land and water, the other seed, dung, and fertilizer, and both contributed labor and equally shared the harvest. Most sharecropping arrangements were limited to one agricultural season. The transmission of sharecropping rights to land still owned by Pampa's former landowner closely paralleled inheritance. With the exception of land still owned by Pampa's former landowner, no formal restrictions barred noncommunity members from sharecropping land in Pampa.[9]

The sharecropping out of land had always been a favorite strategy of migrants away from Pampa for considerable periods of time. For example, the members of the 20 agrarian reform land-grant households who migrated to Santa Cruz between 1959 and 1979 (see chap. 4) were unable to continue cultivating their land in Pampa. Some household reportedly left their land fallow, others "exchanged" usufruct rights, while a few sold off their entire land grants. Most, however, opted for sharecropping their land in Pampa. Their sharecroppers were invariably close consanguineal or affinal kin who had remained behind: siblings, uncles, cousins, and in-laws. The strategy of sharecropping out their land was advantageous, for it allowed migrants to reclaim their land in Pampa at any time, thereby providing themselves security in the event that things did not turn out as expected in Yapacaní. One representative example of these sharecropping arrangements was that undertaken by Silverino, who lived in Yapacaní between 1965 and 1975. During the first five years that Silverino was in Yapacaní his land in Pampa was worked by Cecilio, his father-in-law. In the following five years his land was worked by Leopoldino, Silverino's brother-in-law. In late 1975 Silverino sold his land in Yapacaní, regained access to his land in Pampa, and subsequently acquired a plot of land in the Chapare.

The sharecropping out of land before and during the coca boom was also a favorite strategy by migrants who had not permanently settled in the Chapare. For migrants heavily involved in Chapare commodity production sharecropping their land in Pampa offered distinct advantages. Sharecroppers usually furnished dung and fertilizers, and the owner of the land provided irrigation water (and sometimes labor). Hence, the ever-rising costs of production in a period of hyperinflation were shifted to and assumed by the sharecropper. Moreover, since wealthy and successful migrants no longer viewed crop production in Pampa as essential to their economic well-being, sharecropping permitted them to concentrate time, effort, and resources on lucrative coca production while assuring themselves of a potato crop for consumption.

Some sharecropping arrangements between migrants and others in Pampa appeared very much like a transitional phase toward a permanent alienation of land. This was particularly the case of migrants, like Eufenio, who lived almost permanently in the Chapare. Eufenio had not lived in Pampa on a continuous basis since 1966, when he first acquired a land grant in Yapacaní. After only a few years he left Yapacaní for the Chapare, where he also obtained a land grant. Ever since then his brother Angel has been sharecropping his land in Pampa. Yet Angel retained for himself the entirety of the harvest from the land. Angel insisted that he was the "owner" of the land since Eufenio had "given" it to him, despite the fact that the legal titles are still in Eufenio's name. Clearly what had been given was not the land per se but, rather, the right to cultivate it and the control over its production.

While the sharecropping of land was widespread in Pampa by late 1984, some migrants were having second thoughts about their sharecropping agreements. In large measure this was because of the new agrarian reform law being debated in Congress. Many Pampeños believed that the law would abolish or at least seriously restrict sharecropping arrangements and award sharecroppers permanent rights to the land they worked. Some Pampeños took this perceived threat quite seriously. One migrant who spent most of his time in the Chapare during the previous 10 years had allowed his land to be sharecropped. During my fieldwork in Pampa he reclaimed his land and rescinded his sharecropping agreement, claiming that the sharecropper "wanted to keep the land" (*se quiso quedar con la tierra*). Another migrant had not cultivated his single plot of land in Pampa (one-half hectare of rain-fed land) for 10 or 12 years prior to my arrival. But he also refused to sharecrop it, fearing that he would eventually lose his rights over his land to a sharecropper.[10]

Another means of accessing productive resources in Pampa was *canje*, a temporary but sometimes permanent swap, or exchange, of usufruct rights to land and irrigation water and sometimes labor as well. (In Aymara-speaking communities in Puno, Peru, this practice is known as *uraqipir turkasiña* [M. Painter 1991:82].) While *canje* of usufruct rights usually occurred within Pampa and occasionally between Pampa and migrant colonies in Santa Cruz and the Chapare, the most important point is that it was one mechanism for accessing land in Pampa that surfaced exclusively in the context of intense migration, and only Pampeños could enter into *canje* agreements. A few cases of temporary *canje* of rights to land between Pampa and the Chapare occurred before the 1980s coca boom. None were permanent exchanges, all took place between Pampeños, and most lasted about a year. A typical *canje* of usufruct rights to land would consist of a Pampeño without land in the Chapare exchanging part of his (usually irrigated) land in Pampa in return for a small plot of coca land. For instance, in the early 1970s one Pampeño secured one *cato* of coca land in the Chapare in return for the use of about 2,000 square meters of irrigated crop land in Pampa. These and similar transactions differed from sharecropping in that both parties were entitled to the entire harvest of the newly accessed land. A slightly different variant of this type of *canje* occurred when usufruct rights to land were exchanged for irrigation water. A migrant with land in the Chapare but with an insufficient supply of irrigation water in Pampa would enter in a *canje* agreement with someone in an inverse position, that is, with access to adequate irrigation water in Pampa but with no land, especially coca land, in the Chapare.

The 1980s coca boom, and specifically the high returns to coca cultivation, effectively put a halt to these complementary highland-lowland exchanges of usufruct rights to productive resources. It did, however, set in motion what seemed to be an increase in *canje* exchanges within Pampa itself. The absence of large numbers of Pampeños from Pampa led to many opportunities for temporary exchanges of rights to factors of production—irrigation water, land, and labor. In Pampa *canje* almost always involved access to irrigation water and migrants curtailing crop production but who refused to sharecrop their land. These temporary arrangements, viewed by both parties as highly desirable and advantageous, strongly resembled sharecropping transactions in that both parties provided each other with some factor of production that the other lacked.

One type of *canje* consisted of a temporary exchange of irrigation water and labor. An example was that of my assistant, who, lacking permanent land rights, would exchange one or two days of his labor for a daily allocation of water to irrigate his sharecropped fields. The other party (invariably a migrant) would "collect" the labor due at some other point in time. These and similar transactions were also called *ayni* and "purchase" of irrigation water.

Pampeños had always been permitted to purchase small allotments of irrigation water from neighbors and kin and pay for this in cash. While many nonmigrants were willing and able to continue paying in cash for their irrigation water, by 1984 migrants preferred to receive crops (usually potatoes) in lieu of cash. Such exchanges—essentially a reversion from cash transactions to barter in kind—were also called "*canje* of water." For example, during the 1984 *mishka* potato planting season (and for the third straight season) Enrique, a nonmigrant with considerable land in Pampa, "bought" five days of irrigation water from a migrant at the rate of one-half sack (*carga*) of potatoes per day. (He also claimed to know of 10 or 12 other migrants who were selling or exchanging portions of their water allotments.) Most Pampeños with access to large plots of land and an adequate supply of water usually did not engage in this type of *canje*. As expected, *canje* of water did not occur in times of severe drought (as in 1982–83).[11]

An Incipient Land Market

Land can be and was sold in Pampa (irrigated crop land was usually sold with its corresponding irrigation water allotment). Nevertheless, private property rights, in which land had been transformed into a commodity freely circulating according to supply and demand, did not exist in Pampa. A land sale required the unanimous approval of the *sindicato*. Pampeños and non-Pampeños alike faced numerous restrictions in selling and purchasing land. One important norm stated that Pampeños wishing to sell their land should first offer it to siblings and then to close kin. The most important and jealously defended norm, however, was that cultivable land could never be sold to non-Pampeños.

We saw that relatively little land had been purchased in Pampa by the mid-1980s (see table 5.2). This was due to a variety of reasons. One was that almost all Pampeños migrating to the Chapare had retained jural control of their land in Pampa and also simply that most Pampeños (migrants or nonmigrants) had no desire to sell their land. But another reason that partly accounted for the scarcity of land sales and purchases in Pampa during the mid-1980s was the low returns and high input costs of agriculture in Pampa compared to high returns in coca cultivation. For most Pampeños purchasing and investing in cultivable land in Pampa was simply not a viable economic alternative. This can be illustrated by the attempts of Pampa's former landowner to sell off her land in Pampa in 1984.

In the late 1970s Pampa's former landowner sold almost all her crop land to Pampeños. Most of these sales consisted of small plots of land, often not larger than one-third of a hectare. The largest purchases (from three to six hectares apiece), however, were undertaken by those who had formed part of the wealthy peasant elite before the agrarian reform— the *pefaleros* and the hacienda's *kurakas*. By 1984 the former landowner's holdings in Pampa had fallen from about 153 hectares just after the agrarian reform to about 9 hectares. Seven of these 9 hectares consisted of rocky, uncultivable land covered by eucalyptus trees and pastures, and two were sharecropped.

In late 1984 the landowner returned to Pampa intent on selling her remaining land in Pampa. Pampeños learned of her upcoming visit long before her arrival. Many Pampeños, but particularly some of her share-croppers, seemed genuinely excited about and interested in purchasing the land they had sharecropped, at least until they learned its price. For land currently cultivated under sharecropping arrangements the land-owner asked for U.S. $1 dollar per square meter (U.S. $10,000 per hectare) and U.S. $1,500 for each hectare of rocky and uncultivable land.

A decade earlier Pampa's former landowner encountered little difficulty in selling off most of her land. By late 1984 the overall context had drastically changed. The price she requested for her land was extraordinarily high relative to the low price that one sack of potatoes fetched in the local market, the average cash wage of less than one dollar per day, or the high returns that Pampeño migrants could obtain from coca commodity production. Her crop fields, moreover, were considered "tired" (*cansadas*), and Pampeños balked at the prospects of paying such a high price for crop fields that required ever greater inputs of chemical fertilizers and dung to maintain production levels. But perhaps the greatest obstacle that the landowner encountered in Pampa was the belief by her "Indians" (as she still referred to Pampeños) that available cash could be better invested in other ways, such as in consumer goods, vehicles, etc., that provided an effective hedge against runaway inflation.

By the time of my departure only one Pampeño—my assistant who lacked permanent access to land in Pampa—agreed to buy the land he was sharecropping. The parcel he bought measured about 2,300 square meters. He was able to come up with only U.S. $200 in cash (a good part of this came from the local anthropologist) of the U.S. $2,300 he owed the landowner. Significantly, the remaining U.S. $2,100 was forwarded to him (in U.S. dollars) as a loan by Adriano, the wealthy migrant I have referred to previously (see chap. 4). Adriano's condition for loaning this money was that one-half of all crop harvests from that land be turned over to him until the loan was repaid. Five years later, however, Pampeños and other migrants from surrounding communities purchased from the former landowner almost all her remaining cultivated land in Pampa (see chap. 8).

Although a small, yet growing number of migrant households had accumulated considerable wealth, a process of land accumulation by the outright purchase of land grants had not taken hold in Pampa. Some purchases of agrarian reform land did take place in Pampa. Yet with only two exceptions were entire agrarian reform land grants sold in Pampa. Both took place well before the 1980s coca boom and between close kin. These involved members of two of the three land grant households which were among the first to migrate to and obtain land grants in Yapacaní (Santa Cruz) but who never returned to Pampa. In the first case Rafael, who arrived in Yapacaní in mid-1962, sold his *dotación* in Pampa to his younger brother Sabino. Hernández, also one of the first household heads to arrive with his family in Yapacaní, sold his land grant to his nephew Edgar. Edgar bought Hernández's land in 1980 after having sharecropped it for over sixteen years.

Ten purchases of agrarian reform land plots between 1974 and 1983 are recorded in Cochabamba's office of Derechos Reales.[12] All buyers were Pampeños and eight of these purchases took place between close kin. The largest purchase involved 4.5 hectares while the smallest a mere 300.0 square meters. Eight of the ten buyers purchased land that they probably would have inherited. In fact, the purchase and sale of land among close (and sometimes migrant) kin was not indicative of an open land market in Pampa but, rather, reflected a consistent strategy of consolidating access to land in the face of future potential counterclaims by other kin.

A few examples suffice to illustrate this pattern of land sales among kin and the strategy of consolidating access to land. In 1980 Edgar sold to his son a plot of land (of unknown acreage) to which he had had access for several years. Less than three years later Edgar's son, who had by now begun migrating to the Chapare, sold the same plot of land to Gerónimo, his brother-in-law. Likewise, Víctor, an elderly *dotado* with no surviving children, sold to his adopted son two small plots of land to which he would have been entitled anyway, according to pre-existing rules of inheritance. However, Víctor's son was also a *dotado*, which, given the rule that agrarian reform land grantees should give up their share of inheritance in favor of those who did not receive land, may have cast some doubt on the validity of his claim to inheritance. In one relatively large land purchase that took place in 1974, and one in which migration played an important role, Rosano bought three hectares of land from Valentina, his sister-in-law, whose husband, Hernández, had just passed away (Valentina and Hernández had no living children at the time of this sale.) Hernández had had a land grant in Yapacaní, where he lived from 1958 to 1960. Afterward, like many other Pampeños, he acquired a land grant in the Chapare. He moved there permanently with Valentina in 1980. Valentina was still permanently residing in the Chapare when I arrived in Pampa.

The largest land sale, however, occurred in 1980, when Francisco bought from his father-in-law Primitivo his entire agrarian reform land grant (four and one-half hectares of land) shortly before he passed away. Francisco's wife was Primitivo's only child living in Pampa, had "taken care" of him during his latter years, and no doubt would have inherited her father's land. It is important to note that, despite the fact that the legal title to Primitivo's land was in Francisco's name, it was understood that Primitivo's land "belonged" to his daughter and not Francisco.

I previously mentioned that the most important norm restricting land purchases in Pampa was that cultivable land could not be sold, under any circumstances, to noncommunity members. Although field-work, informal interviewing, and a perusal of land transactions in Derechos Reales failed to uncover purchases of cultivable land by outsiders and a violation of this cardinal norm, some evidence pointed to the fact that the political and economic context within which migration to the Chapare was taking place was slowly undermining the important precept that had until then restricted permanent access to land by noncommunity members.

In late 1984 a serious and potentially explosive situation surfaced in

Pampa, when it was learned that Almaquio, a rich migrant with land grants in both Pampa and the Chapare, agreed to sell part of his rain-fed crop land in the Tuty crop zone to a *compadre*, a non-Pampeño. Almaquio and three of his sons that made up his household each had a land grant in a Chapare colony, a total of 90 hectares of land. *Sindicato* authorities were outraged when they heard of this upcoming land sale and convened an emergency meeting of the *sindicato* membership to deal with this potentially serious transgression. During this meeting Almaquio argued that he had been forced to sell his land as he was unable to repay a loan from the Agricultural Bank. To offset the possibility of forfeiting his land to the bank, Almaquio claimed, he borrowed money from his *compadre* to pay off his bank loan. In return, Almaquio agreed to his *compadre*'s demand that he sell to him the land in question. There was no other way, argued Almaquio, to prevent the bank from foreclosing on his land. The *sindicato* membership questioned Almaquio's reasons— it was well known that he was quite wealthy and had plans to purchase a large truck—and demanded that he rescind the agreement with his *compadre*. Almaquio blatantly refused, claiming that the land was "his" to sell. This first meeting ended in a deadlock.

Tempers also flared during the second meeting that convened several weeks later. Almaquio, flanked by close kin (but not by his *compadre*), continued insisting that the land was "his" to do with as he pleased. In view of Almaquio's defiance the membership, in an angry shouting match, decided that he should forfeit his potato harvest. Dozens of Pampeños then happily trekked their way to his land and proceeded in a festive mood to systematically harvest and appropriate his potato crop. The third and final meeting some weeks later quickly came to an end after the *sindicato* threatened to expropriate and redistribute Almaquio's land if he did not rescind the agreement with his *compadre*. Almaquio quickly agreed to do so, but only after angrily accusing *sindicato* authorities of behaving as bosses and landowners (*patrones*).

It is not at all clear why Almaquio planned to sell his land to his *compadre*. If, as apparently was the case, he had accumulated enough wealth to seriously consider buying a truck, he would not have needed a loan from his *compadre* to pay off the bank loan. Furthermore, his claim that the Agricultural Bank would have foreclosed on his land was quite improbable given the degree of communal cohesion that effectively barred outside interference in internal community affairs, particularly in issues related to land.

Nevertheless, several implications are clear from this example. It appears that an incipient trend undermining a major norm structuring access to cultivable land (i.e., that noncommunity members cannot gain access to this land) had surfaced in Pampa. Yet this norm was still considered sufficiently important to uphold. In addition, wealthy migrants such as Almaquio evidently reached a stage in their careers in which the significance they attached to lowland productive investments and activities far outstripped those in Pampa itself. Almaquio's decision to sell his part of his land in Pampa could, in effect, be interpreted as an attempt to transfer wealth to high-yielding investments in the Chapare. Facing communal ire, and the risk of communal control over his land, was a gamble that Almaquio was partly willing to take.

The incipient erosion of norms structuring access to agrarian reform cultivable land was also taking place with pueblo land plots. When Pampa's pueblo was built in the late 1960s non-Pampeños were strictly forbidden to purchase land plots there. By the mid-1980s, however, and despite the fact that I was repeatedly told by some Pampeños that *ajenos* could not purchase pueblo land plots, some *ajeno* migrants living in the pueblo had in fact recently begun purchasing them. A house and land plot in the pueblo was highly prized by Pampeños because of its proximity to the Cochabamba-Chapare road. But they were especially sought after by non-Pampeño migrants from surrounding communities further removed from the road and who, by living in the pueblo, would have had easy and quick access to the Chapare.

The price of pueblo land was very high and had increased in absolute terms since the late 1960s. While the price of a typical 240-meter land plot in the late 1960s was U.S. $500, or U.S. $2 per square meter, its price in the mid-1980s was far higher. The rise in pueblo land prices was due to several interrelated factors such as rampant inflation and the "dollarization" of the regional economy. But the demand for these land plots by wealthy migrants, and their ability and willingness to offer large amounts of cash for them, undoubtedly also drove up land prices. For example, one non-Pampeño migrant was asking U.S. $3,500 (or over U.S. $14 per square meter) for a *lote* he had purchased the previous year. Another Pampeño was offered the equivalent of U.S. $2,000 for his *lote* by a migrant from an adjoining community. Interested buyers or sellers of pueblo land plots often traveled to the city of Cochabamba to inquire about the latest land values there, which were then used as a yardstick for calculating the asking price of plots of land in the pueblo.

Land plots purchased prior to and during my stay in Pampa were paid in U.S. dollars.

There was a time when all Pampeños would have insisted that non-community members would stand no chance of buying land in the pueblo. In the mid–1980s few insisted in this manner. One Pampeño even told me that "lately anyone" can be sold land in the pueblo (*últimamente a cualquiera*). This statement suggested that noncommunity members had managed to circumvent or otherwise thwart the precept that had recently blocked them from purchasing land in the pueblo and Pampeños from selling land plots to them.

At least 6 of the 13 non-Pampeño household heads in the pueblo, all Chapare migrants, purchased a pueblo land plot four or five years prior to my arrival. Others rented a house in the pueblo and were also interested in purchasing land there. The relative ease with which *ajenos* could move into Pampa and rent a house (or a room within a house) proved a bonanza for those from outlying communities far removed from the paved road to the Chapare and involved in coca production. They not only enjoyed easy access to their lowland crop lands but also the opportunity of using Pampa as a base for drying their coca leaf harvests and for easily transporting them to local markets.[13]

Ten of the twelve male *ajeno* household heads in the pueblo (including the six who had purchased land plots) were married to or living with Pampeñas or daughters of Pampeñas who had originally taken up residence in their community. Jorgelino and his young wife Orudencia, for example, young migrants who spent almost all their time in the Chapare, owned a *lote* in the pueblo. Jorgelino was born north of the *valle alto*, while Orudencia was born in the peasant community of Mayu, as was her mother Aleja. Aleja had moved into Pampa when she and Dionisio, son of a *dotado*, set up a household. They later married, and Dionisio then adopted and recognized Orudencia. Years later Jorgelino and Orudencia met in the Chapare and subsequently married. When they later decided to move into Pampa and purchase a plot of land in the pueblo, Dionisio's kin vigorously endorsed his right to purchase the land.

In other words *ajeno* household heads such as Jorge were capitalizing on past or present affinal ties to current *sindicato* members to move into and/or purchase land in the pueblo. When they petitioned the *sindicato* to buy a *lote* they confidently expected that their spouse's kin would lobby in support of their petition.

One interesting exception to this strategy was that of Geno. Geno was a widow born and raised near Cliza in the *valle alto*, and a migrant who spent almost all her time in the Chapare. In 1980 she rented a house in the pueblo. Soon afterward, and being still single, she gave birth to an illegitimate son in Pampa. Despite her lack of any kinship ties to Pampeños, Geno was permitted to purchase a *lote* in the pueblo after she made a substantial monetary contribution for the construction of the new church and donated a large amount of corn beer to the *sindicato* for the 1982 Pampa fiesta.

Despite these and undoubtedly other purchases, a commoditization of land within the confines of the pueblo had not yet taken hold. A non-Pampeño could not simply walk into Pampa and buy a plot of land in the pueblo simply by virtue of having the money to do so. He or she still needed to at least demonstrate a commitment to the welfare of the community. For instance, Geno made a public statement of her commitment to the community and willingness to abide by its norms by giving birth to a son in Pampa and contributing to the new church and the fiesta. Most of the noncommunity household heads who had moved into and/or purchased land plots in the pueblo legitimized their actions and status within the community by capitalizing on and reaffirming their affinal kinship ties with current Pampeños.

The trend toward the commoditization of land in Pampa, barely detectable at the height of the mid-1980s coca boom, accelerated in subsequent years. As we shall see in chapter 8, by the late 1980s and early 1990s noncommunity members were actively purchasing plots of land in the pueblo (and some were buying cultivable land elsewhere in Pampa), which was now expanding beyond its original boundaries. Furthermore, the all-important and deeply rooted norm restricting access to cultivable land to Pampeños had all but disappeared as noncommunity migrants also sought out and began systematically purchasing cultivable land plots.

Land Accumulation

As mentioned, with the exception of a few former *pefalero* and *kuraka* households that bought land from Pampa's landowner in the 1970s, land purchases (particularly agrarian reform land between Pampeños) have been an insignificant means of accumulating land in Pampa. Yet at the same time a few Pampeños, migrants and nonmigrants alike, encountered and followed up on various (socially sanctioned) opportunities to augment their landholdings in Pampa before and during the coca boom. This still embryonic process of land accumulation surfaced in the context of intense migration, prolonged and sometimes permanent absence of other Pampeños, a waning interest in inheritance, and a sharecropping out of land.

Though members of migrant and nonmigrant households alike accumulated land, this process was particularly pronounced among the latter. Sabino provides a particularly interesting (and the best) example of the different ways in which migration by other Pampeños allowed him to expand his control over a considerable amount of land in Pampa. Sabino was not a migrant and never traveled to the Chapare or Santa Cruz but nevertheless controlled the largest acreage of any Pampeño in Pampa.

After the agrarian reform Sabino, his three brothers (Rafael, Samuel, and Toribio), and their father were all awarded land grants. Sabino, the youngest of the four brothers, took care of and buried his father, thereby inheriting his land grant. We have seen in previous pages that about ten years later Rafael traveled to Yapacaní, never returned to Pampa, and that Sabino purchased his land grant. In the 1970s Sabino also purchased several land plots from Pampa's former landowner. Furthermore, Sabino has been in control for a number of years of another land grant—a nonkinsman who has been permanently living in the Chapare since 1978 with his entire family (and who did not leave behind in Pampa brothers or sisters). Through careful planning and different mechanisms Sabino managed to accumulate a little over 16 hectares of land, making him the largest peasant landholder in Pampa.

Some migrants also accumulated land in Pampa through several connected mechanisms, although none were as successful as Sabino. For example, Joselino's only two brothers moved to Yapacaní in the mid-1960s and never returned to Pampa. Once his father died Joselino inherited his five-hectare land grant. Andrés, Joselino's maternal uncle, also moved to Yapacaní in Santa Cruz with his entire family shortly thereafter. He remained there for a few years but then moved to and acquired land in the Chapare. While Andrés (whose brothers and sisters had by then passed away) was in Santa Cruz, his land was worked by Sabino. Andrés has lived continuously in the Chapare since 1975. Since that year Andrés's land grant in Pampa has been sharecropped by Joselino, who claims that he has by now inherited the land. The two land grants that Joselino has achieved control over as a result of the migration of close kin (that is, his brothers and his uncle Andrés) to Yapacaní totaled a little over seven hectares of land.

Another interesting case of land accumulation consisted of a permanent *canje* over land rights involving one of three migrant households that never returned to Pampa from Santa Cruz in the late 1960s (see also chap. 4). This exchange of property rights over land plots in Yapacaní and Pampa involved two brothers, Justo and José Antonio. José Antonio, but not Justo, obtained a land grant in Pampa after the agrarian reform. Several years later José Antonio's wife passed away. He then remarried and lived in his wife's community from 1955 to 1965. During these 10 years his brother Justo sharecropped José Antonio's land in Pampa. In 1965 Justo traveled to and obtained a land grant in Yapacaní but soon thereafter returned to Pampa and offered his land in Yapacaní to his brother José Antonio. In 1965 José Antonio moved to Yapacaní with his family and worked Justo's land there. Just before José Antonio died (in 1976) he agreed to a legally binding agreement wherein José Antonio and his descendants would remain legal owners of the land in Yapacaní, while Justo would retain property rights over José Antonio's land grant in Pampa. Justo's landholdings in 1984 totaled almost six and one-half hectares.

The examples of Sabino, Joselino, and a few others who amassed considerable land were definitely not, as we have previously seen, representative of other households that gained access to the land of migrants. Nor was this process widespread but was, instead, essentially limited to five or six households. As stressed in earlier pages, access to migrant lands basically consisted of the sharecropping and/or the occasional purchase here and there of tiny plots of land. Nonetheless, the examples of Sabino and Joselino are extremely relevant in that they point to the slow emergence of nonmigrant household heads willing and able to avail themselves of opportunities presented to them to accumulate land and potential wealth, opportunities generated by intense migration to the Chapare.

Chapter 6

Production and Land Use

Pampa's agricultural economy, and the economic mainstay of its population, has historically centered on the cultivation of the potato. We have seen in previous chapters that during the 1980s coca boom large numbers of Pampeños were migrating to the Chapare, many remaining there for prolonged periods of time (and sometimes permanently) and others accumulating significant wealth. How did the cultivation of the potato in Pampa fare under such a context of labor migration and commodity production? A great deal of ethnographic research has addressed the relationship between labor availability, commodity–cash crop production and subsistence cultivation. Kahn (1980:199), for example, referring to rice-producing Indonesian peasants, has stated that

> the growth and decline in peasant commodity production would directly affect the productivity of subsistence rice cultivation. As peasants became increasingly involved in the production of commodities for domestic and world markets they would devote less and less time to subsistence agriculture, often leaving subsistence cultivation to those in economically unproductive age groups. [A] labour drain of the kind hypothesized here would eventually result in less productive rice cultivation, and perhaps a total collapse of the subsistence base of the economy.

In this chapter I argue that, as Kahn has suggested for Indonesian peasants, intense labor migration and a focus toward coca cultivation in the Chapare accounted for a serious disruption in highland and valley crop production during the heyday of Bolivia's coca boom. Such an emphasis on basic food production is an imporant one in the Latin American context, where food production has drastically declined in recent decades; it is an especially relevant issue in the case of Bolivia, which, in 1987, held the dubious honor of being the third highest recipient of food aid in Latin America (Doughty 1991:148).

117

In the first two sections I outline the principal contours of agricultural, but especially potato, production in Pampa. I then pay close attention to and attempt to account for the significant variability in planting and economic strategies by migrant and nonmigrant households. In the fourth and final section I discuss the role that labor shortages played in these differing planting strategies and in the overall drop in potato cultivation.

The Agricultural Landscape

Pampa's land area totals 2,399 hectares, 33 percent of which (804 hectares) were cultivated by the early 1950s. Most of the cultivable land was rain fed. Sixty-two percent of Pampa's land area (or 1,500 hectares) consisted of high-altitude land suited mainly for grazing (*serranías*).[1]

Pampa's climate was marked by two distinct seasons. The rainy season spanned from about the end of August to mid-April, with precipitation heaviest between November and March, while little or no rain fell from about the end of April to August. While median temperatures remained fairly constant throughout the year, they often reached freezing and below-freezing levels during the winter months, and diurnal variability (the difference between maximum and minimum temperatures) was quite dramatic (see apps. 2 and 3).

Pampa's major sources of irrigation water included the lake of Kuyuq Qocha (3,635 meters elevation), two hours' walking distance from the pueblo, and seven streams.[2] In the early 1950s only 18 percent of Pampa's crop lands were irrigated, although the expansion of Kuyuq Qocha a decade later increased the amount of irrigated land. The irrigation of crop fields overlapped with the beginning and end of the dry season.[3]

Pampa's agricultural economy had historically centered on the cultivation of the potato, other tubers such as *papalisa* (*Ullucus tuberosus*) and *oca* (*Oxalis tuberosa*), and grains, root, and leguminous crops—maize, oats, wheat, barley, onions, the broad bean (*haba*), and peas—for consumption and exchange in nearby markets of Sacaba and Cochabamba. Crop fields were dispersed over three partly overlapping production zones, each offering distinct constraints and opportunities for agricultural production. As elsewhere in the Andes (cf. Troll 1968; Brush 1977b; Mayer 1985; Guillet 1983), this multilayered arrangement of crop zones allowed and encouraged complementary crop production, as environmental risks were spread out over a variety of niches, and peak labor demands distributed both within and between these zones. The agricultural calendar in Pampa spanned most of the year (fig. 5).

Pampeños distinguished three partly overlapping crop zones (from 3,050 to 3,850 meters elevation) on the basis of availability of irrigation water, gradient, altitude, temperature, and susceptibility to crop insects. Each crop zone was named after a *lugar,* or neighborhood (see chap. 2), in that zone.[4]

Colpana, the lowest crop zone, lay between 3,050 and 3,380 meters elevation. This zone, one of prized agricultural land, was well irrigated by Kuyuq Qocha and various streams. It was relatively flat and less susceptible to frost than the other two zones, although the warmer temperatures encouraged the spread of crop insects, especially during the rainy months. An added advantage of having land in Colpana was that it bordered the major paved road linking Pampa to the markets of the town of Sacaba and the city of Cochabamba. As a result, Pampeños with land in this zone spent less time and effort transporting their harvest to local markets than others with crop lands in higher (and more distant) zones.

The second zone, Chaupi Pampa, was located east-southeast of Colpana, between 3,255 and 3,530 meters elevation. Chaupi, or "middle," Pampa was not as well irrigated as Colpana. Although its slightly higher altitude entailed greater susceptibility to frost, its more rugged terrain offered a greater variety of niches, such as numerous chasms, that protected potatoes and other crops from freezing temperatures.

The major crops cultivated in the Colpana and Chaupi Pampa crop zones included potatoes, maize, wheat, barley, onions, *quinoa,* the broad bean, peas, *papalisa,* and *oca,* mostly produced for household consumption. Cabbage and carrots were sometimes sown on a few household gardens in Colpana. Crop rotation varied considerably and largely depended on whether fields were irrigated or rain fed and the particular crop zone in which they were located. On irrigated fields in Colpana and Chaupi Pampa the potato harvest was sometimes followed by the planting of broad beans, peas, maize, wheat, *oca,* or *papalisa.* Crops that sometimes directly competed for land with the potato (in the same crop season) were other tubers, such as *oca* or *papalisa,* or grains such as *quinoa.* These were grown almost exclusively for household consumption. None of the household heads I interviewed were producers of large quantities of *oca* or *papalisa,* and those with very small plots of either irrigated or rain-fed land never practiced intercropping. As a result, these secondary crops occupied only a small percentage of the land sown.

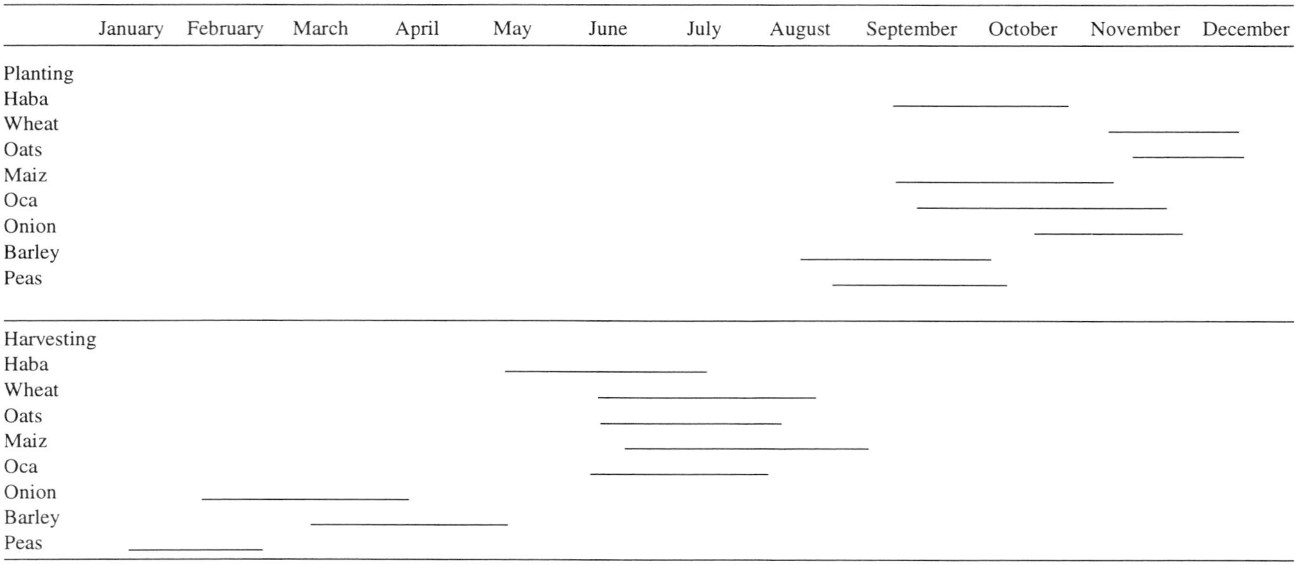

	January	February	March	April	May	June	July	August	September	October	November	December
Planting												
Haba												
Wheat									——————			
Oats										———		
Maiz									————			
Oca												
Onion										—————		
Barley								————				
Peas									———			
Harvesting												
Haba					———————							
Wheat							—————					
Oats							——————					
Maiz						————						
Oca			———									
Onion												
Barley		———										
Peas	———											

See fig. 6 for the planting and harvesting of the potato. *Source:* Field data, 1983–84.

Fig. 5.   Agricultural cycle in Pampa: planting and harvesting of major crops.

Quinoa (*Chenopodium quinoa*), only thin rows of which were sometimes planted in outer rims of the potato fields, occupied an insignificant amount of land.

Other studies in Cochabamba are consistent with these observations and also illustrate the extent to which the production of potatoes in Cochabamba overshadowed other tubers. For instance, during the 1981 season in the peasant community of Chinchiri (province of Ayopaya), 254.6 metric tons of potatoes but only 2.4 metric tons of *oca* and 450 kilograms of *papalisa* were harvested (Dandler, Anderson, León, Sage, and Torrico 1982:87; for comparable national-level data, see Ministerio de Asuntos Campesinos y Agropecuarios 1990b).

Between 3,570 and 3,850 meters elevation lay Tuty, the third and highest crop zone. Most of Pampa's *serranías* and rain-fed crop lands were located here, as was the Kuyuq Qocha irrigation lake. Few trees were present in this high, frigid zone of mostly rolling hills, at almost 4,000 meters elevation, the landscape dotted instead with shrubs and *ichu* grass. Stone and adobe huts here and there were used by Pampeños as shelters when harvesting their midwinter potato crop. Freezing temperatures, which posed the highest risks to crop production, were not uncommon. Aside from a few pockets of irrigated land bordering Kuyuq Qocha, most crop fields in Tuty were rain fed and were generally larger than in the Colpana and Chaupi Pampa crop zones. In Tuty the principal crop after the potato was oats (which was used mainly as fodder for livestock), followed by barley, wheat, *oca,* or *papalisa.* Maize, onions, peas, and the broad bean were too susceptible to the extremely cold temperatures to grow well.

Pampa's three crop zones were not perfectly demarcated zones with clearly delimited boundaries: the mountainous topography ruled out such a neat categorization of the landscape. The boundaries of the different zones blended into one another, with the high ridges of one zone partly overlapping with the lower reaches of another. For instance, though most rain-fed cultivation was carried out in Tuty, tiny plots of land bordering Kuyuq Qocha, as well as parcels of land on Tuty's southeastern fringe irrigated by the stream of Yana Yacu, supported irrigated crops. It was therefore possible for a household to have access to irrigated crop fields ranging in altitude from 3,050 to almost 3,635 meters elevation. Moreover, the advantages allowed by this "vertical zonation" of the landscape was sometimes also partly imitated in horizontal fields in the lower zones by simply sowing at slightly different time intervals.

Finally, it is noteworthy that, despite the range of crops cultivated in Pampa, many Pampeño households did not produce enough of these for their own consumption. It was not unusual to see Pampeños returning Sunday evenings from the town of Sacaba's market with small purchases of carrots, onions, and so forth. Other households produced just enough to satisfy their consumption needs. In Colpana, for example, only two or three households were known for the quantity of onions, *habas,* and/ or peas that they produced beyond their own consumption needs.

Potato Cultivation

The potato is the principal consumption staple of Bolivia's peasantry and urban working class. The period following the agrarian reform was marked by an expansion and intensification of potato production. Between 1963 and 1972 potato production grew 3.3 percent annually, and yields per hectare increased by over 36 percent. These increases were mainly the result of additional land pressed into cultivation and the use of chemical fertilizers (Wennergren and Whitaker 1975:92–93, 123). Some researchers have indicated that between 1970 and 1980 overall per-hectare yields steadily declined (Hoopes and Sage 1982:4). The abolishment of labor and other tribute obligations to absentee landowners, coupled with increased production, yields, and acreage under cultivation, resulted in overall higher peasant income levels after the agrarian reform (cf. Dorsey 1975; Dandler 1984).

The cultivation of the potato, Pampa's consumption staple and the mainstay of its agriculture, marked the initiation of the agricultural calendar, received the greatest care and time, and required the most complex forms of labor recruitment of all crops (see chap. 7). The quantity and quality of the potatoes harvested have long contributed to Pampa's renown.

There were three ways of classifying potatoes in Pampa. The first was in terms of their size, and hence market value, and the uses to which they were put. These ranged from very large potatoes (*chaparas*) to tiny ones (*ch'ili*) too small to be used as seed yet optimal for the making of freeze-dried potatoes (*ch'uno*) in the Tuty crop zone during the winter months.

Pampeños also classified potatoes in terms of their variety. Only two varieties made up virtually all potatoes cropped in Pampa. The first variety, called *imilla blanca,* was similar to a russet potato. It was sown, without exception, on irrigated land in the Colpana and Chaupi Pampa crop zones, and the lower fringes of Tuty. The second, called *runa* and akin in appearance to an Idaho potato, was planted mostly on rain-fed fields in the Tuty crop zone and (to a lesser extent) in the upper reaches of Chaupi Pampa and Colpana. Pampeños claimed that the *runa* variety was more resistant to the extremely low temperatures common in Tuty.

Elder Pampeños stated that "in the past" they sowed a greater variety of potatoes. Potato cultivation in Pampa was undergoing a process of specialization, nowadays depending almost exclusively on the *imilla blanca* and *runa* varieties in response to urban market demands. (Both varieties were very popular among Cochabamba's urban consumers.)[5] Pampeños also suggested that this process of crop specialization entailed not merely a reduction in the varieties of potatoes sown but also an absolute decline in the acreage devoted to other crops, such as wheat and barley.[6] This tendency toward crop specialization was taking place elsewhere as well. Recently Dandler and Sage (1985; Sage 1984) have underscored the increasing specialization of potato production throughout the Department of Cochabamba, with fewer varieties being cultivated over time. According to Brush (1987), a similar process is taking place in the central highlands of Peru.

Finally, potatoes were also classified by the use of terms that reflected the season in which they were sown and harvested. Potatoes sown on irrigated fields were commonly called *mishka* (early) potatoes. *Mishka* sown in the Chaupi Pampa zone and in the lower reaches of Tuty was referred to as *chaupi mishka. Mishka* and *chaupi mishka* potatoes were planted from the latter part of March to late September, although most sowings took place between the first week in June and the latter part of August. *Huata* (new year) potatoes were planted on rain-fed land, mostly in Tuty. The planting of *huata* potatoes was called *jatun tarpuy,* the "big planting." *Huata* plantings took place from early October to late December, although Pampeños preferred to sow between the second part of October and the first part of November (i.e., by the onset of the rainy season). Three complementary potato crops, each corresponding to the three crop zones mentioned above and with slightly overlapping sowing and harvest cycles, were therefore cultivated in Pampa (fig. 6). Potato production cycles are interwoven with the Catholic ritual calendar (see, e.g., Sage 1990:207).

Crop Zone	January	February	March	April	May	June	July	August	September	October	November	December
Tuty	(harvest	mishka	)	(harvest huata) (plant	) mishka)			(plant	mishka)	plant	huata) (harvest	mishka)
Chaupi Pampa			(plant (harvest (harvest	mishka) huata) mishka)				(plant mishka	)	(plant huata) (harvest mishka)	
Colpana	(plant	mishka)	(harvest (harvest	mishka) huata)			(plant	mishka	) (plant huata) (harvest mishka)		

Source: Field data, 1983–84.

Fig. 6. Complementary mishka and huata potato cultivation in Pampa.

Sowing potatoes was a lengthy undertaking requiring considerable foresight, organization, and planning. Land had to be prepared for planting. Weeds, rocks, and stubble were first cleared away. If preparation was done during winter, the land was first irrigated to soften up the soil (*empanto*). The land was then plowed (*arado*) at least twice, almost always with steel-tipped plows drawn by a pair of oxen (*yunta*).[7] Just before planting the field was sometimes irrigated once more.

Long before the sowing got underway, household members were busily at work at other complementary tasks. Dung was prepared (or bought), put into sacks, and, along with seed, evenly distributed throughout the field to be sown. Chemical fertilizer used in planting needed to be purchased. Considerable time was invested in informing relatives and neighbors of the day planting would take place and asking them to participate. Corn beer, cane alcohol, coca leaves, and handmade cigarettes (*k'uyunas*), provided to members of the work teams during the day, were also secured. Households that did not own *yuntas* also had to obtain them, through outright rentals or by exchanging *ayni* labor (see chap. 7).

Sowing, which rarely began before 8 A.M., was usually completed in one day. Participants were organized into teams, each working with one *yunta*. With the exception of the handling of the *yunta,* any other work role was fulfilled by workers of either sex. Furrows (*surcos*) were first opened by a *yunta* driven by a *yuntero*. (The *ch'akitaclla,* the Andean footplow, was not used in Pampa.) Behind the *yunta* another worker deepened and widened the furrow, followed by a *mujiru* who evenly deposited the seed in the furrow. A small boy or girl followed, pressing the seed into the ground with his or her bare feet. A thin layer of chemical fertilizer would then be deposited into the furrow. A *guaniru* then applied an even coating of manure in the furrow. A second *yunta* then came around and closed the furrow. The final major step consisted of leveling the field with a long, heavy log pulled by a *yunta* (*tapada*).

Throughout the day small children and youngsters assisted by replenishing bags of dung and small buckets of fertilizer and providing corn beer to the workers. While the sowing was under way, some women were busily at work preparing food, which was served twice during the day.

Harvest took place about six months later. By this time the furrows would have been weeded several times, the soil between them loosened (*aporque*), and the plants fumigated at least once. If *mishka* or *chaupi mishka* potatoes had been planted, the soil would have been irrigated four or five times prior to the harvest. The harvest began early in the morning and, if necessary, proceeded until nightfall. If the harvest in the Tuty crop zone was completed by nightfall, workers normally passed the night in the *estancias* rather than returning to their homes. Pampeños attempted to complete the harvest in one day, although this was sometimes not possible.

The urgency in completing the harvest was due to two reasons. The first had to do with labor availability. Rarely were households able to provide by themselves all of the labor needed for the harvest (see chap. 7), and, if it was not completed, considerable effort would be required in mobilizing enough labor anew. Some household members may not have been available on the following day, as they may have already made plans to travel to the Chapare. Wage laborers, who often were recruited from nearby communities, would have left Pampa. Furthermore, if reciprocal labor was secured for the following day, this would have required additional labor time to be paid in the future. The second reason why attempts were made to complete the harvest in one day was that mature potatoes spoiled if they remained in the ground, either because of excessive rain (frequent during the *mishka* harvest) or freezing temperatures (often the case in high-altitude *huata* fields).

In Pampa a hectare of land planted in *mishka* seed will yield between 3.4 and 5.5 metric tons of potatoes per hectare (the yield of *huata* seed will be slightly higher).[8] Pampeños usually used mules to haul the harvested potatoes to their dwellings. Wealthy household heads, however, preferred trucks for this purpose, either employing their own or paying a trucker with a part of the harvest. The harvested potatoes were then sorted into different categories. Part of the harvest was set aside for consumption, seed, and for making *ch'uno*. Only the best quality potatoes were sold.

Potato cultivation requires a heavy investment of labor (see chap. 7), and Pampeños and other peasants will use heavy inputs of dung, synthetic fertilizers, and pesticides to maintain production levels. For example, one study (Ministerio de Asuntos Campesinos y Agropecuarios 1983:10–12) maintained that planting one hectare in potatoes required 150 kilograms of chemical fertilizer and 5,520 kilograms of dung.[9] Yet Pampeños stated that, despite its high production costs, no other crop (in Pampa) successfully competed with the potato in terms of revenue obtained per unit of land. Recent studies confirm these statements (table 6.1; see also Jones 1980:174–78).

As with the case of coca (see chap. 3), considerable discrepancies surface in the literature on the net income that peasants can (and do) obtain from their potato fields. Several studies carried out over a considerable time span have concluded that potato production costs have consistently averaged about 50 percent of the harvest's market value (Ministerio de Asuntos Campesinos y Agropecuarios 1965; 1983:10–12; Jones1980:174–78). These production cost figures, however, almost certainly underestimate the real costs that are incurred by peasants in valley and highland crop production (see, e.g., Jones 1980:172–73); therefore, a more realistic estimate of overall potato production costs would be at least 65 percent of a harvest's value. On March 18, 1985, one sack of first-class size and quality potatoes (*primera clase*) fetched U.S. $9 in the markets of Cochabamba and Sacaba. If we assume that a Pampeño harvested and sold a maximum of eight sacks of potatoes for each one of seed planted on one hectare of land (or a total of 120 sacks per hectare) then he or she could have obtained about U.S. $1,080, or almost one-half of the income from one hectare of coca on the same date (see chap. 3).

Of course, a typical plot never produced eight sacks of first-quality potatoes for each sack of seed planted. In addition, peasant households never sold in the marketplace their entire potato harvest as considerable amounts were retained for direct consumption and for seed. The proportion of the harvest sold depended on many factors. Poor harvests (such as in Bolivia during 1983) inevitably led to a smaller proportion sold. Wealth differentiation is also an important factor determining what proportion of the harvest was finally marketed: poorer peasants tend to sell less and consume more (e.g., Abegglen, Mantilla, and Belmonte 1987:76). The degree of insertion of peasant households into wider market circuits also structures the proportion of harvests that are consumed or sold. For instance, in Uchucmarca, a Peruvian peasant community overwhelmingly oriented toward subsistence (at least in the early 1970s), only 7 percent of the harvests were sold beyond the community (Brush

TABLE 6.1   Income from Selected Crops on One Hectare of Land in Cochabamba

Crop	$b	U.S.$
Potato	415,303	933
Broad Bean	232,369	522
Barley	16,601	37

Source: Adapted from Ministerio de Agricultura y Asuntos Campesinos 1983. The U.S.$ equivalent is based on the parallel (black market) rate of 445 pesos *bolivianos* ($b) to the U.S. dollar.

1977b:115). By contrast, in the more commercialized Mantaro Valley between 33 and 43 percent of the harvested potatoes were sold (Werge 1981:19). Lagos (1988:141), whose field research overlapped with mine, has suggested that an average of 40 percent of the harvest in the province of Tiraque (also in Cochabamba) was marketed. Since most peasant households in Pampa (but not in Tiraque) migrated to the Chapare, we can safely assume that the average Pampeño household marketed a smaller percentage of its potato harvest than its counterparts in Tiraque—perhaps 35 percent.

In sum, although a Pampeño household *could have* received from one hectare of potatoes about one-half the amount of cash than from one hectare of coca on the same date, it almost certainly received far less. It is also important to remember that, contrary to potatoes, virtually all of the coca harvested in the Chapare was marketed.[10]

I previously stressed (see chap. 3) that Bolivian peasants have experienced since the agrarian reform an uninterrupted decline in the terms of trade of their major crops and that they have had to intensify production to offset this decline. (For declining terms of trade and of income after the 1985 economic stabilization program, see chap. 8). Both processes were exemplified in Pampa by the decline in fallow cycles. Fallow was virtually nonexistent on irrigated fields in the Colpana and Chaupi Pampa crop zones. According to Pampeños, fallow periods (and the amount of land under fallow) in the higher rain-fed fields of Tuty had also been steadily declining over the years. The decline in fallow has also been documented in other areas of Cochabamba. Over 15 years ago some peasant households in Tiraque, an important potato-producing area southeast of Pampa, placed less than 15 percent of their irrigated and only 20 percent of their rain-fed land under fallow in the 1973 crop season (Dorsey 1975:4:40). And, more recently, Sage (1984:89) has underscored "a reduction in fallow periods" in the Cochabamba province of Ayopaya. Agricultural intensification and the decline of fallow periods are reported for other Andean communities (Orlove and Godoy 1986).

Declining fallow in Pampa was also due to the need to sustain a growing population. In 1954 agrarian reform officials counted 764 peasants living in Pampa. By late 1983 the number of Pampeños, excluding those permanently living in Santa Cruz and the Chapare, totaled 1,427 (see chap. 2). Hence, Pampa's population during these 30 years more than doubled, a rate of increase that exceeded national level estimates (cf. Ministerio de Hacienda y Estadística 1950:7; Instituto Nacional de Estadística 1978:29).

A consequence of both declining terms of trade and rising population is that over time soils in Pampa had been more intensely cropped. Soils, I was told, were constantly "tired" (*cansados*) and year after year yielded less. In order to counteract declining yields Pampeños had been applying to their fields ever-increasing doses of dung (*guano*) and, since the late 1950s, chemical fertilizers (*abono*). While Pampeños preferred a mix of cow, sheep, and chicken dung (they claimed the latter was "stronger"), some had even attempted to increase yields by only applying chemical fertilizers on their irrigated potato fields in the Colpana and Chaupi Pampa crop zones.

Yet, despite these efforts, soils continued to be "tired." Elderly peasants still recalled fallow periods in the Colpana crop zone and when, in the absence of chemical inputs, they would harvest sizable quantities of *chaparas*. Nowadays *chaparas,* consumed only on special occasions, rarely surfaced during harvest time: when they did appear it was a cause for celebration and almost awe. Pampeños had been caught in what Bernstein (1982:165–67) called the "simple reproduction 'squeeze'"—intensification of production (and hence increased production costs) due to increasing needs and deteriorating terms of trade, and falling output, which in turn required ever greater intensification. This "squeeze," magnified by the enormous gulf between coca and potato returns by mid-1985, no doubt underlied the massive migration to the Chapare documented in previous chapters.

Potato Production Strategies during the Coca Boom

By the early to mid-1980s, then, Pampeños had long experienced a progressive decline in the terms of trade of their major crops, were confronting rising input costs, low prices and diminishing yields, and an accelerated fall in living standards as a result of the economic crisis plaguing Bolivia. There seemed, however, no end in sight to the rising value of the coca leaf. Small wonder, then, that some Pampeños told me that "the potato is no longer worthwhile [planting]" (*la papa ya no vale*) or that "the peasant always loses [money planting potatoes]" (*el campesino siempre pierde*). These statements reflected the widespread view among Pampeños, migrants and nonmigrants alike, that the cultivation of the potato was not a viable economic strategy. Pampeños also stated that Chapare coca fields required "less" and "easier" work than cultivating potatoes, which demanded "more" and "stronger" work. One young migrant even told me that potato cultivation was "brute's work" (*trabajo de bruto*).

Undoubtedly, the manual sowing and especially harvesting of potatoes was a strenuous, back-breaking endeavor. Yet the harvest of coca leaves in a hot, humid, and stifling environment was no easy task either. The contrasting cultural appraisements of the worth of labor expended in potato and coca cultivation no doubt reflected the differential economic returns of these two crops. But these appraisals must also be seen in light of a pattern of rising expectations, particularly among younger Pampeños, about what constituted an acceptable standard of living, expectations that could not be solely met from highland agricultural pursuits centering on the production of tubers and grains. These expectations were being generated, fueled even, by the extraordinary (by local standards) purchasing power of wealthy migrants with highly profitable coca enterprises and who engaged in sumptuous displays of wealth (see chap. 4).

What, then, was the impact of the economic crisis and the coca boom on crop production in the highlands and valleys, and specifically in the migrant home communities? Tullis (1987) was perhaps the first to suggest that highland and valley crop production in Peru and Bolivia was declining as a result of runaway inflation, high coca prices, and a shortage of labor. More recently, the postulated drop in Bolivian highland and valley peasant crop, particularly tuber, production in the early to mid-1980s, and especially during 1984 and 1985 (the height of the coca boom), has been disputed by de Franco and Godoy (1990) and others (e.g., Pattie 1988:151; Unidad de Análisis de Políticas Económicas 1990:113–14).

The claim that crop production did not fall during 1984–85 rests on aggregate and survey data mainly compiled by Bolivian institutions (e.g., J. Morales 1990:55–58; Prudencio and Velasco 1987:10–12; Ministerio de Asuntos Campesinos y Agropecuarios 1990b:92). As a result, several caveats need to be raised. First, it should be stressed that agricultural survey data, as government sources themselves admit, are "very deficient" and that conclusions drawn from this data may be "irrelevant" (Unidad de Análisis de Políticas Económicas 1990:114). In particular, other sources using data from the Food and Agriculture Organization (Economist Intelligence Unit 1990:76) point to a drop in potato production of over 20 percent between 1984 and 1985. In addition, there are considerable inconsistencies in crop production statistics—sometimes in the order of 15 to 20 percent—from different government sources (e.g., Ministerio de Asuntos Campesinos y Agropecuarios 1990b:89; Instituto Nacional de Estadística 1990a:5, cf. 1990b). But, even if we assume that Bolivian survey data are remotely accurate—that is, that overall tuber and potato production did not decline between 1984 and 1985—we cannot conclude, as de Franco and Godoy (1990:22–25) have done, that intense migration, rising coca prices, and the spread of coca cultivation had little or no bearing on peasant production and productive strategies in the highland and valley regions.

If we carefully examine recent survey data on aggregate production trends during the 1980s (Ministerio de Asuntos Campesinos y Agropecuarios 1990b:92), we find considerable variability in the production of (and land sown in) potatoes between 1980 and 1988 in Bolivia's seven potato-producing departments.[11] For instance, in 1981 production declined (compared to 1980) in two departments, and by the following year it had fallen in all seven. Although data do indicate a strong overall recovery (with the exception of Tarija) in production levels following the 1982–83 drought, in not one department did 1984 production levels reach those prevalent in 1982. Data for early 1985 suggest even more erratic production trends throughout Bolivia's countryside. Potato cultivation declined in three departments but slightly increased in the remaining four. In only two of these three departments did potato production reach levels prevailing in 1981.

The important point I wish to stress here is the considerable variability in traditional highland and valley production strategies that was certainly taking place in different peasant communities, regions, and departments during the coca boom. This variability no doubt reflected differential (and shifting) degrees of migration, unequal access to subsidized inputs (such as fertilizers), differences in transport costs, and links to and dependence on the coca market. For instance, it is not far-fetched to postulate that in departments, regions, and communities expelling relatively little labor to (and reaping little rewards from) the coca-producing areas of the Chapare and *yungas* of La Paz, some peasant households attempted to increase production in an attempt to offset eroding living standards, while, as suggested by Tullis (1987), production and the amount of land sown remained stationary or even declined in areas and communities such as in Pampa, which were experiencing intense migration. I claim in the following pages that land sown in potatoes was slowly being curbed in Pampa during the coca boom years. But I also argue that the withdrawal of land from cultivation was not uniform across all households and that not all households withdrawing land from cultivation did so for exactly the same reasons. To some extent the steady and well-documented decrease in potato cultivation following the 1985 Nueva Política Económica (see chap. 8) had its roots in this incipient curtailment of crop production.

My analysis of Pampeño household production strategies was grounded on detailed interviews among 42 household heads (29 migrant and 13 nonmigrant) on the amount of cultivable land held and planted in potatoes during the 1984 *mishka* (including *chaupi mishka*) and *huata* planting seasons (March–December 1984). The 42 sample households had access to 73.8 hectares of cultivable land, of which 26 percent (19.3 hectares) were sown. Nonmigrant households had an average of 2.3 hectares of cultivable land, or 65 percent more than their migrant counterparts, and they planted 50 percent more of their land than migrant households (table 6.2).

In general, the average amount of land sown in potatoes by both migrant and nonmigrant households was proportional to the average amount of cultivable land held, that is, the more land available the more of it was planted. However, as tables 6.3 and 6.4 illustrate, the percentage of land sown relative to the amount of available land steadily declined. That is to say, while the total amount of land sown in potatoes increased as more land became available, the overall percentage of available land that was sown actually declined. This decline was more significant among migrant households.

In an economic context marked by high coca prices some migrants opted for redeploying time, labor, and other inputs away from potato cultivation in Pampa to lucrative commodity production in the Chapare. Migrants who accumulated considerable wealth by cultivating coca or participating in the illegal cocaine trade and who had large tracts of

TABLE 6.2   Hectares of Cultivable Land Available to and Sown in Potatoes by Migrant (*N*=29) and Nonmigrant (*N*=13) Households

Household	Total		Average	
	Available	Sown	Available	Sown
Migrant	43.9	11.4	1.5	0.4
Nonmigrant	29.9	7.9	2.3	0.6
Total	73.8	19.3		

Source: Field data, 1984. Includes land sharecropped, inherited, purchased, and agrarian reform land grant.

land in Pampa planted the least percentage of their land and were withdrawing portions of it from cultivation. Conversely, less wealthy migrants with far less land and facing considerable economic risk in the Chapare and Pampa cultivated a greater proportion of their land during the 1984 season. The amount of wealth household heads had amassed and land they had access to in Pampa, the risks that they were able and willing to face by withdrawing land from cultivation, and their ability to recruit sufficient extra-household labor were major factors that structured the productive strategies of migrant and nonmigrant households in different ways.

Adriano, who sponsored the lavish fiesta described in chapter 4, exemplified the case of wealthy migrants who planted little of their land in Pampa. Adriano owned 20 hectares of land in the Chapare settlement of Chimoré and also worked his father's land grant in the colony of Isiboro. (His elderly father never traveled to the Chapare.) During my stay in Pampa he opened a *chichería*, was planning to open a restaurant and cater to travelers to the Chapare, and had plans to travel to Brazil

TABLE 6.3   Average Landholding and Potato Cultivation Pattern of 29 Migrant Households

Landholding	Number of Households	Average Land Held	Average Land Sown (in hectares)	Percentage of Land Sown
< = 1	12	0.7	0.34	49
+ 1 − 2	9	1.4	0.57	41
+ 2 − 3	5	2.4	0.44	18
+ 3 − 4	2	3.0	0.35	12
+ 5	1	5.5	0.63	11

Source: Field data, 1984.

TABLE 6.4   Average Landholding and Potato Cultivation Pattern of 13 Nonmigrant Households

Landholding	Number of Households	Average Land Held (in hectares)	Average Land Sown (in hectares)	Percentage of Land Sown
< = 1	5	0.55	0.37	67
+ 1 − 2	4	1.80	0.60	33
+ 2 − 3	1	2.90	1.30	45
+ 3 − 4	1	3.30	0.87	26
+ 5	2	6.80	1.40	21

Source: Field data, 1984.

to purchase a truck. Adriano also owned considerable land in Pampa. He had purchased 4.2 hectares from the former landowner in the mid-1970s and inherited from his father an additional 1.3 hectares of land. His 5.5 hectares of cultivable land were far more than most Pampeños had access to. In the 1984 crop season Adriano planted 0.63 hectares, or just 11 percent of his total land. He harvested enough potatoes to more than satisfy his household's consumption needs and funneled part of his harvest to the Chapare to help feed his Chapare laborers.

Because Adriano's principal source of wealth stemmed from cultivating coca and not potatoes, he faced little risk of economic hardship by planting only 11 percent of his land in Pampa. His potato harvests could no doubt have failed. Yet Adriano would have easily met an unexpected shortfall of potatoes by harvesting and/or consuming greater quantities of lowland crops (such as rice or cassava) or, as he and other migrants did during the 1982–83 drought, by simply purchasing potatoes elsewhere. It was in the Chapare that he faced considerable economic and political risk in the light of anti-coca and drug campaigns (see chaps. 3 and 8). Nevertheless, by diversifying his economic activities in the Chapare, he minimized the risk to him of these campaigns. Had these campaigns been successful and directly affected him (i.e., his coca crops eradicated or, as had recently occurred, coca prices had fallen below production costs), Adriano would still have been in a position, if he deemed it necessary, to funnel part of his accumulated wealth back into potato production. Since most of his wealth was not tied up in fixed productive investments, he could have also reinvested his wealth in other wealth-generating endeavors, as his desire to purchase a truck illustrated. In sum, the overall economic strategy in Pampa that Adriano was pursuing in the mid-1980s, one deemphasizing potato cultivation, was not seriously endangering his subsistence base.

We saw above that fallow was on the decline in Pampa. In Pampa fallow was expressed by the Spanish word *descanso,* literally "to rest." Yet a plot of land under *descanso* was not necessarily one set aside strictly because of the desire to rejuvenate the soil. Rather, land in *descanso* was simply land "not sown." That is, land in *descanso* had not been planted but was not necessarily under fallow, if by this we mean a conscious decision to set land aside to allow the soil to regain its fertility. Declining yield (or when soils were said to be "tired") was perhaps one reason—but certainly not the major one—some household heads expressed for not planting potatoes. Land was often left idle for many reasons having little to do with the desire to offset declining soil fertility and a great more to do with migration to and coca production in the Chapare. For instance, when I asked Adriano why he had left most of his land uncropped he answered that he wanted the land to rest. When I prodded further he stated, as did other migrants, that he lacked cash to purchase necessary inputs (e.g., chemical fertilizers), that these "could not be found" in time for planting, that they were too expensive, and so forth. Yet clearly, as a rich migrant, he did not lack cash to buy the required inputs and could have easily sown more land in potatoes had he wanted and needed to do so.

Other wealthy migrants also cloaked their disinterest in planting potatoes by recourse to explanations similar to those conveyed by Adriano. By 1984 Emiliano had totally renovated his two-story house by, among other things, installing ceramic tiles on the floors, constructing a brick wall with an iron gate surrounding it, and building a garage for the truck he was in the process of purchasing. I would often observe Emiliano sharing his large house with several of his Chapare sharecroppers and laborers, some of whom would spend weeks at a time there. Emiliano decided not to plant a *mishka* crop in 1984, claiming that he did not have "enough money" for chemical fertilizers and dung. Besides, he said, the land was too tired and needed rest. Rather, he traveled to Colomi, where the price of recently harvested potatoes was lower, and purchased potatoes necessary for his household's (and laborers') consumption.

Valeriano, a very successful migrant, pursued a strategy similar to that of Adriano and Emiliano. Valeriano and his brother and nephew had 80 hectares of land and several coca fields in two Chapare colonies. (Valeriano obtained land grants in Isiboro and Ichilo, and his brother and nephew each had a land grant in Ichilo). Valeriano owned a television and a car and was shopping around for another vehicle at the time of my departure. Valeriano and his brother and nephew jointly worked 1.6 hectares of cultivable land in Pampa, which Valeriano had inherited from his father. Of this amount Valeriano planted 0.18 hectares in *mishka* and *huata* potatoes, 11 percent of his total cultivable land, as did Adriano. Valeriano did not plant more land because he expected to harvest "just [enough] to eat" (*mik"ullapaq*). He harvested 22 sacks—almost 5,000 pounds—of potatoes from his *mishka* planting. He did not sell any portion of his harvest. Instead, he set aside part of it for his household's consumption and transported the rest to the Chapare for his (and his brother's and nephew's) laborers. As with Adriano, Valeriano and his kin not only had little interest in expanding potato production but utilized part of the harvest that they might otherwise have sold in local markets to subsidize their coca operations in the Chapare.

The relatively little interest in potato cultivation that wealthy migrants displayed was also manifested and compounded by a lack of attention to other tasks necessary for an adequate potato harvest. For instance, in the 1984 *huata* planting season Juan, who, as we observed in chapter 4, spent prolonged periods of time in the Chapare, planted only one sack of potato seed (one-fifteenth of a hectare). Since he spent considerable time away from Pampa with his wife and some of his eldest children, he failed to return to weed and fumigate his crop. (Other members of Juan's household who had been left behind included his smallest children and Juan's elderly aunt, who took care of them.) As a result, he harvested only two sacks of potatoes, far less than that required to completely satisfy his household's consumption needs.

Other migrants sowed significantly higher percentages of their land than the wealthy migrant household heads who controlled large tracts of land in the Chapare and in Pampa. They were generally younger and less wealthy household heads with smaller land plots in Pampa and only tenuous access to small coca fields in the Chapare. Marcialino, with far less land in Pampa and the Chapare than Adriano or Valeriano (see also chap. 4), was representative of these young migrant household heads who planted more of their land. Marcialino's household consisted of himself, his wife and father-in-law, and three small children all under the age of five. Marcialino's cultivable land in Pampa amounted to one hectare. Of this amount he inherited from his father 0.87 hectares and purchased the rest. In the Chapare Marcialino sharecropped from kin a small plot of (exclusively) coca land (see chap. 4). He did not invest money in remodeling his home or purchasing a vehicle. In the 1984 crop season he planted 39 percent of his available cultivable land. Two other migrant household heads, who, like Marcialino, sharecropped small plots of coca in the Chapare but who inherited only one-fifth of a hectare of land in Pampa, sowed over 85 percent of their land.

The economic and political risks faced by Marcialino and other less wealthy migrant household heads with less and tenuous access to land in the Chapare and in Pampa were far greater than those faced by rich migrants who enjoyed greater options for maneuvering within an overall risky environment. None had accumulated wealth comparable to that of their rich counterparts, and they normally had access to just one tiny coca plot in one Chapare settlement. They were therefore far more vulnerable to repressive actions by the state, and a successful coca eradication program would have quickly put them out of business. Marcialino and his fellow coca sharecroppers also faced the risk of eventually losing their sharecropper status.[12] In addition, their small potato fields in Pampa barely yielded enough to satisfy their households' consumption needs. Completely abandoning (or greatly reducing) their acreage devoted to potato cultivation would, then, have put these young and less wealthy household heads at far greater risk of economic hardship if coca were eradicated and major droughts, such as the one in 1982–83 and the more recent 1988–89 drought, hit Pampa once again. These migrant household heads constantly strived for a delicate balance between economic rewards and risks in Pampa and the Chapare. They were clearly cognizant of the disincentives to potato cultivation but were also wary of the high risks in hinging their livelihood soley on coca production.

In sum, wealthy and successful migrants—and it is important to remember that these were only a small minority of all of Pampa's migrants—deeply involved in multiple facets of the coca economy and with large tracts of land in Pampa pursued a strategy of systematically sowing only small percentages of their land. Migrants not able to amass as much wealth because of their smaller and less diversified economic base in the Chapare and who had smaller land plots in Pampa faced considerable more economic and political risk. As a result, they planted a greater proportion of their land in potatoes than their wealthier counterparts.

The critically proximate factors that nonmigrants coped with as they decided to sow their potato fields were rising input costs and availability of labor. Nonmigrant household heads typically had access to and planted more land than migrants. Yet, like many migrants, the percentage of land sown by nonmigrants was inversely proportional to the extent of their landholdings. Wealthy nonmigrants—defined in Pampa partly in terms of the amount of land they held—generally sowed a lower percentage of their crop fields. Poorer nonmigrants with less land faced higher risks to their livelihood and planted a greater percentage of their land.

Baltazar was representative of wealthy nonmigrant household heads who generally planted far more of his land (but a smaller percentage of it) than migrants but less so than nonmigrant Pampeños. He never traveled to nor obtained land in the Chapare. Baltazar had 5.1 hectares of cultivable land, all from his original agrarian reform land grant. In

1984 he planted 1.2 hectares, or 23 percent. Enrique, another nonmigrant with a slightly larger household but with less cultivable land than Baltazar (2.9 hectares) planted 43 percent. Both stated that they wanted to plant additional land but did not do so because they wished to leave some land in fallow and because input costs at the time were too high. Both also claimed—as did other nonmigrants with considerable land—having had difficulties in procuring extra household labor—an issue we shall return to shortly. By allowing land to stand idle in the face of considerable environmental uncertainty, hyperinflation, and the declining value of highland crops, nonmigrant household heads such as Baltazar and Arturo avoided a continuous infusion of ever more costly inputs with little guarantee of a good harvest and often with virtually no prospects of at least recovering production costs.

The poorest of nonmigrants with the smallest amounts of land planted the greater proportion of their available land. Miguel, who has never held land in the Chapare (he did, however, once have a land grant in Santa Cruz), was one of the poorest household heads in Pampa. Denied his share of inheritance from his father's land (see chap. 5), Miguel eked out a precarious existence by sharecropping small plots of land from primarily migrant household heads who had left their land idle. He planted all of the land available to him (one-third of a hectare) during the 1984 planting season with the help of his children and wife. Poor nonmigrant household heads such as Miguel could not pursue a strategy analogous to that of rich migrants and nonmigrants such as Adriano and Baltazar, who left considerable amounts of land uncropped. With little land and facing the greatest risks to their livelihood, it is not surprising that they tilled most of their land.

In general the planting strategies of nonmigrants paralleled that of migrants: the lowest percentage of land was sown by those with greater wealth and/or larger crop fields. Similarly, among nonmigrants those with access to more land—and thereby facing less risks of economic ruin—left a greater percentage of it uncropped. Yet migrants and nonmigrants grappled with slightly different constraints. In deciding to leave a percentage of their land idle, migrants took into account the risks that they faced in the Chapare (e.g., loss of their coca fields or harvests as a result of state eradication efforts), while the planting decisions of nonmigrants were determined by the risks to their livelihood in Pampa. Moreover, while rising input costs and high coca prices potato prices undoubtedly were major reasons why migrants opted to leave tracts of land untilled, these loomed more critical for nonmigrants. Above all, nonmigrants faced the heavier burden than migrants of accessing sufficient labor in a context of massive emigration.

The Shortfall in Labor

Claims that traditional subsistence production was largely unaffected in highland areas and communities with high levels of migration to the Chapare partly rest on key assumptions regarding labor availability. For instance, de Franco and Godoy (1990:23) state that cocaine production "did not cut the number of laborers in traditional agriculture because traditional agriculture enjoys abundant workers." This view—that highland regions are characterized by a surplus of unproductive labor or, what is the same, suffer from massive underemployment—is reminiscent of earlier views held by development planners encouraging migration to the eastern lowlands (see chap. 3). Yet, as Brush (1977a, 1977b:117–32) and more recently J. Collins (1988:121–30) have convincingly argued, claims of underemployment are often based on faulty premises and are usually misleading. Nor is seasonal migration and complementary highland-lowland production necessarily indicative, as de Franco and Godoy also claim (1990:24), of a surplus of labor. Rather, production complementarity entails a stringent and carefully balanced allocation of labor to successfully satisfy the complex productive requirements of highland and lowland agriculture. A skewed allocation of labor, one directed at crop intensification and expansion in the lowlands will almost inevitably siphon away labor required to adequately sustain highland production (Rasnake and Painter 1989:43; J. Collins 1987, 1988:142–50; Platt 1982b:49–51; Mitchell 1991:34, 73, 114).[13]

In chapter 4 I stressed that a full 80 percent of Pampa's households were expelling labor to the Chapare, permanent migration was on the increase, and that many migrants who were still engaged in seasonal migration were nevertheless spending an increasing amount of time in the Chapare. The availability of labor during the potato sowing and harvest periods was a critical issue with which nonmigrant household heads constantly grappled. As we saw, nonmigrants with considerable land in Pampa claimed considerable difficulties in securing enough labor during the 1984 agricultural season. Seasonal labor shortages during critical periods of the agricultural cycle as well as various mechanisms to insure access to extra-household labor during these periods have, of course, always been commonplace in Pampa and elsewhere in the Andes. The outflow of Pampeños to the Chapare, however, was a qualitatively different type of labor shortage—one progressively acute and absolute—for which no precedents existed. This labor shortage proved to be an insurmountable obstacle for many households, despite the variety of ways of recruiting labor in Pampa (see chap. 7).

Migration before the 1980s coca boom did not adversely affect household production at home. The migration of Pampeños to Yapacaní in Santa Cruz (see chap. 4) did not result in severe labor shortfalls, as the outflow of Pampeños to the Chapare did by the mid-1980s. Over a 20-year time span (1959 to 1979) the number of migrants traveling from Pampa to Santa Cruz averaged a mere six persons annually, and most migrants remained in Santa Cruz less than three years and many less than one. Households that temporarily lost young males were able to compensate for the labor differences by relying to a great extent on reciprocal labor practices or by recruiting seasonal laborers, particularly during the harvests. Production on land belonging to the land grant households that abandoned Pampa was quickly taken up by kin and neighbors who gained temporary or permanent access to their land (see chap. 4). In addition, no crop cultivated in Yapacaní at the time displayed the economic and agronomic advantages that coca does today in the Chapare.[14] Moreover, migration to Santa Cruz did not occur at a time of such a deep economic crisis that recent migrants to the Chapare were experiencing. The terms of exchange of major highland crops, furthermore, were not as adverse to peasant cultivators as they were by the 1980s. It is also unlikely that early migration to the Chapare affected production in Pampa, despite the fact that coca was, even then, a profitable cash crop (Henkel 1971). Migration to the Chapare, especially during the first 10 or 12 years, was predominantly of a seasonal nature. Coca was planted early on in the Chapare, but migrants also devoted time and effort to other annual and perennial crops both for subsistence and cash sale (see chaps. 3 and 4).

By the early 1980s the nature and context of outmigration had dramatically changed, and migration to the Chapare was leading to a shortfall of labor that affected the ability of many nonmigrant households to sustain production. These household heads constantly claimed that they "no longer planted as much (as before)" because household members (usually young sons) "are in the Chapare," "no longer work (in Pampa)," "do not want to work (the land)," or "are too busy (working in the Chapare)." Nonmigrants with large tracts of land—and, hence, in need of proportionately greater amounts of extra-household labor—confronted severe difficulties in recruiting labor due to the flow of Pampeños to the Chapare. On the other hand, very poor nonmigrants who cultivated miniscule plots of land were by and large able to recruit from their own households the labor they required.

Labor scarcity was a problem for virtually all nonmigrant households, but it was an especially severe problem for households in a late stage of their developmental cycle attempting to maintain production levels. Elderly heads of these households often claimed that they would have planted more of their land in potatoes had it not been for their difficulties in obtaining an adequate labor supply during crucial periods of the agricultural cycle. These household heads often complained that younger migrant members of their households were no longer returning to Pampa to participate in agricultural tasks. They also claimed that young migrants were unwilling to assist them in purchasing inputs such as dung and chemical fertilizers.

The outflow of labor from Pampa to the Chapare was also intertwined with changing intra-household authority, traditionally predicated upon the right of the household head to award or restrict usufruct rights to the means of production. Young household members wishing to secure a resource base through inheritance for their own future households within the community had been obliged to demonstrate deference and obedience to their parents and, particularly, to take an active role in the reproduction of the household. Migration to the Chapare and the possibility of accumulating wealth there, however, assured many young migrants of a fund of resources independent of domestic boundaries and, in many cases, control. This was in turn paralleled by a waning interest in inheritance by many young and successful migrants (see chap. 5). The result was a slow erosion and undermining of authority patterns within the household domain, evidenced by the case of elderly household heads who seem genuinely unable to entice or force younger members to fully cooperate with them in tasks directly related to the economic survival of their households.

For nonmigrant household heads such as Jacobo, Rudecindo, and Cayetano, in which the late developmental stage of their households and the lack of labor were major determinants of the extremely low acreage of land they were able to sow, the coca boom was no blessing. Jacobo and his wife, both in their mid-80s, lived alone and barely above a subsistence level in the lower Colpana crop zone. They were too weak to actively participate in agricultural tasks and, to make matters worse, they had difficulties in securing outside help in the planting and harvest of potatoes. According to Jacobo, Mario (his only son), a migrant who spent most of his time in the Chapare, "did not want" to plant more potatoes in Pampa for him. Mario almost never appeared in Pampa, and I never encountered him during the more than two years I carried out research in Pampa. Jacobo recognized that his household's consumption needs were minimal, but he also suggested that he would be willing to put more land under cultivation if he had access to additional labor. Jacobo, with his wife's and a nephew's assistance, sowed only 5 percent of his two hectares of cultivable land in 1984.

For Rudecindo, an 89-year-old widower, coca "was not good" (*perjudica mucho*). In the late 1970s he parceled out part of his agrarian reform land grant among his two grandsons (see also chap. 5). Rudecindo allotted to his eldest and favorite grandson (and the one Rudecindo hoped would "bury" him) about one-half of his land grant and awarded a smaller portion of land to his second grandson. The first grandson obtained a land grant in the colony of Chimoré the same year that he received land from Rudecindo. In 1983 (the year I carried out the household census in Pampa) Rudecindo's two grandsons stated that they were spending more time in the colony of Chimoré than in Pampa. When I interviewed Rudecindo he bitterly complained to me that neither of his grandsons had been helping him sow his potato fields. "They do not," Rudecindo complained, "plant (potatoes) as they used to (before)." Very upset (*rabioso*), Rudecindo talked about the possibility of selling his land grant in Pampa, and the last time I spoke to him he had arranged for a nephew to sharecrop his elder grandson's land. (I never learned how that arrangement would have worked out, for Rudecindo died about a month later, shortly before I left Pampa.)

Cayetano, in his late 60s, was caught in a similar bind. He headed a household that included his wife, two teenage sons, a grandson, and a daughter-in-law. Yet both his sons traveled continuously to the Chapare to work with their two other brothers, who were permanently residing there. The latter two, Cayetano's eldest sons, rarely visited Pampa, and his two youngest sons were often away when Cayetano was about to plant or harvest his potato crops. His four sons, Cayetano claimed, were "very busy" in the Chapare. As the case of Valeriano, a wealthy migrant, Cayetano claimed that he planted "very little." Although both planted just "enough to eat," they did so for radically different reasons: the first was far more interested in channeling time and effort into his coca fields in the Chapare, while the second was unable to recruit sufficient labor for crop production in Pampa.

Chapter 7

The Deployment of Agricultural Labor

In previous chapters I have examined the intensity of migration by Pampeños to the Chapare, the accumulation of wealth by prosperous migrants, and the overall decline of potato cultivation in Pampa during Bolivia's coca boom years. In what ways were these processes intertwined with the deployment of agricultural labor in Pampa? Was wage labor replacing nonwage forms of deploying and recruiting labor? In this chapter I argue that nonwage patterns of labor recruitment in Pampa, far from disappearing as Pampeños became more tightly integrated with the cocaine market, were actually being strengthened. The central argument of this chapter is that the noncommoditization of labor in Pampa was precisely one outcome of the integration of Pampeños to an increasingly commoditized regional economy centered on coca production. In the first section I first briefly review the different explanations that have been put forth to account for nonwage and reciprocal labor patterns in the Andes and then examine the different yet complementary modes of recruiting labor in Pampa. I then present a detailed, quantitative account of the amount and type of labor deployed and mobilized in the planting and sowing of Pampa's potato crops. In the last section of this chapter I offer various explanations that account for the labor patterns prevalent in Pampa.

Why Nonwage and Reciprocal Labor?

The study of nonwage and reciprocal labor in the Andes has been a recurrent thread in the ethnographic literature. Over a decade ago Guillet (1980) surveyed existing ethnographic research on labor recruitment patterns in the Central Andes. He noted that, while some observers were claiming at the time that reciprocal (and, in general, nonwage) labor was on the decline, others were asserting precisely the opposite. For instance, at about the same time that Guillet (1980:157) himself asserted that "reciprocal labor is flourishing," J. Weil (1980a:393) stated that

"Andean cooperative institutions have fallen into disarray." This debate is far from over, as ethnographers continue to debate the importance of reciprocal and other forms of nonwage labor in the economic organization of Andean communities (cf. M. Painter 1985, 1991; Brown 1987; Chibnik and Jong 1989; J. Weil 1989).

The recurrent controversy over nonwage and reciprocal labor in the Andes has had two intertwined—and not always discernible—dimensions: documenting and explaining the survival or demise of these labor patterns.

One major reason for this controversy (and confusion) is that few researchers arguing for or against the persistence or demise of reciprocal and other nonwage forms of labor recruitment in the Andes have offered quantitative evidence of the relative weight of different labor arrangements in the productive process, as J. Weil (1980a, 1989) has done among migrants from the Cochabamba highlands on their homesteads in the tropical Chapare. That is, virtually all claims of the persistence or decline of reciprocal and nonwage labor have largely consisted of generalizations based on informants' (normative) statements but seldom have researchers systematically gathered quantitative data on the deployment of labor with the objective of confirming or refuting their informants' views.

Furthermore, not all ethnographers who have collected quantitative data on labor arrangements have grappled with the same problematic in identical ways, which has impeded comparisons and generalizations. Some ethnographers have been interested in ascertaining the number of individuals who used to, but no longer, engage in reciprocal labor; others in the number of households that have shifted from recruiting reciprocal to nonreciprocal, including wage, labor (e.g., Brown 1987); some in days in which reciprocal labor practices were observed taking place (Chibnik and Jong 1989); and still yet others in the extent to which the presence of wage labor compares to that of other forms of nonwage labor recruitment.

In addition, claims for or against the survival of nonwage labor are often cast against a backdrop of an absence of diachronic, historically grounded field research. Related to this is an

illusion that, as we travel across space to reach the peasant populations we study, we are also moving back in time. In so doing, we have reconstructed a traditional peasant society based on what we imagine institutions would look like if they were not beseiged by the changes occurring in the larger society. This vision of traditional society then serves as a platonic ideal against which we hold our observations in order to assess the magnitude and significance of the changes that are taking place. (M. Painter 1985:6-7)

A relevant example of the transformation of "traditional"—but not timeless and unchanging (cf. Roseberry 1989a:75-76)—social arrangements in novel contexts and meeting new exigencies is the well-known Andean *mit'a*. An institution with deep historical roots, the *mit'a* consisted of seasonal and periodic labor services, couched within an ideology of reciprocity, that Andean households provided to their communities and ethnic lords. The Incas later adopted and extended the *mit'a* (as well as other local Andean social and economic institutions) to underwrite imperial needs, such as to colonize new lands, provide labor to state-supported agriculture, and augment their armies. In turn, Spanish colonial officials "transformed the mit'a tradition into a colonial institution of forced labor" (Stern 1982:82) to serve in the mines (cf. Stern 1982:82-89; Spalding 1984:26, 82-95; Larson 1988a:28-30, 58-64; Rasnake 1988:106-13). According to this perspective, then, nonwage, reciprocal, and traditional social arrangements are contemporary manifestations of a long and sustained contact with wider social and economic processes, some of which superficially appear to have remained the same but which have had their meanings and functions drastically altered (e.g., Wolf 1982; cf. Hobsbaum 1983; see also chap. 1). Roseberry (1989b:118) puts it nicely when he states that anthropologists

need to pay close attention to the complex interplay of external pressure and internal response over time and need to be aware of the possibility that those features of peasant life that seem most traditional or customary may be the results of past impositions, responses, or accommodations. It may be that the traditional peasant is part of a modern history, a history that has placed the peasant in a wider world.

A set of explanations for nonwage and reciprocal labor has stressed its importance for Andean peasants extracting a livelihood in a harsh environment and with low levels of technology. One explanation relates nonwage labor to features of the Andean ecology, seasonal imbalances in household labor availability, and attempts to gain access to land. For example, labor-short households require access to additional labor to fully exploit their dispersed crop lands, and land-poor households will offer their labor in order to gain access to land and crops to which they would not otherwise have access. Labor exchanges are, in other words, an important means of optimizing the use of and access to land and labor (Guillet 1983:563; Brush 1977b:106; Figueroa 1984:21; Golte 1980:73–74).

Reciprocal and other modes of nonwage labor have also been explained as mechanisms for gaining access to resources in a context of socioeconomic inequality. The central idea here is that peasants may and will engage in reciprocal labor for reasons other than labor shortages. Sons may help their fathers because they want to avoid forfeiting their inheritance, and rich peasants will turn to reciprocal arrangements, not because of a shortage of family labor or cash but as a way of obtaining cheap labor (Sánchez 1982; Orlove 1977a; Long and Roberts 1978:314–21).

An additional interpretation is that Andean peasants are normally short of cash and that wage labor is far more convenient and expedient than other forms of labor recruitment. Consequently, the absence of wage labor is believed to be a manifestation of an acute shortage of cash within peasant households and communities (Guillet 1978:10–13; 1980:159; Brush 1977b:105–6; Golte 1980:74). A logical corollary of these arguments is that rural areas in which cash is readily available will display higher indices of wage labor and a concomitant decline in reciprocal and nonwage labor practices.

There is little doubt that the different ways of recruiting labor in the Andes do not "represent remnants of 'traditional' behavior but are some of the basic means by which the continuity and survival of the peasant household system is ensured" (Long and Roberts 1978:308). In the specific case of the Chapare, J. Weil (1980a, 1980b, 1989) has offered perhaps the best analysis of how traditional Andean labor recruitment patterns were molded to meet new environmental and economic needs in the tropical frontier.

However, many (if not most) authors who would agree with Long and Roberts's statement on the contemporary relevance of Andean nonwage labor patterns appear to jump to the conclusion that these should be foremost or solely explained in terms of internal (household and community) needs. The persistence of these labor patterns, according to this perspective, is to be primarily explained by the lack of multiple linkages to wider economic, social, and political forces beyond household and community boundaries. The implication here, of course, is that, as capitalist production and exchange relations spread throughout the countryside, traditional and nonwage labor will give way to wage relationships (e.g., Erasmus 1956; Alberti and Mayer 1974; Golte 1980; Brown 1987). As we saw in chapter 1, this interpretation is wholly consistent with the "differentiation" perspective shared by some scholars of different theoretical persuasions.

One glaring exception to this line of analysis is Guillet's (1980) view that reciprocal labor may also be explained by the function that it fulfills for capitalist enterprises (i.e., lowering the costs of production). He writes that "because of the structure of peripheral capitalist social formations, one can expect the socioeconomic attributes of peasantry to persist" (1980:163), an explanation wholly compatible with the perspective that the "survival" of peasant socioeconomic forms is a functional requirement of capitalism (see also chaps. 1 and 9). While this interpretation has the obvious advantage of situating local-level phenomena within the context of wider social and economic processes, Guillet provides little data to adequately support his conclusion that reciprocal labor is "flourishing" partly because it fulfills certain "needs" of capitalism. It may very well be, as I will argue, that reciprocal and nonwage labor may indeed thrive in certain contexts in which peasants are more intensely intertwined with broader economic processes but having little or nothing to do with directly satisfying or meeting the needs of capitalism.

Some of the methodological and theoretical difficulties in assessing the pervasiveness of reciprocal and nonwage labor are illustrated by Brown's comparison of migration and labor recruitment patterns in two Peruvian villages (Brown 1987). Following the argument originally expounded by Erasmus (1956) in a well-known essay, Brown claims that increasing links with a cash economy led to a "breakdown of reciprocal labor" (Brown 1987:226). In support of his claim Brown noted that in Utani, the village more closely linked (through seasonal wage migration) to the cash economy and experiencing the most intense outmigration to the Peruvian coast, 46 percent of households did not recruit *ayni* labor, while 64 percent of the households employed wage labor at some point in time during the agricultural season (Brown 1987:236).

Brown's analysis based on the percentage of households that recruit labor through various means does not reveal the total amount (and type) of labor recruited through different labor arrangements and subsequently deployed by these households. It is possible, for instance, that in Utani the total number of peasants engaging in reciprocal labor may have risen over time, while the number of households recruiting labor (through, say, *ayni*) may have remained constant. An equally serious difficulty in Brown's analysis is that he draws diachronic conclusions from essentially synchronic field data. We simply do not know the prevalence of wage recruitment or *ayni* exchanges nor enough of the local and extralocal context within which these take place in Utani prior to the seasonal migration of household heads to the Peruvian coast. Last, Brown's conclusions presume an inevitable unidirectionality of change—from isolated to less isolated households, more to less modern, reciprocal to wage labor. Nevertheless, other courses, contexts, and outcomes of change are certainly possible.

In the following sections I present a quantitative account of the type and amount of labor deployed in the cultivation of the potato by a small sample of Pampeño migrant and nonmigrant households. (See app. 1 for the methods employed for quantifying labor inputs.) My central argument is that, although nonwage and reciprocal labor recruitment patterns were certainly related to local exigencies, they were also to a large measure the result of new demands sparked by migration to the Chapare, increasing linkages that Pampeños were forging with the wider coca market, and the collapse of the national economy, all of which impinged upon local productive decisions, including the deployment of labor.

Patterns of Labor Deployment

In the previous chapter I examined different strategies undertaken by Pampeño household heads in the cultivation of their irrigated (*mishka* and *chaupi mishka*) and rainfed (*huata*) potato crops. In this section I provide a quantitative account of the amount and type of labor, expressed in terms of person-days, mobilized and deployed for the sowing and harvest of *mishka* (including *chaupi mishka*) and *huata* potato crops by 47 household heads. The following analysis rests exclusively on tasks carried out at the day of the planting and harvest. During planting these tasks included, for instance, opening furrows and planting seed but excluded land preparation, the transport of guano and chemical fertilizers to the fields, and other activities necessary for sowing. Likewise, the analysis of the labor deployed during the harvest was limited to the actual digging up of the crop but excluded other crucial tasks, such as weeding, the sorting of the harvested potatoes into different categories, and its transport back to the dwellings.[1]

The agricultural season in Pampa, as noted in the previous chapter, was marked by the planting and sowing of the potato. Potato cultivation required a considerable investment of labor, far more than other highland crops (table 7.1). The cultivation of the potato also demanded the most varied means of labor recruitment. In Pampa, as in many other Andean (and non-Andean) peasant communities, households were generally unable to muster by themselves all the labor they required to cultivate their potato fields, given the time and ecological constraints under which the sowing and planting took place. For example, during the 1984 agricultural season 47 households mobilized 1,180 person-days for sowing and harvesting their potato fields, but they required an additional 1,711 person-days (59 percent of all labor deployed) of extra-household labor (table 7.2). The total contribution of household labor

TABLE 7.1   Annual Labor Invested in Cultivating Selected Crops on One Hectare of Land in Cochabamba

Crop	Person-Days
Mishka potato	218
Huata potato	197
Irrigated broad bean	109
Nonirrigated broad bean	79
Irrigated barley	86
Nonirrigated barley	68

Source: Adapted from Lagos 1988:130.

TABLE 7.2   Labor Use, Harvest and Sowing all Potato Crops, 1983–84, in Person-Days

	Ayuda	Ayni	Paga	Jornal	Tarpuja	Total	Percentage of Total
Kin	155.8	421.1	262.7	15.4	49.0	904.0	52.8
Nonkin	23.4	146.2	544.0	58.2	35.2	807.0	47.2
Total	179.2	567.3	806.7	73.6	84.2	1711.0	—
Percentage of Total	10.5	33.2	47.1	4.3	4.9	100.0	100.0

Source: Field data, 1984.

declined during the harvest, which required a greater investment of labor (including extra-household labor) than during the planting stage of the agricultural cycle.

Extra-household labor was mobilized through five complementary mechanisms. *Paga* (payment in kind) accounted for the most significant mode of recruiting labor in the cultivation of both crops (47.1 percent). The second and third most important ways of recruiting additional labor beyond household boundaries consisted of *ayni* (33.2 percent) and *ayuda* (10.5 percent). These latter two inter-household labor exchanges, which did not entail payments in goods or cash, totaled 43.7 percent of all labor deployed in the sowing and harvest of both potato crops (table 7.2).

Ayni refers to carefully documented reciprocal prestations of (primarily) labor, usually between close kin and/or neighbors. In an *ayni* labor exchange the party receiving labor has the responsibility of reciprocating with an equal amount of labor at a future date. The "debt," however, can be repaid in other ways, such as by a daily loaning of a pair of oxen or by reciprocating with an allotment of irrigation water.[2] *Ayni* can also entail labor exchanges between Pampa and the lowland colonies.[3] For example, a migrant may incur *ayni* obligations while sowing or harvesting his potato crop in Pampa and repay that obligation in the Chapare, either with his own labor or that of his lowland laborers. Likewise, an *ayni* obligation incurred in the Chapare can be repaid in Pampa. Most *ayni* labor exchanges between Pampa and the Chapare colonies surfaced during the potato harvest.

Ayuda refers primarily to labor exchanges in which household members freely cooperate with each other and contribute their time and labor to the wide range of tasks necessary for the maintenance and reproduction of their households. Because of the strong obligation within the household for members to cooperate and reciprocate labor, *ayuda* can, strickly speaking, be classed with *ayni* as reciprocal labor (cf. Brush 1977b:105). At the same time *ayuda* in Pampa also referred to and included enduring and recurrent labor exchanges between different households. (This is the sense in which most of the ethnographic literature refers to reciprocal labor.) Examples of inter-household *ayuda* labor exchanges included the labor provided by the owner of the land for his sharecropper or, more commonly, donations of a day's labor by migrants temporarily in Pampa to other kin. Unless otherwise noted, reciprocal labor as used in the present discussion will refer to inter-household *ayni* and *ayuda* exchanges.[4]

The least important modes of recruiting labor in the sowing and harvest of Pampa's potato crops during the 1984 season consisted of *jornal*, or wage labor (4.3 percent), and *tarpuja* (4.9 percent). *Tarpuja* referred to an exchange of the harvest of one furrow of land for labor. In some Quechua-speaking Peruvian communities this pattern is called *arimsay* (Webster 1981:620). *Tarpuja* typically involved someone who, lacking sufficient land and/or labor, planted one furrow of someone else's land with his or her own seed for one crop season. In return for irrigation water and the full harvest of that furrow, he or she would provide labor during sowing and the harvest of the owner's entire plot of land, regardless of the length of time it may take. The owner of the land was assured of one day of *tarpuja* labor during planting and as many days of labor as he or she required to complete the harvest on the entire plot of land. Sage (1990:212–13) has recently described a virtually identical mode of labor recruitment in the Cochabamba province of Ayopaya.

In the *mishka* and *huata* sowing (tables 7.3 and 7.4) the overwhelming percentage of extra-household labor (68.2 and 61.7 percent, respectively) was recruited through *ayni*. *Ayni* and *ayuda* jointly constituted over 73

TABLE 7.3   Labor Use, Mishka Sowing, 1984, in Person-Days

	Ayuda	Ayni	Paga	Jornal	Tarpuja	Total	Percentage of Total
Kin	19.6	183.8	3.2	11.6	26.0	244.2	64.6
Nonkin	6.0	74.0	3.0	31.2	19.8	134.0	35.4
Total	25.6	257.8	6.2	42.8	45.8	378.2	—
Percentage of Total	6.8	68.2	1.6	11.3	12.1	100.0	100.0

Source: Field data, 1984.

TABLE 7.4   Labor Use, Huata Sowing, 1984, in Person-Days

	Ayuda	Ayni	Paga	Jornal	Tarpuja	Total	Percentage of Total
Kin	17.6	91.6	1.0	3.4	14.6	128.2	53.1
Nonkin	10.4	57.2	10.2	20.0	15.4	113.2	46.9
Total	28.0	148.8	11.2	23.4	30.0	241.4	—
Percentage of Total	11.6	61.7	4.6	9.7	12.4	100.0	100.0

Source: Field data, 1984.

percent of the labor. *Paga* labor was virtually insignificant, while wage labor and *tarpuja* accounted for about 22 percent mobilized during the sowing of the *mishka* and *huata* crops.

Planting was a predominantly kin-based undertaking. Kin (*parientekuna, familiaresnikuna*) included cognates and affines, those sharing the same paternal surname, and fictive kin. Nonkin were referred to as *ajenos*, the same term used to designate a noncommunity member. Cognates sharing an identical paternal surname but with whom an exact genealogical link could not be ascertained were termed "distant kin" (*parientes lejanos*). At the core of this category of *parientes* was an ego-centered kindred of a first-cousin range (sometimes called by Pampeños a "parentela") comprised of cognatic descendants of ego's two sets of grandparents.[5]

Over 64 percent of the labor deployed in the sowing of *mishka* and 53 percent of the *huata* labor was provided by kin. Kin also contributed most of the *ayni* and *ayuda* labor, while nonkin (recruited mainly from neighboring communities), significantly enough, provided most of the wage labor. During the *mishka* sowing five household heads employed 15 noncommunity laborers; four of these (two of whom worked for *ayni*) lived in the Chapare. Kin and nonkin provided *tarpuja* labor in roughly equal amounts.

Considerably less labor was needed to sow the rain-fed *huata* crop than the irrigated *mishka* (241.4 person-days vs. 378.2 person-days). This was because of the relatively flat yet higher terrain in the Tuty crop zone (where most *huata* plantings took place) compared to that of the other crop zones, the fact that most households had only one crop of *huata*, and the absence of rains, which usually interrupted the *mishka* sowing. These factors appeared to permit a greater efficiency in the allocation of labor during planting.

The harvest of the *mishka* and *huata* potato crops (tables 7.5 and 7.6) required over 50 percent more labor than their sowing. The most striking characteristic of the potato harvest, when compared to the sowing, is the overwhelming weight of *paga* labor (more than 65 percent of the labor recruited for both crops). Conversely, reciprocal labor (*ayni* and inter-household *ayuda* combined) made up only 32 percent of the total labor during the harvest of *mishka* and just 22 percent for the *huata*. In sum, wage and *tarpuja* labor was meager during the sowing and virtually nonexistent throughout the harvest of both potato crops.

The increase of *paga* labor investment during the harvest was paralleled by a corresponding rise in the percentage of nonkin employed as
laborers; as suggested, payment in kind continued to be undertaken
primarily by nonkin recruited from beyond Pampa. Some of these nonkin
also worked for Pampeño migrants in the Chapare. All of the nine non-
Pampeños from the Chapare who labored in Pampa during the *mishka*
and *huata* harvests were remunerated with payment in kind.

Pampeño households were therefore able to mobilize a significant
percentage (41 percent) of the labor they required to cultivate their potato
crops during the 1983–84 agricultural cycle. Their ability to do so, however, is almost certainly related to an incipient decline in land area sown
in potatoes as a result of intense migration to the Chapare (see chap.
6). That is, it is possible that many households would have had to recruit
additional extra-household help had they not curtailed potato production.

When we examine the amount and type of labor deployed in the
cultivation (sowing and harvest) of both potato crops, *paga* looms as
the most important mode of recruiting labor, followed by *ayni, ayuda,*

TABLE 7.5   Labor Use, Mishka Harvest, 1984, in Person-Days

	Ayuda	Ayni	Paga	Jornal	Tarpuja	Total	Percentage of Total
Kin	59.6	73.8	126.6	0.4	3.2	263.6	56.8
Nonkin	3.0	12.2	178.0	7.0	.0	200.2	43.2
Total	62.6	86.0	304.6	7.4	3.2	463.8	—
Percentage of Total	13.5	18.5	65.7	1.6	0.7	100.0	100.0

Source: Field data, 1984.

TABLE 7.6   Labor Use, Huata Harvest, 1984, in Person-Days

	Ayuda	Ayni	Paga	Jornal	Tarpuja	Total	Percentage of Total
Kin	59.0	71.9	131.9	0	5.2	268.0	42.7
Nonkin	4.0	2.8	352.8	0	0	359.6	57.3
Total	63.06	74.7	484.7	0	5.2	627.6	100.0
Percentage of Total	10.1	11.9	77.2	0	0.8	100.0	—

Source: Field data, 1984.

wage labor, and *tarpuja*. Significant differences from this general pattern emerge, however, when the labor deployed during the sowing and harvest phases are analyzed separately. In the harvest *paga* loomed far more important than *ayuda* and *ayni* combined. During the sowing, by contrast, *ayuda* and *ayni* accounted for the greater part of the labor mobilized, while *paga* was almost totally absent.[6]

It should be stressed that I have not shown that more, or an equal number, of Pampeños sought out, and/or engaged in, reciprocal and nonwage labor relationships than in previous years. As I have argued, such a conclusion would have required a diachronic analysis of labor deployment over a number of crop seasons, an analysis that I did not undertake. Nevertheless, given the intensity of migration from Pampa to the Chapare and the diminishing role of seasonal migration (see chap. 4), and the trend to withdraw land from potato cultivation (see chap. 6), the total number of Pampeños actively engaged in agricultural tasks in Pampa, and therefore in any mode of labor arrangement, was probably far less than at the onset of Bolivia's coca boom.

My goal so far has been to demonstrate the overwhelming weight of nonwage and reciprocal labor in a community in which large numbers of its members and households were tightly intertwined with commodity production centered on coca in the Chapare. In the next section I will argue that the importance of these traditional labor patterns in Pampa was precisely one outcome of the integration of Pampeños to an increasingly commoditized regional economy.

As noted, I have excluded from my calculations of labor inputs the amount and type of labor devoted to major complementary tasks (*labores culturales*). This exclusion does not in itself invalidate the conclusions reached thus far. This is because most of the labor required in almost all these tasks was primarily provided by household members with little or no use of outside help. For instance, during the planting of the *mishka* crop, all but 4 of 32 households carried out the *empanto* (land irrigation prior to planting) by relying on their own labor, and 38 out of 47 households relied solely on their labor to plow their fields just before planting (*arado*). In addition, the productive activities that I have focused on during the planting and harvesting probably occupied most of the households' time and labor. Brown (1987:231), for instance, has calculated that in Peruvian peasant communities these activities required 87.7 percent of a household's time.

An Interpretation of Labor Patterns

Some of the explanations of the presence of nonwage labor patterns in the Andes that I briefly discussed at the beginning of this chapter, particularly those stressing the role of ecology, dispersed crop fields, and the need for a flexible (and efficient) allocation of labor, no doubt seem appropriate for an understanding of the structure of labor deployment in Pampa. For instance, we have seen (see chap. 6) that the sowing and harvesting of the potato takes place in a tightly constrained time span and that Pampeños will attempt to complete these tasks in one or two days. In the case of the harvest the dominant role of *paga* labor was partly due to the fact that it nicely complemented household labor in as much as most kin were also simultaneously engaged in harvesting their own crop. Furthermore, the reason why most *paga* laborers were recruited from neighboring valley-floor communities was partly because the harvest cycles (and therefore labor needs) in their communities only partially overlapped with those in Pampa. During sowing, on the other hand, the prevalence of *ayni* is partly explained by the fact that households enjoyed considerable leeway in the planting of their crops and, hence, had less difficulties in recruiting additional labor from among other kin and households in Pampa. The labor patterns documented above are also related to uneven resource distribution: in Pampa, as elsewhere, land-rich peasants attempted to seek out and receive, but usually not give, reciprocal labor. They were also unlikely to offer to others *tarpuja* and *paga* labor.

As I also mentioned earlier, an often unstated assumption of the explanations stressing the adaptive role of Andean recruitment patterns is that these are to be primarily explained in terms of needs internal to the community and households studied. A fieldworker in Pampa would almost certainly have been struck by the overwhelming role of kin-based, nonwage, and reciprocal forms of labor deployed throughout the agricultural season. If convinced that labor deployment in Pampa was to be understood solely within the confines of Pampa's agricultural economy, he or she would perhaps have remained unaware of the multiple linkages that Pampeños had forged with wider market forces and thereby also concluded that Pampa was a "traditional" community—socially, geographically, and economically "isolated" from, or only minimally integrated to, the "outside" world.

Such a conclusion, however, would have been mistaken and far from accurate. Pampeños buy and have bought in the past much of what they need from regional markets: clothes, cooking gas, consumption staples, agricultural inputs such as fertilizers, and so forth. We have seen in chapters 3 and 4 that, by migrating to and cultivating and selling Chapare coca, most Pampeño households were tightly integrated with and responding to the demands of the cocaine market. We have also examined in the previous chapter the different ways in which the surge in the price of and demand for coca was directly intertwined with the crop production strategies of virtually every Pampeño household.

The predominant weight of nonwage and reciprocal patterns of labor recruitment and deployment in Pampa is precisely one outcome of the linkages that Pampeños have forged with an increasingly commoditized regional economy centering on coca cultivation. We saw in chapter 3 that the early 1980s witnessed an acute inflation rate that severely depressed the purchasing power of cash wages and living standards alike and that this was paralleled by a massive migration, regional and local, to the Chapare. The almost total absence of wage labor during the cultivation of Pampa's potato crops was not simply the result of a shortage of cash or an inability or unwillingness of Pampeños to engage in monetary transactions. Better still, the availability of cash was perhaps a necessary but certainly not a sufficient condition for the presence of wage labor. The purchasing power of cash, the absence or presence of other economic options, and the ability and willingness of land-based peasants in the Chapare to hire wage laborers at quite high wage rates (or offer other, more valuable forms of compensation) were other important factors that structured particular labor recruitment patterns and decisions in Pampa during Bolivia's the coca boom.[7] In particular, the negligible role of wage labor demonstrates the profound resistance by many Pampeños to work for the prevalent cash wage *in Pampa,* and the inability of some nonmigrant (and the refusal of migrant) household heads to offer wages for the cultivation of the potato comparable to those prevalent in the Chapare. The result of both factors was increasing difficulties to attract and retain (primarily young) laborers.

In Pampa corn beer formed part of a "local model" (Gudeman 1986, esp. chap. 1) from which Pampeños gauged broader agro-economic trends. Fluctuations in the price of corn beer would alert them to changes in the availability of corn and sugar in local markets as well as to fiscal policies that affected the prices of these products. In the present discussion the importance of corn beer within the local agricultural economy pivoted on its intimate relationship to wage labor. In Pampa and surrounding communities wage labor was usually, and still is, compensated at the rate of the monetary equivalent of five liters (*media lata*) of corn beer—the equivalent to about one U.S. dollar—in addition to food, coca leaves, and drink. The extraordinary rate of inflation that gripped Bolivia shortly after my arrival soon upset these terms of equivalence. Runaway inflation and acute shortages quickly led to skyrocketing prices of sugar and corn, creating havoc with agreed upon wage rates, the centerpiece of which was corn beer. Almost all Pampeños who processed corn beer had decided to replaced unrefined blocks of sugar (*chankaka*) by refined sugar manufactured by Santa Cruz agribusinesses. Furthermore, few Pampeños cultivated enough corn of their own for beer, and most were forced to travel to Punata or Cliza (in the *valle alto*) to buy additional corn at inflated prices. (Some *chichería* owners would buy corn beer at wholesale prices in Punata, Cliza, or the town of Sacaba, transport it back in former oil drums, and resell it at higher prices.)

As a result of the increase in the prices of sugar and corn, and the lack of cheaper *chankaka* and of a sufficient supply of corn in Pampa, the price of corn beer also rose dramatically. Nonmigrant household heads soon claimed that it was too costly to peg wage rates to the price of corn beer—much less offer wages or other types of compensation comparable to those that laborers received in the Chapare—given the overall low returns from potato cultivation. Instead, they opted to offer the average daily minimum wage set by the national government (about one U.S. dollar), a rate that always trailed inflation. Not unexpectedly, they found few other Pampeños willing to work for such a low pay in Pampa when the prevailing daily wages and other payments in the Chapare, particularly in the illegal sector, were much higher.

Wealthy migrant household heads (and some relatively wealthy nonmigrant household heads with large tracts of land) recruited most of the wage labor in Pampa. But even these migrant household heads mobilized predominantly nonwage labor in the cultivation of their potato crops. The case of Valeriano, a wealthy migrant who along with his brother and nephew controlled considerable land in two Chapare settlements (see chap. 4), is revealing of how even wealthy migrant household heads failed to recruit a large number of wage laborers. In sowing his *mishka* crop, Valeriano employed no wage labor, while during his *huata* planting he mobilized three times more labor through *ayni* and *ayuda*. He would have preferred to hire, and had the cash to pay for, additional wage laborers. But Valeriano refused to pay higher wages comparable to those in the Chapare, given the low prices of each sack of potatoes he harvested, despite the fact that he had no intentions of selling any portion of his harvest. Sánchez's (1982:170) statement that "the availability of finance (i.e., cash) [is a determinant factor] in peasants' choice of wage labour over other forms" presumes a lack of a competing market for labor and an ample supply of peasants willing to and needing to work for established wage rates. Both conditions, however, were absent in Pampa.

In another case Enrique, a nonmigrant household head with considerable land in Pampa, constantly faced difficulties in securing help from his kin for the cultivation of his two potato crops. He was successful in recruiting some wage laborers at the established daily wage rate, but they accounted for less than 36 percent of all the labor he deployed during the sowing and less than 25 percent in the course of the harvest. Enrique was unsuccessful in recruiting additional wage or *paga* laborers and hence unable, he claimed, to sow as much land as he had wanted to.

Other nonmigrant household heads unable to offer high wages comparable to those in the Chapare confronted similar difficulties in recruiting labor. Many household heads were also unable to enter into reciprocal labor arrangements with their kin. This was because many of their kin would often be in the Chapare during the critical harvest and sowing periods or else planting and harvesting their own crops. Elderly nonmigrant household heads unable to mobilize sufficient labor to maintain former levels of production (see chap. 6) were becoming more isolated from both former household members, other kin, and other Pampeños who were away in the Chapare. While they primarily relied on *ayuda* and *ayni* to meet their labor needs, they too faced difficulties in mobilizing labor, for often household members and other kin were away in the Chapare during critical periods of the agricultural cycle. To these nonmigrant household heads coca, as they explained to me, was "not good."

Pampeños who occasionally worked for cash wages in Pampa were often youngsters or others whose immediate need for some cash was not great enough to warrant an extended (and expensive) trip to the Chapare. For those Pampeños in need of cash and who lacked access to coca land there, the Chapare also provided other, far better alternatives than seeking out wage labor in Pampa. These options included working for *paga* and getting paid in coca (which could be subsequently resold or processed into coca paste with far higher returns) or entering the lucrative business of buying and selling coca leaves. These alternatives to wage labor in Pampa led to an absolute decline of the number of persons with a need to work for cash wages.

The virtual absence of wage labor in Pampa contrasted with the importance of payment in kind. As we have seen, *paga* was a significant means of recruiting extra-household labor, especially from neighboring communities, when most Pampeños (and their kin) were occupied in their own harvests. But the predominance of *paga* over wage labor cannot be attributed soley to the distribution of crop fields over the physical landscape and the subsequent need to optimize the allocation of labor. The importance of *paga* also illustrated the different ways in which processes beyond Pampa's physical boundaries exerted a powerful role in structuring the organization of agricultural labor. The overwhelming import of *paga,* when compared to wage labor in Pampa, did not reflect the community's isolation from the market, the wider cash economy, or lack of cash. Conversely, the marginal presence of wage labor is better explained by the widely recognized preference of opting for agricultural products in an economic environment in which the purchasing value of cash constantly and quickly dropped in relation to agricultural goods.

Pampeños, especially nonmigrants, and others who offered their labor for *paga* did so in order to meet an unexpected shortfall of cash or of potatoes for consumption (a common concern and need, especially at the beginning of the harvest). *Paga* was compensated at the daily rate of 50 pounds (two *arrobas*) of potatoes, regardless of their current market price, plus meals, drink, and coca. The overwhelming role of *paga* compared to wage labor in Pampa points to the fact that the 50 pounds of potatoes that a laborer received by working for *paga* was a far better return for a day's work than a daily wage, given the rapid depreciation of cash in a hyperinflationary context and wildly fluctuating state fiscal policies. Depending on the rate of inflation and the often sudden rise and fall of potato prices, the monetary value of these two *arrobas* of potatoes would easily be worth many times the daily cash wage. For instance, on September 30, 1983 the daily wage in Pampa was a mere 700 *pesos bolivianos*; by contrast, 50 pounds of first-quality potatoes (*de primera clase*) were worth close to 8,000 *pesos bolivianos*. It also made little sense to want to be paid such low cash wages in an inflationary period when the value of cash would erode overnight. Payment in kind also offered other options and advantages. For instance, a Pampeño in need of cash could secure potatoes through *paga* and hold onto them for a while and, given the high inflation rate, could later sell them for a far higher price.

Despite its remunerative dimension, a *paga* labor relationship cannot be reduced to a mere exchange of labor services for agricultural goods, as a simple variant of a cash wage (on this point, see Platt 1982b:61–63, for northern Potosí).[8] Among Pampeños and other Andean peasants (Brush 1977b:109)—as well as Guatemalan coffee-cultivating peasants, who paid each other wages (Swetnam 1989:107)—*paga* transactions involved considerable expectations to reciprocate in the future. Moreover, many Pampeños entered into a *paga* arrangement with nearby friends and neighbors, past *ayni* partners, and kin. That is, those who recruited and offered *paga* labor to each other were enmeshed in a web of mutual social obligations that transcended its purely remunerative aspects and which were continuously recreated in other social contexts. These reciprocal obligations embedded in a paga relationship are so significant that Sánchez (1982:172) goes so far as to view payment in kind as a variant of reciprocal labor.

The refusal by most Pampeños to work for cash wages and to opt instead for *paga* did not, then, reflect their inability to clearly recognize the value of their labor and production—quite the contrary. As with other Andean peasants (e.g., Martínez-Alier 1973:7–37; Brush 1977b:107; Long and Roberts 1978:310; Harris 1982:89; Mallon 1983:210; Figueroa 1984:65; Brown 1987:237; Rasnake 1988:274), Pampeños clearly recognized work in agriculture as far more attractive (at least in Pampa) than work for cash wages, especially in a context of runaway inflation. In addition, some peasants in Pampa who preferred to be paid in kind during the sowing and harvest of the potato would later travel to the Chapare and engage in wage labor there. Clearly, in the 1980s most Pampeños wanted to circumvent cash transactions in local currency within the confines of Pampa's agricultural economy. Yet this has not always been the case. According to respondents, in periods of monetary stability Pampeños did not evade but, rather, when it was advantageous to them, actively engaged in cash transactions. These periods were also when, for example, land rentals were commonplace in Pampa (see chap. 5).

Mallon's (1983) research in the central highlands of Peru at the turn of the century provides a fascinating parallel with the issues I am raising here. In 1917 peasants resisted cash wages in lieu of payment in kind. According to Mallon (1983:210) "the peasants did not resist payment in cash out of attachment to their traditional rights, but because prices were going up extremely rapidly. Not only was the cash they were offered insufficient, but continuing to receive payment in kind would serve as insurance against further inflation." Martínez-Alier (1973:7–37) has likewise noted that tenants in central Peruvian haciendas obtained far higher incomes from cultivating desmesne land and managing small herds than by engaging in wage labor. Consequently, they resisted, often successfully, attempts by the landlowner to transform them into a wage-earning proletariat.[9] Similarly, R. G. Williams (1986:55–65) has demonstrated how the shift to wage labor in Central American cotton plantations resulted in the loss of land and a sharp drop in living standards and how this shift was vigorously, but unsuccessfully, resisted by peasant tenants.

The fact that Pampeños, as well as other Andeans and peasants, often engaged in wage labor and cash transactions does not necessarily mean that they do so willingly (or happily) or that strong cultural norms against wage labor or cash/labor exchanges do not exist. Allen, for example, explains the absence of wage labor in Sonqo, a Quechua-speaking community near Cuzco, in the following way: "their rejection of money is a refusal to bypass human reciprocity" (1988:219). S. Skar (1984:93) similarly explains the virtual lack of wage labor within the Peruvian peasant community she studied on the basis of the "strong emotive quality based upon reciprocity." These norms, in and of themselves, however, are insufficient to explain the seeming absence of wage labor within many Andean peasant communities and especially in Pampa.

The amply documented "resistance to cash" (Harris 1982:79) by peasants throughout the rural Andes cannot be necessarily interpreted as an innate desire to isolate themselves from wider economic (or political) processes, nor as a mere result of admittedly powerful cultural norms favoring or encouraging reciprocity. I would argue, instead, that Pampeños and other Andean peasants engage in, or retreat from, specific forms of market circulation and wage labor arrangements, within and outside of their communities, according to the advantages to be reaped or disadvantages to be evaded by a particular economic strategy in a specific socioeconomic context, *regardless* of the presence or absence of cultural norms against wage labor. Pampeños operated in—and constantly moved between—two distinct yet interrelated economic spheres, each spawned by the convergence of political, agronomic, and economic trends and each with its own rationale: the Chapare, where commodity production was profitable and increasingly widespread, and in Pampa, where the production of highland crops was being curbed due to adverse economic conditions. An analogous interpretation has been provided by Rasnake (1988) for northern Potosí, far from Bolivia's centers of coca production. Among the Yuras inflation and deteriorating real wages during the 1980s led to a renewed emphasis on subsistence agriculture and, with it, probably a "renewal of traditional cultural forms and practices" (Rasnake 1988:274).

Nonwage labor patterns in Pampa were related in other ways to the migration of Pampeños to the Chapare. *Ayni* labor exchanges between Pampa and the Chapare are a case in point. This variant of *ayni* was especially advantageous in a highly mobile population, given its remarkable flexibility for mobilizing labor. Additionally, these *ayni* labor exchanges led to intense and lasting economic cooperation between kin-linked households, which was otherwise difficult to attain. For instance, some migrants more or less permanently settled in the Chapare found it difficult for many reasons to cooperate with their parents' harvests in Pampa. Nevertheless, when in Pampa they offered *ayni* to other households, whose members then pledged to reciprocate to the latters' fathers when they required it.[10]

These nonwage land reciprocal labor patterns in Pampa were also mechanisms that both generated and consolidated social ties, which in turn facilitated access to land and other resources in the Chapare. (Owners of land in the Chapare in need of labor in turn assured themselves of a reliable work force.) For example, youngsters or other nonmigrants in Pampa working for *ayni, paga,* or even cash wages on the land of migrants in Pampa could slowly demonstrate that they were reliable, trustworthy, and hard workers. Over time relationships of trust would arise between them and the migrants they work for. At some point they could be asked to travel to the Chapare and work there as laborers, either in the coca harvests or in activities related to the processing of coca paste. Eventually, some were offered land to sharecrop. While in the Chapare, they had the opportunity of consolidating relationships with other migrants and to learn of land opportunities in the area. The goal of most, of course, was to eventually gain permanent access to land there. Joaquín provides a good example. Joaquín began traveling to the Chapare in 1970, when he was only 12 years old. He was invited to work there as a laborer by a neighbor in Pampa for whom he had worked for *paga* many times before. He was, in his own words, "a good worker." In subsequent years Joaquín worked in various Chapare settlement as a laborer and was finally offered a sharecropping arrangement by one of his brothers. Years later, while in the Chapare, he learned of a new nearby settlement that was being colonized. The head of that colony was his brother's *compadre*, who subsequently played an important role in helping Joaquín obtain a land grant there.

One upshot of intense migration to the Chapare, and of the tight integration of Pampeños into a lucrative commodity market, was the predominant role of nonwage and reciprocal labor patterns in Pampa. From the vantage point of the "traditional" interpretation of Andean labor practices, nonwage labor patterns in Pampa paradoxically surfaced within a context of regional and national commodity production and solid linkages to regional and global economic circuits generated by the transnational drug trade. Time-honored, or "traditional," labor practices underlying the organization of productive relations in Pampa were far from being markers of isolation or economic irrationality, and their apparent "traditionalism" were in fact a matter of surface appearance generated by the integration of Pampeños into a regional commodity market.

Chapter 8

Epilogue: 1985-92

I left Pampa in June of 1985, two months before a new government imposed severe measures to restructure the Bolivian economy and amid ominous signs of increasing repression of coca cultivation and trade. I returned to Pampa for several weeks in June 1991 and again in the summer of 1992. Coca prices have nose-dived, and the "boom" has, at least for now, turned to "bust." Far from quietly fading away, however, the "coca problem" will most likely persist as a central political and economic issue for Pampeños and many others, in and outside of Bolivia, for many years to come.

Taming Inflation: The 1985 Economic Program and
Its Impact

At the end of 1984, in the midst of deepening economic chaos, political turmoil, and escalating social unrest, the government of Hernán Siles Suazo and the Bolivian Congress called for general elections for June 16, 1985. The administration of the newly elected president Víctor Paz Estenssoro assumed power on August 6, 1985, and quickly followed up on its pledge to tame Bolivia's inflation and restructure the country's chaotic economy. Within weeks it launched the severe "New Economic Policy" (Nueva Política Económica) designed to profoundly and irreversibly reshape Bolivia's economic structure (and which Paz Estenssoro himself had played such a prominent role in forging after the agrarian reform). The key features of the Nueva Política Económica included the shift away from state intervention in the economy toward neoliberal, free-market principles; a greater emphasis on economic stabilization and capital accumulation; and the opening of domestic markets to international market forces (Malloy and Gamarra 1988:195-97).

Bolivia's Nueva Política Económica was part of a wave of neoliberal, free-market economic thinking that swept the Andean countries at the time (Conaghan, Malloy, and Abugattas 1990; see also Mann and Pastor

1990). The economic program was strongly supported by all of Bolivia's major, and traditionally rival, political parties and implemented by a team of ministers and economic advisors strongly aligned to (and supported by) powerful capitalist sectors. The fact that the major outlines of Bolivia's 1985 "economic package" (*paquete económico*) have changed little despite successive governments and political alliances between traditionally rival elites points to the remarkable cohesion among and convergence of interests by Bolivian capitalists during this period (Conaghan 1991), which in turn signaled the emergence of a more powerful state. In fact, a widespread view and deep concern shared by top state officials was that the legitimacy—and, indeed, the very survival—of the state depended on a firm and unwavering implementation and rigid enforcement of these economic policies, the most severe and orthodox of any of the neighboring Andean countries (Conaghan, Malloy, and Abugattas 1990:17–18.)

The economic policies that were carried out were truly draconian. The Bolivian *peso boliviano* (which was replaced by a new currency, the *boliviano*, in January of 1987) was devalued by 1,500 percent. Salaries, especially in the public sector and state corporations, were immediately frozen. Massive layoffs were ordered in the public (but especially in mining) enterprises. Tariffs and other restrictions on the importation of foreign goods, including agricultural products, were lifted. State-owned mines were restructured, and most of the deficit-ridden ones shut down. Many state-owned enterprises were privatized, and fiscal subsidies to other public corporations were suspended. Equally critical was the lifting of state subsidies for popular urban consumer staples. The monetary supply was sharply restricted, as was additional credit to state enterprises. The foreign currency black market was quickly undermined through the free floating of the peso and, later, the *boliviano* (see, e.g., Dunkerley and Morales 1986; Bailey and Knutsen 1987; Cole 1987; Sachs 1987; Aguirre, Pérez, and Villegas 1990:10–24; Conaghan, Malloy, and Abugattas 1990).

By most accounts these economic measures were incredibly successful. The state's deficit declined from 28 percent of gross domestic product (GDP) in 1984 to a mere 3.8 percent in 1986. Moreover, inflation came to a virtual halt shortly thereafter, and Bolivia quickly regained access to international credit lines (Pattie 1988:3; Jameson 1989). The social costs of this "recovery" program were nevertheless extremely high, and already low living standards worsened even more.

Unemployment and underemployment reached massive proportions. For instance, 20,000 miners, almost 75 percent of the state mining corporation's work force, lost their jobs by mid-1987, and hunger was reported widespread in quickly vanishing mining towns (*Latin American Weekly Report* 1987c; Crabtree, Duffy, and Pearce 1987; Jameson 1989:97; Mann and Pastor 1990:14).

The freezing of wages and the doubling or tripling of the prices of consumer staples, partly due to the lifting of government subsidies, led to a drastic fall in real income. Between 1970 and 1980 there was "no change in real wages: the gains up to 1978 were eroded with the onset of the economic crisis." By 1986, and especially as a result of the economic stabilization program, real wages were "41% or less of their value in 1980 (and hence also 1970)" (Horton 1991:13, 14). By late 1987 the real income of an average peasant household in the department of Cochabamba (but excluding migrant households in the Chapare region) declined by at least 34 percent from 1980 (Maletta 1988:106; see also Mann and Pastor 1990:14). In March of 1988 the minimum monthly wage hovered at only U.S. $24 (*Latin American Weekly Report* 1988a). The gap between the poor and the rich also quickly widened (Bailey and Knutsen 1987:49). In addition, the economic program also accelerated the consistent trend in the deteriorating terms of trade of major peasant crops noted earlier (chap. 3). According to Healy (1991a:8) the "price index of agricultural products declined by 29% from the stabilization to the end of 1988 relative to overall consumer prices."

As expected, the economic program led to a steep contraction in demand (cf. Antezana 1990:105) and production, from which the economy has yet to recover. Interestingly enough, despite the fact that the Nueva Política Económica seems to have been endorsed by most capitalist sectors, by and large they have consistently refused to engage in productive investments in Bolivia, preferring instead to invest their capital overseas or to maintain it in Bolivia in U.S. dollar accounts and engage in speculative transactions (see, e.g., Conaghan 1991).

The economic program also significantly raised costs for peasant producers. Potatoes, the key agricultural staple and cash crop of Cochabamba's valley and highland peasantry, were especially hard hit by the fall in prices and rising costs. For example, one week after the new economic program went into effect "the price of potatoes in Tiraque dropped from $b 24 million to $b 15 million while transport costs for manure increased from $b70,000 to $b 120 million" (Lagos 1988:206).

The gulf between costs and prices for peasant households worsened in subsequent years. During 1988–89 potato prices in Cochabamba decreased by 9 percent, while the costs of chemical fertilizers more than doubled (Healy 1991a:18–19). Another study emphasized that potato prices (in U.S. dollar terms) in Cochabamba fell by 49 percent, while transport costs and inputs rose 33 and 15 percent, respectively, between 1987 and 1989 (Healy 1991a:20).

To make matters worse, a key provision of the new economic program consisted of lifting restrictions on agricultural imports. As a consequence, less expensive agricultural staples from abroad, including large quantities of potatoes from Argentina, apparently flooded local markets precisely when Bolivian peasant producers were being squeezed by higher costs and drastically lower prices (Healy 1991a:12). Last, the new economic program replicated previous credit and other fiscal policies (see chap. 3) that largely benefited agro-industrial elites in Santa Cruz and reduced in absolute terms the amount of credit channeled to peasant producers (Healy 1991a:24–26). Not unexpectedly, overall agricultural production fell by 17 percent between 1985 and 1988 (Healy 1991a:7–8). Potato production declined throughout Bolivia and has yet to reach levels prevalent in the early 1980s (J. Morales 1990:55–58; Prudencio and Velazco 1987:10–12; Ministerio de Asuntos Campesinos y Agropecuarios 1990:89; Economist Intelligence Unit 1990:76; Instituto Nacional de Estadística 1990:5).

Miners, urban workers, and peasants alike—who confronted an increasingly repressive and cohesive state—vigorously but unsuccessfully resisted the *paquete económico* (Malloy and Gamarra 1988:197; Walton 1988; Nash 1992; Walton and Ragin 1988). The immediate and drastic decline in living standards generated by these economic measures led to a renewed migration of peasants and former miners and other unemployed workers to the Chapare, an increase in coca cultivation, and almost certainly an ever greater infusion of drug-related wealth into the country. Shortly thereafter coca leaf prices would begin a slow yet sustained decline—as a result of antidrug operations in Bolivia and Colombia that apparently disrupted trafficking circuits and an oversupply and decline in consumption of cocaine in the North American market (see, e.g., Johnson, Williams, Dei, and Sanabria 1990). Not until mid- to late 1990, however, would the expansion of coca cultivation show some signs of slowing down.

Repression and Coca Eradication

The long and bitter debate on the effects of coca chewing by Andean peasants and the unhappy tendency (still evident in some circles of the United States government) to equate coca chewing with cocaine addiction shaped what Burchard (1976:21) years ago called the Andean "coca problem."[1] From a political and economic standpoint Bolivia's contemporary "coca problem" has been of a different nature altogether. It has consisted of the ever greater expansion of and increasing economic dependence of peasants on coca production; the concomitant increase of cocaine-related activities throughout the countryside; and the political, economic, and military response to both by the Bolivian and United States governments.

Bolivia's "coca problem" is riddled with contradictions. Most of the wealth generated by the cocaine market ultimately escapes Bolivia. Yet the coca economy was, and to some extent has been, an important and consistent source of hard currency—fleeting but nevertheless real—that dampened the effects of the 1980s economic crisis for significant sectors of the population as well as for the country's financial system. At the same time the coca boom and the influx of "coca dollars" contributed to Bolivia's high inflation rate, vastly increased the economic and political power of the lowland capitalists and an emergent urban commercial class heavily involved in contraband (Doria Medina 1986), but benefited only a small proportion of Bolivia's peasantry. The Bolivian state has exercised little control over and cannot tax the wealth generated by the coca industry and is ostensibly committed to undermining the narcotics trade (*narcotráfico*).[2] But the state has also systematically encouraged a "compenetration" (Henman 1985:155) of the cocaine industry with the country's political, financial, and legal spheres and has repeatedly attempted to lure illicit funds into the formal banking system. Some notable examples of the legitimization of the cocaine industry include the mid-1985 Central Bank's "no questions asked" policy in purchasing dollars on the open market (Economist Intelligence Unit 1986:23) and the similar policy of luring illicit funds into the banking system as part of the Nueva Política Económica (*Latin American Weekly Report* 1985; Maletta 1988:98; Jameson 1989). This legitimization of the cocaine industry, which, once again, has paralleled and contrasts with attempts to limit and repress coca cultivation and marketing by peasant producers, has pervaded all levels of government.[3] Finally, the "coca problem" has angered the United States government, which has consistently threatened to cut off economic and military assistance if coca cultivation is not curtailed and a determined assault on drug traffickers not carried out.

Cocaine, along with other drugs, was outlawed in the United States at the turn of the twentieth century in the midst of profound social and economic transformations.[4] Since then Bolivian governments have signed various international agreements—never fully implemented—designed to interrupt the commerce of cocaine and limit the cultivation of the coca leaf.[5]

In the mid-1980s, however, under increasing pressure from the United States, Bolivian authorities intensified a cautious, twofold approach designed to stem the increased cultivation of coca and the processing of its by-products (and, indirectly, halt the flow of peasants to the Chapare). First, they escalated acts of repression. Antidrug raids by narcotics police (Leopardos), the 1984 military occupation of the Chapare, the 1986 deployment of United States troops (Henkel 1988; Healy 1986), and the stationing of large contingents of Drug Enforcement Administration (DEA) agents and other United States military personnel currently in Bolivia (United States House of Representatives 1990a) clearly were directed at small-scale cocaine-related operations, while frontal confrontations with the cocaine kingpins centered in Santa Cruz and the Beni during the 1980s were for the most part minimal.[6] As expected, peasants were and have been blamed for the current "coca problem" and have received the brunt of proposed "corrections."

The second and related approach toward solving the "coca problem" has consisted of a two-pronged effort—a "carrot and stick" strategy—designed to directly or indirectly force migrants in the Chapare to take up production of other tropical crops.

The first has consisted of research into alternate crops that can successfully compete, economically and agronomically, with coca. These efforts, underway since at least the early to mid-1960s and closely tied to attempts at eradicating the coca plant (e.g., Figueras 1978; USAID 1978; Parkerson 1989:290) have yet to pinpoint crops that can provide as much cash income and return on investments as coca and display its other advantages, such as low weight and high value, and strong and secure demand. Research into alternate crops has been based on the premise that repression and forced eradication, which will reduce the demand for and price of coca, will be implemented on a significant scale. The following statement by the United States' leading development organization is clear on this point: "A major assumption made in the project design is that the Bolivian government will pass legislation to limit the area of coca planting and will effectively enforce regulations against illicit traffic and cocaine production, thus making coca production less lucrative" (USAID 1981:2).

The objective of the second strategy is the forced elimination of coca. While the goal of police and military antidrug raids has been to undermine the immediate demand for coca leaves by dismantling coca paste and cocaine operations and interrupting the marketing of coca leaves, the repressive dimension of coca eradication and substitution programs aims at eliminating (often by force) coca growing altogether and supplanting it with other crops. This strategy was especially endorsed by the Paz Estenssoro government, which "demonstrated a strategic shift away from emphasis on the futile strategies of marketing control to raw material reduction, and subsequently, to coca leaf eradication" (Healy 1988:113–14).[7]

Indeed, these two approaches form the cornerstone of the United States' Andean narcotics policy. This policy, clearly spelled out by the Office of National Drug Control Policy's "Andean Initiative" (cf. United States House of Representatives 1990a:10–14; Levitsky 1990), is to increase military operations/interdiction against coca paste/cocaine processing facilities and distribution networks, undermine the production and marketing of coca leaves, and at the same time offer large sums of "development aid." The goal of this "supply-side" approach to the North American drug problem is to depress coca prices below production costs by undermining the demand for coca leaves by cocaine traffickers, either by imprisoning them or making it more difficult for them to secure an adequate amount of leaves. Once this goal is achieved, the argument goes, coca-producing peasants, faced with drastically low coca prices, will be more prone and willing to switch to alternate crops. It is at this juncture that development assistance—consisting of research into crop substitution and improvements in infrastructure and marketing arrangements in the lowlands and, more recently, an infusion of development funds in the highland and valley regions where migrants originate—come into play (United States House of Representatives 1990a:71; Rasnake and Painter 1989; Bostwick 1990:28). It is expected, furthermore, that the fall in coca leaf prices and levels of cocaine processing will in turn lead to higher cocaine prices in the United States consumer market and a subsequent decrease in demand.

After August of 1985 coca cultivation and eradication trends and policies entered a radically different phase. This was one marked by a precipitous drop in coca leaf prices from their early to mid-1980s peak levels, the destruction of thousands of hectares of coca, an increase in coca-inspired military and economic assistance, a new and bold coca eradication law, and an escalation of military and police interdiction and repressive efforts. The United States' Andean Initiative seemed well on the way toward achieving its goals.

A major objective of the United States antinarcotics strategy—a fall in coca prices and an absolute decline in the income to peasants from coca leaf cultivation—has, at least temporarily, been achieved. Coca leaf prices have declined drastically since the 1984–85 peak years (Ministerio de Asuntos Campesinos y Agropecuarios 1989, 1990 [n.p.]; Bostwick 1990:32–35; *Latin American Weekly Report* 1988b; Lee 1989:84–85, 159; United States House of Representatives 1990a:68). An oversupply of coca leaves due to the disruption of trafficking networks in Bolivia and Colombia and the decline of cocaine consumption in the United States are some of the explanations offered for the fall in coca leaf prices (United States House of Representatives 1990a:73).[8]

Some reports further claim that in the late 1980s coca prices barely covered production costs (cf. Bureau of International Narcotics Matters 1990:110–11). The decline in coca leaf prices has not been steady nor without strong upswings but, in fact, has fluctuated considerably. Average yearly prices between 1986 and 1989 remained, nevertheless, rather constant at about 150 *bolivianos* (or about U.S. $50) per *carga* (Bostwick 1990:32–35; Ministerio de Asuntos Campesinos y Agropecuarios 1989, 1990 [n.p.]). More intense fluctuations in leaf prices occurred during 1990.[9] In June 1991 coca prices were again on the rise.

There is also little doubt that thousands of hectares of coca have been eradicated since 1984–85, mainly in the Chapare. For example, according to DIRECO (Dirección de Reducción de la Coca), the Bolivian government agency directly responsible for carrying out the destruction of coca shrubs, slightly over 11,000 hectares of coca were eradicated between September and December 1987 and September 12, 1990 (Ministerio de Asuntos Campesinos y Agropecuarios 1990 [n.p.]). Other sources (e.g., Tolisano 1989:57; Bostwick 1990:34; Bureau of International Narcotics Matters 1990:113, 1991:80–81, 1992:92–94) also confirm • that thousands of hectares of coca have been eradicated in recent years.

The destruction of coca has not, of course, taken place in an economic and political vacuum. By 1988 the Bolivian economy was firmly "under control," a more powerful state apparatus had emerged, and coca leaf prices were rapidly declining. Bolivia was also receiving an influx of economic development assistance, including USAID funds to partly offset Bolivia's balance of payments deficit (Bureau of International Narcotics Matters 1991:83).

Military and economic assistance directly tied to and contingent upon successful drug control (including coca eradication) efforts was pouring into Bolivia at perhaps an unparalleled rate. Between (fiscal years) 1990 and 1994 Bolivia will have received as much as U.S. $837.7 million from the United States alone in narcotics-related funds. Sixty percent of this amount will be slated as "economic assistance," the rest as military and law enforcement monies (United States House of Representatives 1990a:17; see also *El Diario* 1991b; *Presencia* 1991d; *Los Tiempos* 1991a). Many more millions were being funeled into Bolivia by other international agencies (Colin Sage, pers. comm.; Tolisano 1989:12). Bolivia, and especially the department of Cochabamba, was and is being flooded with "aid" from abroad that it otherwise might not have received—yet another unexpected "benefit" of the coca trade. This "aid" was giving birth to a plethora of Bolivian government agencies, bureaucracies, and repressive institutions often at odds with each other but which owed their very existence to the coca economy (Bostwick 1990:23–26; Rasnake and Painter 1989:17–21; Bureau of International Narcotics Matters 1990, 1991, 1992). As has occurred with much of past development assistance (see chap. 3), current narcotics-targeted "aid" from abroad will almost certainly augment the country's already high foreign debt and contribute little to the overall well-being of Bolivia's peasant population.

One important coca-inspired development program was the Chapare Rural Development Project (CRDP). Funded in mid-1983 but fully operational by 1987, the CRDP was a direct response by USAID to stem the growing coca boom (for an overview of this project, see Rasnake and Painter 1989; Bostwick 1990). The original rationale for this project was not novel—integrated rural development efforts in the Chapare, including ongoing research into the viability of alternate crops. In late

1987, in the midst of declining coca leaf prices, the length of the project was extended, funding increased, and development activities (especially improvements in irrigation systems) expanded to the southern Cochabamba provinces of Mizque and Campero. The later CRDP focus on some valley and highland communities of Cochabamba was intended to improve living standards in migrant home communities and hence do away with conditions fostering outmigration in the first place. The CRDP, originally scheduled to last through 1994 but phased out in the summer of 1992, would have invested a quarter of a billion dollars—a large sum but still only "2.5% of [the] income generated by [the] coca economy" (Bostwick 1990:31). The Bolivian state will have borne the burden of just over half of this amount.

It is in this economic and political context that the Bolivian government approved (and, more important, followed up on) a major coca eradication program—the famous "Ley 1008." In return for hundreds of millions of dollars in loans and other types of economic aid, as well as preferential access of Bolivian products to the United States market, the government committed itself to restricting new coca plantings, eventually eliminating all coca in the Chapare, curtailing the number of coca hectares in the *yungas* of La Paz (now considered the only legal coca-producing area of Bolivia), and quickly and forcefully eradicating illegal coca plantings in other regions (e.g., Yapacaní in Santa Cruz).

Chapare peasants voluntarily eradicating their coca were, at least according to published reports, promised payments equivalent to U.S. $2,000 (U.S. $350 in cash, the rest in the form of inputs to plant other crops) for each hectare taken out of production as well as technical assistance with alternate crops. Furthermore, the Chapare Regional Development Project also reportedly began awarding large loans—up to U.S. $20,000—to peasants eradicating part of their coca and planting other crops (Bostwick 1990:84; Rasnake and Painter 1989:17–22). In reality many Pampeños who "voluntarily" eradicated their coca often did not receive the full equivalent of the U.S. $2,000 promised them, and, as of the summer of 1992, not one Pampeño migrant who applied for one of these loans received it despite the fact that they had begun eradicating coca plots in their settlements.[10]

The decline in coca leaf prices, the destruction of thousands of hectares of coca, and the 1988 coca eradication law were paralleled and bolstered by increasing military and police operations. Between 1988 and

1989 almost 8,000 coca paste processing pits and cocaine "laboratories" were reported destroyed in Bolivia (Bureau of International Narcotics Matters 1989:9-10). Thousands of Bolivian police, army, and naval troops were poised for large-scale antinarcotics operations and were "sealing off" the Chapare and other coca-producing areas. For its part the United States permanently stationed sizable contingents of Special Forces, DEA agents, and other military personnel in the Bolivia. DEA agents have taken part in, and have often been in operational command of "search and destroy" operations against coca paste and cocaine pits and processing laboratories (Bostwick 1990:28; United States House of Representatives 1990a:23-27; *El Diario* 1991a; *Hoy* 1991). In late 1991 elite Bolivian military units trained in guerrilla warfare were given the green light to begin sweeps against drug traffickers (*narcotraficantes*). Interestingly enough, this strategy coincided with new Bolivian legislation that guaranteed drug traffickers immunity against extradition to the United States if they surrendered to Bolivian authorities. Supposedly because of this legislation, in September of 1991 several self-proclaimed traffickers turned themselves in (*Presencia* 1991a, 1991b, 1991c). There may be, however, other reasons for this recent rash of powerful traffickers peacefully "surrendering" to authorities.[11]

The bulk of official reports emphasizes that military and police operations have focused on capturing traffickers and disrupting coca paste/cocaine processing facilities and operations. These reports also stress that peasants themselves have destroyed most of the coca eradicated, or "reduced," in recent years. But what is often overlooked, and downplayed by official reports, is that the militarization of the Chapare is not merely directed against traffickers. Increasingly, repression is also being directed against coca-producing peasants whose everyday lives are punctuated by coercion, arbitrary arrests, physical abuses, threats and intimidations, confiscation of personal belongings, cash, and coca, and a variety of other actions carried out with near impunity by the narcotics police, members of Bolivia's coca eradication agency (DIRECO), and the recently organized Dirección Nacional de Control de la Coca (DINACO).

It is in this context of systematic repression—always backed by the threat or use of force—that the "success" of eradication efforts are better understood. It is also this context that explains the widespread rage and anger brewing and soaring in the Chapare, the variety of ways that peasants are successfully resisting state drug policies, and the potential for widespread violence in the near future (see Sanabria 1992).

Eradication and Alternative Development: A Success Story?

Optimistic claims to the contrary notwithstanding, state drug policies and strategies have been far from successful. And, despite escalating repression, peasants in the Chapare have managed to resist, thwart, and undermine these policies and strategies in a variety of ways.

In spite of low coca prices, repression, and the apparent success at coca eradication, the number of hectares sown in coca actually rose between 1985 and mid-1990, and only in late 1990 and early 1991 did overall coca hectarage apparently decline (United States House of Representatives 1990a:68; Bureau of International Narcotics Matters 1991:88–89). Between 1987 and 1990, for instance, coca leaf cultivation expanded from about 40,000 to 55,000 hectares, an increase of almost 40 percent (Bureau of International Narcotics Matters 1990:114). Since official estimates of coca cultivation are often lower than what they are in reality, the increase in land planted in coca during this period was probably far higher.

Furthermore, the amount of coca paste and cocaine processed in Bolivia continued to rise, almost paralleling the influx of economic development aid and the intensification of repressive efforts. There was also evidence that coca paste/cocaine processing was spreading to other, new parts of Bolivia (Bureau of International Narcotics Matters 1989:9; United States House of Representatives 1990a:19, 68). Last, highland peasants continued to migrate to the Chapare, and some reports indicated that coca-cultivating migrants were "encroaching" into previously unsettled areas (Bostwick 1990:50). Tolisano (1989:13, 40) has recently emphasized that because of "population pressure" many migrants are cultivating steep upland slopes with considerable damage to soils.

There is also no solid evidence that research on and funding of alternative development (or crop substitution programs) was having a lasting impact. Despite historically low coca prices, other crops still cannot match coca's advantages—such as the ability to grow well in the Chapare's 7 to 10 agro-ecological zones; early, abundant, and continuous harvests; and low weight in relation to value. There is no convincing data that confirms that Chapare peasants are massively taking up other alternative crops in lieu of coca (Pattie 1988:46), which, until quite recently, has expanded at a faster rate than most other Chapare crops.

Crops other than coca are reported to currently provide a far higher net return to Chapare migrants. According to research sponsored by

USAID in late 1989, for example, pineapple was at the time the most profitable crop in the Chapare, said to yield almost 25 times the income of coca. These claims, as Bostwick (1990:72) perceptively notes, are, however, "supiciously high" inasmuch as detailed analyses on production costs, market potential, and so forth are absent in these reports. More recently, USAID has been pushing for widespread planting of soybeans as a replacement crop for coca (United States House of Representatives 1990b). How Chapare peasants will successfully compete with highly capitalized farm enterprises in Santa Cruz that also grow soybeans is but one of many questions that have yet to be fully explained.

Statements on the profitability of alternative crops should be greeted with deep skepticism, for they are clearly generated in a context of intense political pressures to demonstrate viable alternatives to coca, given its currently low prices. In addition, claims of the relative profitability of other crops do not take into account the wild fluctuations of coca prices, with which peasants are obviously aware, and especially the consistently low prices of other lowland *and* highland crops. If pineapple is, indeed, such an attractive and lucrative crop, why haven't thousands of Chapare peasants eagerly taken up its cultivation?

Pampeño migrants I spoke with in 1991 and 1992 laughed when I told them that researchers had claimed pineapples to be so profitable that they should perhaps think of going into large-scale pineapple production. They did complain of low prices for other crops: according to Pampeños in the settlement of Ichilo, 100 oranges or one stem (*racimo*) of plantains would fetch them only two *bolivianos*—about U.S. $0.57 at the prevalent exchange rate—not enough, they said, to even offset transportation costs to nearby Villa Tunari. Coca prices, Pampeño migrants admitted, had been low, but so were the prices of other crops. Besides, coca prices had been steadily rising in recent months, surpassing a respectable 200 *bolivianos* per *carga* in June 1991.

Pampeños ridiculed plans to substitute other crops for coca. It was obvious to them in the mid-1980s—and again when I spoke with them in 1991 and 1992—that no other crop rivaled coca in its adaptability to the Chapare environment, demand, and in terms of the revenue obtained (cf. J. Weil 1980a, 1980b, 1989). Equally significant was the fact that Pampeños were deeply skeptical of coca substitution programs, for they hinged on unreliable state promises of varied types of financial and technical assistance. Despite some official statements of price supports for crops supposed to replace coca, Pampeños were keenly cognizant of damaging past state policies that, by maintaining artificially low prices for traditional agricultural commodities, have worked in favor of urban consumers and to the detriment of the rural peasantry (see chap. 3). Moreover, and as Pampeños were painfully aware, Bolivia's long history of political instability, abrupt changes in political alliances, broken promises, and contradictory Bolivian and United States policies, all worked against coherent and trustworthy agricultural and economic policies that would benefit them. The cultivation of coca in the Chapare, as J. Weil (1980), has correctly pointed out, has always hinged on the successful intersection of ecological, economic, and political processes.

A particularly relevant example of the risks that Pampeños and other Chapare peasants constantly confronted by placing too much faith in substitution programs has surfaced in a recent report (USAID 1988). Oranges were proposed by USAID as one of several long-term alternate crops in lieu of coca. Presumably, the idea was to have Bolivian oranges enter the United States market at favorable prices. Members of the U.S. Congress in Florida, however, eager to protect the Florida citrus industry, sternly objected to this plan. USAID officials were forced to look for another (as yet undisclosed) potential market for Bolivian oranges. In effect, Pampeños correctly realized that acceptance of coca substitution programs would dangerously increase their vulnerability to the uncertain ebb and flow of Bolivian and United States politics. In a very real sense survival hinged on not trusting or depending on government officials. Therefore, while the risks associated with migration, coca cultivation, and participation in the illegal cocaine industry were indeed high, the short- and long-term political and economic risks that an acceptance of the substitution programs entailed were far greater while the immediate rewards were, at best, meager.

One tempting explanation entertained by some antinarcotics planners for the spread of coca cultivation is that coca leaf prices have not fallen enough, and that a further and sustained drop in coca leaf prices, to be achieved by increasing repression, is necessary for peasant cultivators to realize finally the futility of cultivating coca and the desirability of taking up the production of other crops on a mass scale (see, e.g., Bureau of International Narcotics Matters 1992:93–94). The difficulty with this explanation is that it assumes that migrant economic strategies are primarily determined by current (short-term) price levels and that there is an absolute minimum level of income under which peasants will cease to cultivate coca.

Both assumptions are clearly mistaken, for they rest on incorrect views of peasant perceptions of prices and production costs and clearly reflect a fundamental misunderstanding of peasant production and survival strategies. Pampeños and other peasants were clearly cognizant of the fact that coca leaf prices had been marked by sharp downspins and upturns and retained expectations that prices (as well as demand) would stabilize at a higher level in the near future. Indeed, during my visits in June 1991 and again in 1992 these expectations seemed to be paying off: rising prices were leading some Pampeños to state that "it is not worthwhile to cut [i.e., eradicate] coca" (*no conviene cortar la coca*). These expectations, coupled with coca's still-strong advantages over other crops and the added benefits of eradication income, were translating, as we shall see, into a strategy of planting new coca.

Reports suggesting that current coca prices barely reflect production costs assume that there is a clear-cut income threshold under which peasants will refuse to cultivate coca, that peasant households place a monetary value on all (or at least most) of the labor they deploy, and that peasants share or agree with stated cost-benefit analyses.

In fact, peasant cultivators' view of coca's "real" production costs substantially differed from those held by development/agricultural experts. This was especially the case when we realize that an important objective was to maximize overall income (or compensate for income loss due to low coca prices). As in the case of potato production in their highland home communities, peasants stated that coca prices were "too low," and yet at the same time, and for different reasons, they increased its cultivation. The costs of maintaining or expanding coca cultivation was indeed high in a context of low prices and the infusion of ever greater amounts of labor, but the benefits—the ability to attempt to stem the decline in living standards—was clearly perceived as even higher. Some Pampeños argued that the further coca prices dropped the more compelled they felt to continue harvesting their coca. One Pampeño told me that he could not afford to discontinue his coca harvests, even if prices fell below 10 *bolivianos* (slightly over U.S. $2) a *carga*. It was far preferable, I was told, to earn those at least 10 *bolivianos* than to allow leaves to fall from the shrubs and rot on the ground. Pampeños were, of course, aware of the declining marginal returns to their labor, but this in and of itself was not a sufficient reason for giving up coca cultivation and harvesting. Finally, the costs and benefits of coca cannot be construed in isolation from that of other crops cultivated by Chapare migrant peasants in their home communities. What exactly constituted acceptable costs and/or benefits in the Chapare was also a function of the totality of livelihood strategies undertaken and risks borne by peasant households. From this perspective both the absence of truly competitive lowland crops and the low returns of highland agriculture translated into acceptable returns to coca cultivation, despite low prices.

Resistance

In previous pages I have stressed the increasing repression taking place in the Chapare and that thousands of hectares of coca have been destroyed in recent years. How have peasants resisted repression and state policies that are posing such a severe threat to their livelihood and security? Are state coca policies as successful as they might appear to be?

In recent years Chapare peasants have consistently employed different strategies to resist coca eradication policies. Frontal and open confrontations with the increasingly powerful Bolivian state usually have had disastrous results and, not unexpectedly, have been uncommon. Before and after the signing of the 1988 eradication law, for example—described in a United States government report (Bureau of International Narcotics Matters 1988:34) as a "voluntary" program—powerful coca-producing peasant organizations (cf. Healy 1991b) carried out massive and bloody protests in 1987 and 1988 that were quickly put down by police and army troops.[12] In June 1991 a peaceful march by several hundred Chapare peasants, including several Pampeños, protesting the militarization of antidrug efforts and the powerful role of United States officials in shaping local drug policies and clamoring for "dignity," was violently stopped by the army (e.g., *Aquí* 1991; *Los Tiempos* 1991b; *Opinión* 1991a, 1991b, 1991c, 1991d; *Ultima Hora* 1991). By and large, Chapare peasants have painfully learned that open, frontal confrontations with the state, at least in the near future, are futile at best.

It is not by directly and openly confronting the state and its repressive institutions that peasants have successfully resisted state coca policies. Rather, peasants in the Chapare have striven to constantly maneuver around these policies and stubbornly pursue an array of short-term tactics (but with long-term implications) that have nipped away at the ability of the state to fully attain its coca policy goals. The fact that thousands of hectares of coca have been destroyed in recent years is undeniable.

But the fact that Bolivia has consistently failed to meet coca eradication goals agreed upon with the United States (Bureau of International Narcotics Matters 1990, 1991, 1992), despite massive economic and military assistance, points to the vitality and ingenuity of forms of peasant resistance. It is first important to recall that between 1987 and 1990 coca leaf cultivation expanded by almost 40 percent, despite record numbers of coca hectares eradicated, declining leaf prices, and increasing repression. How can we best explain this seeming paradox of increasing coca cultivation despite rock-bottom leaf prices and increasing success at coca eradication during this period? And what are we to make of other reports that suggest a recent decline in land planted in coca?

I suggest that this seeming paradox is partly the result of an intricate strategy undertaken by peasant migrants consisting of destroying old and/or diseased coca shrubs and planting new shrubs in other settlements. Both are designed to minimize risk, diversify economic options, and strive to maintain living standards that still cannot be achieved through traditional agriculture, either in the highlands or lowlands. Indeed, the absolute drop in the amount of land planted in coca is almost certainly a temporary lull fully consistent with this strategy, and reports in the near future will almost certainly once again record rising levels of coca cultivation.

We learn from official reports that "farmers" are eradicating coca or other "farmers" are planting food crops, but we know little else about them: we are simply not informed about who is eradicating coca plants and why. Statements that "farmers are eradicating coca" gloss over important socioeconomic differences among Chapare peasants (chap. 4) and thereby mistakenly assume that all "farmers" are following identical economic strategies (e.g., cutting their plants because of low coca prices). A more poignant explanation for the destruction of coca shrubs and the spread of coca cultivation between 1985 and 1990 would hinge on the sharp differences in access to wealth, land, and labor among Chapare migrants, diversification and investment decisions by these migrants, and the role of prices in their decision making.

The first migrants to gain land in the Chapare in the foothills west of Villa Tunari were almost certainly those who provided the first "success" stories in coca eradication efforts in the late 1980s (Bureau of International Narcotics Matters 1988:8). After 20 or 30 years their land plots were probably quite small (due to inheritance or sales) and their coca shrubs old, relatively unproductive, and disease ridden. In such a context, the fall in coca prices and promises of cash payments or credit loans for eradicating their coca could not have come at a better time, as the cash inflow for destroying their coca probably more than compensated them for the income they would have received from diminishing fields. As we shall see, many of those cutting their coca shrubs did not necessarily get out of the coca business altogether.

Migrants with old and unproductive land plots were not the only ones eradicating their coca. Their more wealthy land-based counterparts were doing so as well—those with a considerable amount of fertile coca land, land plots in different settlements (and at various stages of land use and varying levels of fertility), access to a large labor force, and engaged in diversified coca-related activities (see chap. 4). These Pampeños also had much to gain and little to lose by destroying part of their coca. While some may have given different reasons for cutting their coca shrubs, "voluntary" eradication clearly constituted the core of a long-term strategy to accumulate wealth and capital, "weather out" the current slump in coca prices, and survive the increasingly repressive environment generated by antinarcotics efforts.

During my June 1991 visit to Pampa I learned that many, if not most, Pampeño migrants with land in the colonies of Ichoa, Isiboro, and Chimoré (see chap. 4) had cut their coca; I was told over and over again that "there is no longer coca" (*ya no hay coca*). Some Pampeños claimed that coca prices had dropped to such low levels that it was no longer worthwhile at the time to continue planting (although they continue to harvest their shrubs). Some also claimed that they were also destroying their coca because most coca shrubs in Colonia Pampa had been infected with *estalla*—and, interestingly enough, apparently *estalla* only spread to coca fields whose owners had been harvesting yet immature leaves, that is, intensifying cultivation (see chap. 4; see also SUBDESAL 1988:10). It made sense to many Pampeños to eradicate their coca, given low prices, the spread of *estalla*, and monetary payments offered by DIRECO. Other Pampeños claimed that *estalla* had not affected their fields but that they decided cut their coca anyway, fearful that DIRECO would soon carry out forceful eradication without compensating them.

This is not all that we need to know about who was eradicating coca and why. Many Pampeño migrants had access to several land plots in different colonies (for a similar pattern elsewhere in the Chapare, see

C. Weil 1983). Many Pampeños who eradicated their coca in Colonia Pampa simultaneously planted coca seedlings in Ichilo (near Santa Cruz) or in other colonies. Part of the money they obtained from destroying their old coca was diverted into hiring wage and contractual workers to plant coca elsewhere, while other Pampeños recruited sharecroppers to clear new land and plant crops and coca.

The prevailing expectation among Pampeño migrants pursuing this stategy was, of course, that coca leaf prices would soon rise to more profitable levels. In the meantime voluntary coca eradication seemed a solid economic strategy to pursue by some land-based migrants in the context of rock-bottom prices (and, in the case of others, of spreading *estalla*), as it almost guaranteed them a solid, although small, income despite falling demand for and prices of coca. In fact, the government's eradication program may have set into motion a cycle of expanding coca production, and recent reports of an absolute drop in the amount of land sown in coca has probably not taken into account recent plantings in new, more fertile land. In the summer of 1991, for instance, some Pampeños who had just cut their coca in one settlement already knew how much coca they would plant in another, how soon they would cut the newly planted shrubs, and how large a payment they expected to receive from DIRECO. (One Pampeño migrant was said to have eradicated at least nine hectares of coca in at least four settlements and received payments totaling over U.S. $18,000. I was unable to verify this statement, however, during my short visit to Pampa in 1991.) These migrants claimed that the payments they obtained by eradicating their coca in one settlement outstripped the labor costs (e.g., hiring wage/ contractual workers or employing sharecroppers) they incurred in clearing land and planting new coca and other crops elsewhere. (The move to the Chapare by highland and valley peasants fleeing drought-stricken regions in the late 1980s suggests that a shortage of labor may not have been a significant problem for these wealthy migrant households pursuing this strategy.)

Eradication programs may have allowed many to cope partly with heightening risk—and increasing risk for coca-producing peasants has been a major goal of the United States narcotics strategies. Other reports (e.g., United States House of Representatives 1991a:26) suggest that government officials themselves have acknowledged that peasant migrants used eradication payments to expand their coca plantings and therefore have intentionally stopped paying out large credits and loans to Chapare peasants. Some sources (cf. United States House of Representatives 1990:36) have also acknowledged that new coca plantings have expanded in eastern Bolivia, and other reports have stressed the fundamentally contradictory effects of state eradication efforts (see Rasnake and Painter 1989:19; Bostwick 1990:87). In sum, the government's coca eradication program has been good coca business, at least for some wealthy land-based migrants. But what of the less fortunate migrants in the Chapare, the sharecroppers and landless workers?

Most Pampeño sharecroppers worked only minute plots of coca owned by wealthier migrants, they often had access to very small plots of land in Pampa, and they therefore confronted greater risk to their livelihood (see chaps. 4 and 5). As a result, it is almost certain that these sharecroppers were not among those who eradicated their coca but, rather, who lost their land (and sharecropper status) as the owners of the land they worked for opted to uproot or cut their coca. While some sharecroppers may have obtained their own land elsewhere in the Chapare, it is more likely that they were deployed by land-based migrants to expand coca cultivation into new areas or diversified into coca paste/cocaine processing endeavors.

Landless wage and contractual workers probably confronted an analogous situation. Rasnake and Painter (1989:34) have recently suggested that

> effective Chapare development will almost certainly force large numbers of rural workers to seek alternative migratory destinations. Given the lack of economic opportunity in Bolivia, and given that coca may be grown anywhere in Bolivia's humid tropical lowlands, the most likely result of successful development and interdiction in the Chapare is that the geographic center of narcotics production will shift to another region, and that the rural poor will continue to provide an ample supply of cheap labor.

This is precisely what occurred. Land-based Pampeño migrants told me in 1991 that they employed wage workers and sharecroppers to expand coca cultivation into new areas and dismissed many of them once they cut their coca. The narcotics policy endorsed by the United States was not only leading to spreading coca cultivation but also contributing to demographic instability and almost certainly resulting in sharper differentiation in the Chapare.

According to official reports, peasants themselves and not the police or other repressive institutions (such as DIRECO and DINACO) have eradicated the greater part of coca in recent years. For instance, less than 1 percent of the slightly over 11,000 hectares of coca reduced between September 1987 and September 1990 were forcefully eradicated by DIRECO (Ministerio de Asuntos Campesinos y Agropecuarios 1990 [n.p.]). Other data point to similar trends: "The GOB [government of Bolivia] paid compensation to growers for eradication of a record of 7,760 hectares in 1990. In addition, the GOB eradicated 312 hectares of illegal coca without paying compensation" (Bureau of International Narcotics Matters 1991:81).

The peasant strategy outlined above—destroying coca and replanting in other areas of the Chapare—only partially accounts for the "voluntary" eradication of coca in the Chapare. Far more important and insightful is the fact that, given the escalating repressive milieu in which they find themselves, Chapare peasants are constantly and systematically being coerced and intimidated in many ways to "voluntarily" eradicate their coca. United States–funded reports (e.g., Bostwick 1990) suggesting that voluntary eradication is taking place in a coercive and conflict-free context in which peasants are freely choosing to undermine their subsistence base because it is in their best interests to do so are wholly misleading (Sanabria 1992).

Pampeños and other peasants are also resisting, often successfully, these continuous pressures to force them to "voluntarily" eradicate their coca. One particularly good example of successful peasant resistance that has undermined the ability of the state to fully implement and achieve its eradication policies and goals is what is known as *concertación* (roughly equivalent to *agreement*). *Concertación* typically occurs when, instead of descending on and forcefully razing a coca field, DIRECO teams "ask" its owner to recruit his or her own workers and voluntarily eradicate it. Afterward DIRECO pays the owner the total number of daily wages (*jornales*) that he or she required to carry out the task of destroying the coca.

Despite the fact that Pampeños "agreeing" to *concertación* receive a payment far below the U.S. $2,000 promised them under the 1988 eradication law, I have argued elsewhere (Sanabria 1992) that *concertación* is essentially a negotiated standoff between peasants and DIRECO teams. Pampeños, almost invariably faced with the threat, and very real possibility, of having all their coca eradicated without receiving any compensation, at least manage to cling to and avoid the destruction of their "old" coca (i.e., that sown prior to the 1988 eradication law), and they receive some income. DIRECO officials, while they often fail in their attempts to destroy all the coca they originally had hoped for, are at least able to demonstrate that they are partially succeeding in carrying out their tasks. Equally important, they avoid the threat of peasant reprisals and assaults in the short term, to some extent.

In fact, DIRECO and other eradication officials have very good reasons to be constantly concerned about their safety. In 1991 Pampeños and other migrants organized "defense committees" (*comités de defensa*) in an attempt to block the forced eradication of coca fields. Armed clashes between DIRECO teams, Leopardos, and peasants soon followed (*Presencia* 1991e, 1991f). Members of these defense committees were admittedly no match for the well-armed and mobile Leopardos. Nevertheless, lore in the Chapare is rich with stories of how peasants have consistently, stubbornly, and ingeniously pursued a wide spectrum of hit-and-run tactics, violent or otherwise, which have slowed down and nipped away at the capacity of the state and its repressive institutions to fully carry out its objective of eliminating coca cutivation (Sanabria 1992). Indeed, peasant efforts and strategies to resist attempts by the state to eradicate coca shrubs and undermine their livelihood have been systematic and massive (cf. Scott 1986, 1991).

Claims of "voluntary" eradication mask the anger and rage widespread in the Chapare, Unites States–backed coca policies are inevitably intensifying political polarization and increasing the potential for escalating violence, and the recent appearance of armed guerrilla groups in Bolivia is an ominous sign of worse scenarios yet to come. Since "the elasticity of demand for cocaine in the United States with respect to the price of [the coca] leaf is essentially zero" (United States House of Representatives 1991:11, 28), coca eradication policies and the ensuing violence in Bolivia is a high price to pay for a policy that will do little to offset America's "drug problem."

Assessing Change: Pampa in 1992

Between June 1985 and 1992 several notable events occurred in Pampa. The massive stone church still being built in 1985 was finally completed, and a large two-story dwelling next to it now houses a team of Brazilian nuns; mass is now offered every Sunday in Pampa. All but one of Pampa's *lugares* now has potable water, and a new concrete irrigation canal from the irrigation lake to Colpana was constructed with Bolivian government development funds. In a community in which scarcely 40 years earlier the *hacendado* had prohibited a school and teachers for his "Indians," Pampa now boasts its first university student, the eldest son of a Chapare migrant studying agronomy at Cochabamba's Universidad Mayor de San Simón. More dwellings and television sets are clearly visible in the pueblo, and a few Pampeños now even own stereos with compact disk players. The government's Nueva Política Económica has virtually generalized the U.S. dollar as a commonly held and traded currency in Bolivia, and many Pampeños now regularly save, invest, and purchase goods in U.S. dollars.

Pampeños presently enjoy even easier transportation links to Sacaba, Cochabamba, the Chapare, and Santa Cruz than ever before. Taxis now offer daily service to and from Pampa and Sacaba, and in Cochabamba trufis (14- to 18-passsenger minivans) can be boarded for Pampa and Colomi several times a day. Traffic through Pampa has intensified after the construction of the Chapare-Santa Cruz road in 1988, and modern long-distance buses (*flotas*) now pass by Pampa day and night en route from Cochabamba to Santa Cruz. Pampeños currently own more vehicles than in the mid-1980s—one major strategy has been to use coca eradication income to further diversify into transport services—and Pampeño taxi owners were planning to organize their own *sindicato*, which would compete with other taxi owners offering daily service between Sacaba and Pampa.

In these ensuing seven years non-Pampeños (*ajenos*) established a firm foothold in Pampa, and the slow undermining of communal land tenure norms I had noticed earlier (see chap. 5) was now fully under way. The *propietaria* sold most of her remaining land in Pampa (including all her cultivated fields) by the late 1980s, despite her high asking price—but only after she threatened to sell her land to outsiders if no Pampeño buyers came forth. *Ajenos* have begun to regularly buy land in the pueblo as well as cultivable crop land, from which they had been firmly barred several years earlier. A large segment of cultivable land purchased from the former landowner in the Colpana crop zone (specifically the land bordering the newly constructed church and facing the Cochabamba-Chapare road) will now be set aside for a new pueblo. Here non-Pampeño Chapare migrants have eagerly bought up most of the land plots (especially after the construction of the Chapare–Santa Cruz road). In the process they have driven up local land prices: land sold by the *propietaria* for U.S. $1.00 a square meter now sells for U.S. $5–8 per square meter. While some kinship (especially affinal) relationship to a Pampeño was absolutely essential to buy pueblo land plots in 1984–85 (see chap. 5), this was no longer necessary by 1992. The most significant change in land tenure norms occurred with cultivable crop land. Whereas no *ajeno* had been previously allowed to purchase crop land, at least 10 *ajenos* had done so by 1991 and several more in 1992. All land purchases still had to be approved by the *sindicato*, but it is clear that a fully developed land market was under way and that the "closed corporate" features that characterized Pampa were mostly a thing of the past.

Significant developments also took place among Pampeño migrants in the Chapare. The 1985 austerity measures, the drop in coca prices, and coca eradication efforts jointly contributed to a wider spatial dispersal of Pampeños throughout the Bolivian humid tropics. For instance, for the very first time several Pampeños now live in the department of Beni. More significantly, as most Pampeños eradicated their coca fields in the settlements of Ichoa, Isiboro, and Chimoré (Colonia Pampa), they began abandoning these settlements altogether and moving on and spreading coca cultivation to Ichilo. Right on the Chapare–Santa Cruz road, Ichilo is only three to four hours away from the city of Santa Cruz, the commercial, financial, and narcotics hub of the eastern lowlands. With about 113 Pampeño *afiliados* in the mid-1980s, Ichilo currently has close to 200. In June of 1991 over 350 Pampeños were said to be in Ichilo at any given period. Crop cultivation, virtually nonexistent in 1984 (chap. 4), has also expanded in Ichilo in recent years. While many Pampeños had about one hectare of coca by mid-1991, others had three or four hectares, far more land than that sown in other crops. Significantly enough, some Pampeños had already "voluntarily" eradicated part of their coca in Ichilo. From Ichilo other Pampeños were moving on to nearby colonies to the east and north. And for the first time since the 1950s Pampeños began moving into colonies in the department of Santa Cruz, and a few had taken up residence in Yapacaní, precisely where their parents and grandparents had first trekked to in search of better prospects following the agrarian reform.

Prospects for the Future

The cultivation of coca, and the processing and marketing of coca paste and cocaine hydrochloride, is and has been a two-edged sword. While it has allowed some peasants and other impoverished segments of Bolivia's population a certain degree of respite from devastating and periodic economic (and political) crises, the long-term structural consequences are far from ideal.

By accepting short-term palliative, although admittedly massive, development aid designed supposedly to counter the coca problem, Bolivian authorities have acquiesced to and complied with the whims of politicians in Washington. For instance, it is possible that United States government research into effective herbicides against the coca plant (*New York Times* 1988) will lead to massive spraying of these herbicides in Bolivia. At the national and local levels the surge in the cultivation of coca in the 1980s, and especially the trend toward specialized cultivation and the processing of its illegal by-products, increased the peasantry's vulnerability to and dependence upon foreign market demands. Bolivia is, in other words, a more, not less, dependent country subject to the unpredictable boom-and-bust Latin American economic cycles (see, e.g., Tienda, Schurman, and Booth 1987).

Bolivia has long been known for its political instability. Although recent years have witnessed the formation of a remarkable alliance among political and economic elites, Bolivia has been marked historically by endemic factionalism—with one class failing to achieve a solid and enduring control of the state. The cocaine market promises to intensify this deep-seated factionalism and potential for conflict. At the local and regional level the peasantry and the unemployed will likely be caught in the middle of this power struggle, one from which they will probably not benefit in the long run.

The prosperity generated by the cocaine market has been an illusory one. While it provided some concrete and short-term benefits to a segment of the peasantry—and to the suddenly impoverished unemployed—it was a facade of prosperity, one not leading to long-term, structurally sound development.[13] Little if any resources generated by the cocaine market were reinvested in productive activities, basic crop production was on the decline and economic polarization on the rise, and the differential accumulation of land and wealth had strongly taken root. Meanwhile, caught between a desire for a better life for themselves and their children and facing conditions over which they have little control, such as the 1992 drought, Pampeños will likely continue to travel to the Chapare and make the best of whatever options they have. In the end disillusionment is the most likely outcome, something they have faced many times before.

Chapter 9

Local Actions and Global Paradigms

Analysis of the organizational aspect of social action is the necessary
complement to analysis of the structural aspect. Social organization
has usually been taken as a synonym for social structure. [I]t is time
to distinguish between them. The more one thinks of the structure
of a society in abstract terms, as a group of relations or of ideal
patterns, the more necessary it is to think separately of social
organization in terms of concrete activity.
—(Firth 1961 [1951]:35–36)

The *active* agents in any sociological explanation must be
microsituational. Social patterns, institutions, and organizations are
only abstractions from the behavior of individuals.
—(R. Collins 1981:989)

Forty years have passed since the anthropologist Raymond Firth—
reacting against Malinowskian functionalism and British structural social
anthropology—made his now classic distinction between social structure
and social organization and called for studies grounded on the "concrete
activity" of individuals. Recent years have witnessed a surge of attempts
and approaches in anthropology, sociology, history, and other disciplines
aimed at addressing two long-standing, related, yet analytically distinct
concerns, both often subsumed under the rubric "micro-macro link."
The first centers on the process whereby "larger systems" or social
entities are reproduced over time. Here the problematic is often expressed
in terms of multiple, encompassing "levels of analysis"—individuals or
social actors, households, communities, regions, the state, and the international (or global) level—and key questions center on how patterns
and activities at one level account for, generate, or translate into patterns
at another. The second related issue, couched in terms of the dialectic
between "individuals and society" (Leacock 1985), "agency and structure," or "how does the system shape practice?" and "how does practice
shape the system?" (Ortner 1984:152, 154), centers on explaining specific

193

behavioral patterns or strategies in terms of broader social constraints, contexts, or processes. Here the issue at hand is that of the relative autonomy of social actors—the opportunities for and constraints on behavior and action—and how by pursuing goals and strategies social actors knowingly or unknowingly erect subsequent barriers to or constraints on, and create new opportunities for, other goals and strategies.

At the centerpiece of these (often quite different) attempts to grapple with the micro-macro link has been an emphasis on actors, subjects, individuals, individual decision making, micro situational behavior, and so forth—what Ortner has referred to as "practice" (1984:144–61). In anthropology these attempts have quite different roots, such as Firth's dissatisfaction with British structuralism and the transactional studies in the late 1960s and early 1970s. The increasing relevance and popularity of neo-Marxist world systems, dependency, and modes of production frameworks and the unfortunate trend within part of this stream of work to downplay individual and local strategies in favor of reified and teleologically construed global processes have also spurred interest in contextually situated practice approaches (Ortner 1984:146–47; C. Smith 1983; Roseberry 1988, 1989a).[1] In sociology practice and other actor-centered approaches—what Layder (1989:136) has called "strategic conduct"—surfaced against the backdrop of the dominant structural paradigm represented by Parsons, which had also submerged "concrete activity" (to use Firth's terms) within "systems" and similar constructs (see Hazelrigg 1991; Layder 1989; Coleman 1986; R. Collins 1981; Sewell 1987; Denzin 1986). And from the field of Latin American social history Stern (1988a:861) has recently talked of "the options, constraints, and opportunities faced by the 'world system.'" More forcefully, in this fascinating debate with E. Wallerstein, Stern (1988b:892, 896) has convincingly argued that

> Wallerstein seems unable to accept the possibility that even if, from the point of view of "origins," inclusion in the world-system dramatically altered the disease environments, social relations, and power conflicts of colonized American regions, these (changed) conditions of life and labor could quickly take on a dynamic or life of their own. The human geography of frontiers, and the uneven spread of social control, are not reducible to a mere phenomenon of the world-system. [The people of Latin America] have had major importance as historical agents and causes of their own experience. This agency should not be idealized or overstated, but it has not been limited to futile

resistance against the onslaught of the capitalist world-system. A full analysis of such agency—its history, explanation, accomplishments, failures and limitations—requires serious study of America-centered social dynamics and structures as well as world-system dynamics and structure.

Despite the great deal of work carried out to date on the micro-macro link, the anthropologists DeWalt and Pelto (1985:7) have recently stated that "there is no magic formula for integrating the many possible levels of analysis. There is no single set of linking concepts, nor is there a particular methodological key that will unlock the doors of understanding." From other quarters, such as sociology, we hear similar cries of despair:

> If the problem of scope is "the means by which purposive actions of individuals combine to produce a social outcome," or social structure, then we have apparently reached agreement on what an "individual" is and of what "social structure" is-inter alia, that they are separate and distinct-and we are in search of the operation, combinatorial or otherwise, that has them in linkage. But we really have little agreement on the basic terms of a point of departure for such a search. Shifting our vocabularly from "individual and social structure," or "self and world," to "micro-level and macro-level" substitutes the appearance of one set of questions for "another" set of questions. The persistence of difficulties "to bridge the dichotomy between agency and structure" has been one of the most remarkable features of our theorizing, even in the midst of some notable changes in vocabulary. (Hazelrigg 1991:232, 234)

I would argue that, despite the undeniable lack of a "magic formula," there do in fact exist "basic terms of a point of departure" that allow us tentatively to go about studying the constraints and options faced by individuals and, for lack of a better term, "structures" or "systems." This departure hinges on simultaneously undertaking several methodological strategies.

The strong thrust toward historically informed anthropological (and sociological) research constitutes one important and necessary strategy to adequately grapple with the mutually reinforcing, and limiting, interactions between individual (or local-level) strategies and broader socioeconomic and political constraints and alternatives for action (see, e.g., C. Smith 1983; Ortner 1984:158–59; Sewell 1987; Kertzer, Silverman, Rutman, and Plakans 1986; Roseberry 1988:163–64, 1989a, 1989b; O'Brien and Roseberry 1991).[2] This historical perspective not only entails recognizing that broader processes are embedded in "local" events but also examining specific sequences of past decisions and actions (Sewell 1987:170) and the ways in which they cumulatively hinder or enable future decisions, options, and goals (see esp. Roseberry 1989a:88–90).

In addition to paying close attention to sequential and cumulative impacts, an analytic movement "back and forth" (Coleman 1986:1323; see also Sewell 1987:168–69; Stern 1988a, 1988b) between past and present local and broader options, actions, and strategies is also necessary. This does not mean that actors have available to them, or necessarily pursue, neat, clearly articulated blueprints for actions. Nor does it imply that the results or outcomes of whatever actions or strategies they do pursue are consistent with the goals or results social actors originally hoped for or had in mind. Strategies, options, and goals are not merely contingent (at least partially) on past actions that limit and generate novel opportunities; they are also powerfully conditioned by unexpected, unintentional (and quite often unwanted) effects, results, or outcomes (e.g., Ortner 1984:149; Marcus 1986:182; Marcus and Fischer 1986:92; Sewell 1987:170–171; cf. Roseberry 1989a). These in turn generate and shape new contexts and circumstances—and additional possibilities and constraints—within which subsequent behavior, goals, and strategies are reevaluated and pursued.

A historically grounded approach that construes local events in terms of broader and cumulative processes (and vice versa), marked by competition and differential access to power, must also be placed within a context of specific dimensions of *material* production and reproduction. These dimensions would minimally include the ecological settings and technical requirements of production, demographic processes and imperatives, and labor and other social arrangements.

As suggested, a further strategy for grappling with the micro-macro issue consists of downplaying the sharp analytic wall often erected between the local (or "internal") and extralocal (or "external") and systematically construing one in terms of the other. What this means is that attention should focus on the interrelatedness of local and external events and processes—the multiple ways in which they embody and shape each other—without necessarily assigning analytic or causal priority to one over another. This strategy clearly underlies Stern's call for the study of "America-centered social dynamics and structures as well as world-system dynamics and structure." It also lies at the root of Cardoso's notion of "internationalization of the internal" (1977:13, qtd. by Roseberry 1989a:88), Knorr-Cetina's (1981:31) statement that "micro transactions *always in principle* transcend the immediate situation [or] that many micro-situations *appear only to exist in virtue of other such situations,*" and Marcus and Fisher's claim (1986:78) that "cultural situations [are] always in a state of resistance and accommodation to broader processes of influence that are as much inside as outside the local context."

Finally, an approach or strategy focused on the demand for and competition over commodities or strategically valued resources is also critical for understanding specific actions or strategies in different and shifting contexts. This focus should be informed by a recognition that competition over resources is an eminently economic and political undertaking, one grounded on ongoing relationships marked by unequal access to and differential deployment of resources and power, which inevitably reshape and redefine the contexts under which such relationships are continuously recreated (Wolf 1990). Any attempts at grappling with micro-macro linkages without clearly recognizing and attaching due importance to the issues of power and inequality (such as, e.g., in DeWalt and Pelto 1985) seriously undermine their explanatory value. What this suggests, of course, is that, as in the case of coca, different historical periods have been marked by competition and struggle over the production, distribution, and consumption of a seemingly identical resource or commodity, but that the nature of this competition (e.g., who is competing, why, and why now; over what; how is this struggle is played out in the ground, what is to be gained or lost, and what is the specific constellation of social, political, and economic features that mark or imbue this competition?) may be radically different. Therefore, an important task consists of teasing out the multiple strands that permeate relationships marked by competition and struggle that converge in a specific context and over a particular commodity.

Coca and the Bolivian Peasantry

In the previous chapters I have relied on these methodological strategies in order to unravel and understand the contemporary significance of coca for Bolivian peasants. I began this volume by outlining its four major and interrelated aims. These were to: (1) explain some fundamental and intertwined social and economic ramifications for Bolivian peasant migrants who have been increasingly drawn into far-flung economic circuits generated by the global drug trade; (2) account for and understand the unfolding of Bolivia's coca market and the ongoing competition for and struggle over coca (and its by-products); (3) examine the different ways and contexts in which peasant migrants actively contributed to the emergence of this market; and (4) offer a critique of current development and narcotics policies in Bolivia.

As I have shown, the meanings to Pampeños (and other Bolivian peasants) of their deepening integration into an international market through the production of a lucrative commodity—the different ways it has shaped their lives, relationships with others, and their livelihood—cannot be adequately understood without first examining the pivotal roles (social and cultural, economic, and political) that coca has historically played in the Andes.

Coca, as other authors have consistently stressed, has occupied an important role in Andean social and cultural institutions. But equally important, and far more important in the context of this volume, is that the production and distribution of coca has consistently been a key arena through which conflicting (and conflictive) political and economic concerns have historically converged. In the Andes access to coca and coca fields was probably the object of dispute, competition, and rivalry ever since the shrub was first domesticated and almost certainly intensified during periods of state imperial expansion. In previous pages I mentioned that coca was an important medium through which the Incas expanded their political (and probably hegemonic) control over the Andes. Coca also loomed as a prominent and hotly contested political-economic issue in the vastly different colonial period. Mining was the fiscal backbone of the early colonial state (and throughout most of republican Bolivia), adequate supplies of labor were essential to mining, and fears that (despite the obligatory labor drafts) miners would not work without adequate supplies of coca were paramount in the decision by colonial authorities not to outlaw coca cultivation in Bolivia and Peru, despite strong opposition from certain quarters of the church and the state. The demand for coca ultimately destined to Potosí spurred increased production in the *yungas* east of La Paz in Spanish-owned plantations as well as in coca fields under the control of Aymara corporate communities. And it was this region, the *yungas* east of La Paz, that would, until quite recently, supply most of Bolivia's internal demand for coca.

The long-standing interest in "developing" Bolivia's eastern lowlands—and, more specifically, the interlocked and successive political and economic steps and decisions undertaken by those in control of the state to achieve this goal—would be decisive in the subsequent rise of the coca/cocaine market. Viedma's interest in developing the vast eastern lowlands in the 1700s—and his concerns were rooted in the context of a deep economic and agricultural slump that afflicted Cochabamba (and that probably eroded landowner control in this region)—would later be echoed by republican governments, which also viewed the resource-rich eastern territories as a panacea for all sorts of social and economic ills that plagued Bolivia. By the turn of the twentieth century, and especially by the 1940s, huge grants of state-claimed land in the vast eastern lowlands were awarded to nonpeasant settlers, policies that would lay the foundation for the agricultural enterprises that would later spring up, particularly in Santa Cruz. Timid attempts were also carried out at resettling highland and valley peasants to these territories, directly anticipating large-scale resettlement efforts after the agrarian reform.

Economic and political policies carried out after the 1952 MNR rise to power would also intersect with and further these goals and previously enacted policies. While the agrarian reform was indeed an event of immense economic, social, and political significance, the primary economic goal of the dominant wing of the MNR (and of the governments that followed), especially after 1964, was to spur agricultural investment and large-scale agricultural capitalism (and capital accumulation) in the eastern lowlands. The lion's share of the state's fiscal resources was funneled to the *latifundia* that had emerged as a result of the huge land grants awarded during prior decades. Agricultural investment in the eastern enterprises also reflected and was made possible by the easy availability of capital from international agencies and banks eager to lend and invest billions of dollars during the 1960s and 1970s.

In the meantime peasant agriculture in the Bolivian highlands and valleys languished as a result of scarce fiscal resources and overall neglect, conscious and systematic state policies to hold down urban food prices (Dandler 1984:126–27), and deteriorating terms of exchange.[3] Simultaneously, state officials—with the blessing and solid financial backing of leading international development organizations—began vigorously promoting migration to the eastern Andean slopes, a policy that, again, was not novel but, instead, emulated and built upon earlier ones. The Chapare area in the department of Cochabamba, where two centuries earlier Viedma had praised the small coca plantations he encountered,

was designated a priority area of colonization, and an especially pro-
pitious one, from an ecological standpoint, for the growing of coca.

Eroding living standards, rising population, and land fragmentation
plagued the heavily populated highlands and valleys. In and of themselves
these circumstances did not account for either the intense migration to
the Chapare that would later take place nor the deep commitment by
peasant migrants to coca cultivation. These processes intersected with
the state's resettlement (and other major political and economic) pri-
orities, major features that included awarding of land grants to incoming
migrants and constructing the major road from Cochabamba to the
Chapare in the early 1970s. As in Viedma's time, one cash crop promoted
by government extension agents was coca. By the mid- to late 1970s tens
of thousands of peasant cultivators, most from Cochabamba's central
valleys, had land in and were seasonally migrating to the Chapare, and
coca was their major cash crop. It is the intersection of these and other
processes during different historical periods (on this point, see esp. Roseberry 1989a) that best explains Bolivia's contemporary coca problem and
makes the sharp distinction between local and external events difficult
to accept.

It was at this time, the late 1970s, that a new constellation of economic, political, and social processes—concurrently local, regional, and
international—converged, heralded the emergence and consolidation of
Bolivia's cocaine market, and ushered in far-flung transformations of
peasant communities. North America, and especially the United States,
underwent profound transformations in its economy and social structure
in the late 1970s that reflected and were intertwined with a shifting global
division of labor and of new capital flows (cf. Frank 1988). This was
paralleled by the now mass consumption of cocaine and the appearance
and escalating consumption of new and powerful cocaine derivatives
such as crack. These global changes had profound consequences on and
in Bolivia, which were in turn molded by other local processes. Bolivia
in the late 1970s witnessed an end to an era of apparent prosperity. By
the end of this decade the economic foundations of the state would be
severely shaken. State mining enterprises were in bankruptcy, and the
demand for traditional exports (minerals and agricultural commodities)
plummeted as a result of a global economic slump. Equally important,
international credit lines, which by then had helped transform eastern
agricultural estates into highly capitalized agro-industrial concerns (Gill
1987; Arrieta, Abrego, Castillo, and de la Fuente 1990; Reye 1970),

essentially disappeared. These enterprises prospered from and formed the political backbone of the authoritarian regime of General Hugo Bánzer (Malloy and Gamarra 1988:71–116), under which large-scale military involvement in cocaine trafficking emerged. And Bolivia was saddled with a multibillion dollar debt. Fiscal bankruptcy, runaway inflation, and economic chaos inevitably followed.

By the early 1980s, then, the wealthy and politically powerful eastern lowland agrarian capitalist class that emerged as a direct sequel to economic assistance programs and under the tutelage and protection of the state quickly consolidated, with the active support and collaboration of segments of the state apparatus and an urban commercial class, coca paste and cocaine trafficking as a response to the surging demand for cocaine by North American consumers and the economic chaos that loomed ahead.

Bolivia's peasantry did not passively sit back in the face of these events. Cochabamba's peasants, Pampeños among them, quickly and decisively responded to the immediate and grave threats to their livelihood. They did so by rapidly perceiving available goals and potential risks, pursuing different strategies appropriate to swiftly shifting political and economic contexts, and drawing on (and remolding along the way) a repertoire of traditional organizational forms and practices with which they were familiar (see esp. J. Weil 1980: chap. 8, 1989). Facing and overcoming numerous obstacles (many stemming from antinarcotics state policies), in a matter of years they expanded and intensified coca cultivation and helped provide a steady supply of the raw material required to meet the consumption needs of North American consumers thousands of miles away. Bolivian peasants, however, were not so much passively "drawn into" the coca and cocaine market as they were, and continue to be, primary and decisive actors in this political and economic arena. Well organized and constantly striving to outmaneuver policies they considered deleterious, coca-cultivating peasants have in different ways powerfully shaped but (probably to their own disadavantage in the long run) the course of new and ongoing development and narcotics policies, programs, and discourse in Bolivia and in the United States.

By pursuing different yet intersecting goals and strategies, Chapare peasants have no doubt enriched and enhanced the political power of trafficking organizations and other capitalists. Their active and quite diverse types of engagement, however, cannot be explained in terms of a passive response to the demands or dictates of external, structural factors or forces or (local or global) capitalist "needs." That the goals, needs, and opportunities of Bolivian peasants differentially inserted into the coca economy happened to have converged at one particular period with that of agrarian capitalists and other elites is undeniable; that convergence occurred *because* Pampeños and other coca-cultivating peasants fulfilled the needs of agrarian capitalists and cocaine elites is quite a different story.

The "window of opportunity" that Pampeños and other Chapare peasants seized upon and continually reshaped in the face of shifting circumstances (sometimes favorable, other times not) was, as I have tried to show, the result of a concatenation of events originally having little to do with coca. Yet, in large measure because of these unintentional events (and opportunities), Pampeños were in an advantageous position to quickly respond to the challenge of the economic crisis. For example, they were located relatively close to the Chapare, and during previous decades many had already begun to migrate there, as a result of state-sponsored colonization programs, and to grow coca. The paved Cochabamba-Chapare road, constructed with development aid funds to spur agricultural colonization of the Chapare, also provided Pampeños with the unforeseen advantage of quick and easy mobility to the Chapare.

In a concerted drive essentially meant to offset rapidly declining living standards, Pampeños and other peasants were flowing to the Chapare in the 1980s, expanding and intensifying coca production, despite increasing levels of economic and political risk. While in the past Pampeños produced a variety crops in their home community first for consumption and then exchange at local and regional markets, coca production—the key thread through which Pampeños were directly linked to the international drug market—was almost exclusively for cash exchange: a commodity *par excellence*. The drug market's international scope and the production of a prized commodity centered away from the traditional foci of livelihood in Pampa critically distinguished this mode of integration by Pampeños from that of local and regional markets in the past. And the production of this commodity embodied a host of cumulative and intersecting policies and processes, as did some of their aftermaths.

Socioeconomic inequality grounded on differential access to land and labor was quite evident in the Chapare during the 1980s, and there is strong evidence that this process can be traced to at least the early to mid-1970s, if not earlier (see, e.g., J. Weil 1980:406, 1989:333). Inequality was not so much the result of "population pressure" (although relative land scarcity based on access to strategically located land had no doubt emerged) as grounded on differential access to land, labor, and wealth. The coca boom and the intense migration did not engender inequality but, rather, intensified a process deeply rooted in the past.

Wealthy, enterprising, land-based migrants with considerable land in coca and able to recruit and retain a large work force through various mechanisms were clearly at the pinnacle of the social and economic hierarchy; sharecroppers and others with less land, labor, and wealth were the second major category of migrants; at the bottom of the hierarchy were landless workers providing the bulk of labor.

In some Chapare settlements this trend toward increasing inequality was temporarily arrested due to the "voluntary" uprooting of coca, the appearance of disease that afflicted coca shrubs, and the virtual abandonment of some settlements and the move of many Pampeños to new ones. This in turn coincided with bold and politically charged state policies designed to halt the spread of coca cultivation. There were few signs of traditional, nonaccumulating peasant migrants in the Chapare, although a variety of contexts, including state repression, limited the ability of many migrants to accumulate significant wealth. Nevertheless, a small group of Pampeño migrants were able to accumulate wealth. Quite aware of economic opportunities and constraints in an environment of great risk and high inflation, these wealthy migrants invested their wealth in different ways, some that functioned to generate additional wealth, while others surfaced in ceremonies and in other contexts that validated success and prestige.

Not only were large numbers of Pampeños migrating to the Chapare, but virtually all of Pampa's households were expelling labor by the mid-1980s. Although migration to the Chapare remained largely seasonal, increasing numbers of Pampeños were spending a greater amount of time in the Chapare. In a volatile and rapidly changing context marked by a greater amount of land pressed into coca cultivation, an intensification of production, and increasing political and economic risk (including escalating repression), the outflow of labor to the Chapare would in turn have ramifying consequences for land use, the deployment of labor, and access to productive resources in Pampa.

Pampa, a former hacienda, shared many characteristics often ascribed to corporate peasant communities, including strict rules on membership and means of accessing productive resources. Interlocking norms restricted usufruct rights to community members and specific categories of kin and structured socially sanctioned means of gaining access to land and irrigation water. A commoditization of land had not yet taken hold in Pampa at the zenith of Bolivia's coca boom, and land purchases made up only a fraction of land held by most Pampeño households. Pampeño migrants and nonmigrants ingeniously drew upon a variety of well-known ways of gaining access to land, labor, and irrigation water in Pampa (such as *canje,* sharecropping and rental arrangements, and highland-lowland labor exchanges) and redeployed them with new goals in mind during the first wave of migration to Santa Cruz and later to the Chapare. Nevertheless, by the mid-1980s intense migration from Pampa and the possibilities of accumulating wealth in the Chapare were slowly resulting in profound changes in Pampa's land tenure system. Especially noteworthy was the fact that a cardinal land tenure norm in Pampa—one that emphasized that noncommunity members were not allowed to gain permanent usufruct rights to land—was slowly eroding and that an incipient land market loomed on the horizon. By the early 1990s this land market was fully under way.

Another important outcome in Pampa of intense migration to the Chapare were the opportunities that surfaced for some Pampeños who remained behind to accumulate land. In effect, a small number of nonmigrant household heads, relying on various socially sanctioned ways of gaining access to usufruct rights, cleverly seized upon these opportunities to extend their control over a significant amount of land, despite the absence of a developed land market in Pampa. These opportunities surfaced as a result of the declining interest in inheritance by many younger migrants, prolonged absence from Pampa by increasing numbers of Pampeños, and an overall decline of land under cultivation.

Intense migration to the Chapare and the expansion and intensification of coca production for the global drug market were closely intertwined with—partially the outcome of and determinant factors in—crop production trends and evolving productive strategies in Pampa. These in turn were also shaped by a collapsing national economy beset by runaway inflation and systemic agricultural policies that had resulted in deteriorating terms of trade. By the mid-1980s both had drastically undermined the real value of major peasant subsistence and cash crops. In Pampa these processes intersected with differential access to land, labor, and wealth—the result of unequal land distributions after the agrarian reform, rising population and a declining land base, and the ability of migrants to successfully confront risk and accumulate wealth in the Chapare.

The result of these processes was the emergence in Pampa of distinctive production strategies. In the realm of potato cultivation the wealthiest migrant household heads—those with significant amounts of coca land and access to labor in the Chapare and far more capable of weathering out economic, environmental, and political risks in the Chapare and in Pampa—planted an insignificant amount of their land in Pampa. Less wealthy migrants, sharecroppers and others at far greater risk, sowed greater percentages of their land.

By and large nonmigrants pursued a strategy of sowing significantly greater amounts of their land in potatoes than migrants. But even among nonmigrants important differences loomed large. The important productive strategies among nonmigrants stemmed from differences in wealth gauged from the amount of land they held in Pampa, declining returns, and difficulties in securing adequate labor for the sowing and harvesting of the potato crops. While migration and coca cultivation improved the economic lot of many migrants, other Pampeños left behind were not as fortunate. The labor drain from Pampa and the difficulties in securing labor were especially significant problems for households in a late stage of their developmental cycle. In some cases their very economic survival was endangered by their inability to secure much needed labor. A context of intensified commodity production for global markets was in many respects dysfunctional for a country such as Bolivia, which periodically faced chronic food deficits. These different crop production strategies during Bolivia's coca boom, clearly intertwined in manifold ways with the mosaic of processes outlined in previous pages, resulted in an overall drop in the amount of land sown in potatoes, Pampa's consumption staple and major cash crop, and almost certainly of other crops as well.

Labor availability, then, played an important role in crop production strategies in Pampa. But the labor drain from Pampa—the reployment of labor away from basic crop production toward coca commodity production—was also important for other reasons. Less labor was no doubt deployed in overall agricultural activities in Pampa than prior to the coca boom because of the curtailment of crop production in Pampa. Yet high levels of migration, the tighter integration of Pampeños with the coca commodity market, and the increase of monetary wealth within Pampa was not leading to the demise of nonwage labor arrangements. In fact, wage labor was almost totally absent during the sowing and harvesting of Pampa's major potato crops during the 1983–84 agricultural season. The numerically most important ways of recruiting and deploying agricultural labor, as we saw in chapter 7, consisted of inter- and intra-household labor exchanges, followed by payment in kind. Almost paradoxically, "traditional" ways of mobilizing and recruiting labor emerged paramount in a region in which the major economic mainstay pivoted on coca production for a global market, a regional economy clearly pervaded by cash exchanges and a seemingly inexorable trend toward a commoditization of labor.

During the economic and political context of the 1980s the almost virtual absence of agricultural wage labor in Pampa or, in other words, the preference of most Pampeños to work for each other by sidestepping the cash domain was undoubtedly the result of the variety of wider linkages that different Pampeños—migrants and nonmigrants, wealthy and not-so-wealthy—had forged. The presence of many Pampeños in the Chapare during periods of peak labor demands in Pampa, the comparatively higher incomes, wages, and other payments that coca-cultivating migrants and those engaged in other coca-related activities obtained there, and the high rates of inflation that made payment in kind far more valuable than a rapidly depreciating currency were some of the major variables that accounted for patterns of nonwage labor in Pampa.

In the latter part of the 1980s a powerful drive was undertaken by the Bolivian government to restructure the national economy, root out coca paste and cocaine trafficking, and effectively drive back the cumulative increase in coca cultivation that had been taking place for years. The economic restructuring plan, outlined in greater detail in chapter 8, achieved its goal of controlling inflation and setting up the conditions for the free play of market forces. But it did so at a high social cost that undermined income, consumption, and production throughout different sectors of the economy. Shortly thereafter state officials began carrying out new and vigorous policies to limit new coca plantings and eventually eradicate all coca in the Chapare. This bold new move toward coca eradication was partly in response to intensified political and economic pressures brought to bear by the United States, including ongoing threats to cut off economic assistance that the state required to bolster and continue its economic stabilization program.

Coca eradication programs and policies in the late 1980s and early 1990s, bolstered by the large-scale deployment of police and military forces, were also shaped by the successful ways in which peasant migrants had consistently outmaneuvered policymakers and essentially undermined previous coca policies. The basic assumptions and underpinnings of coca policy strategists—that peasants would cease to plant coca once prices drastically fell as a result of intensified interdiction against coca paste and cocaine trafficking and an undermining of coca leaf marketing and when supposedly economically viable alternate crops became available—proved untenable. Despite drastically low coca prices, peasants employed to their own advantage specific programs designed to entice them to grow other crops in order to continue to expand coca plantings. One upshot of this recent interplay of antagonistic forces has been the wider dispersal of new coca plantings and of Pampeños throughout the Chapare and neighboring Santa Cruz. In fact, if we interpret *community* as a complex and ongoing web of social and economic relationships between and among a specific category of individuals and households, and not a reified entity, then the boundaries of the community of Pampa extended to include the Pampeños and the Chapare settlements they were living and producing in during the 1980s.

An almost inevitable confrontation and escalating violence looms ahead as Bolivian and United States officials seem determined, and confident enough, to carry out their plans to eliminate coca in the Chapare—and essentially undermine the livelihood of tens of thousands of peasant households. Although massive and frontal confrontations with the state are presently unrealistic, peasant organizations no doubt will still put up a fight, particularly when they are reminded, as they have been during the recent droughts, of how precarious earning a livelihood from highland agriculture has become, especially after the 1985 economic program. Attempts by government officials to portray this persistent and growing opposition to their plans as a strategy by drug traffickers to protect their own interests—that is, the view that drug traffickers are troublemakers arousing what would otherwise be a docile and acquiescent peasantry—are clearly not convincing and, in fact, run counter to the documented historical experience of Bolivian peasant movements. A growing sense of nationalism, ethnic pride, and antiforeign feelings cutting across class lines and increasing political polarization and deepening class cleavages—all within the context of increasing repression, militarization, and economic recession—are on the rise and foreshadow increasing violence in the Chapare. At the same time we need not uncritically accept government claims that acts of violence and confrontations in the Chapare are the result of traffickers somehow "stirring up the masses" to acknowledge that traffickers too will exploit this explosive situation to their own benefit. Indeed, the prognosis for a peaceful settlement of the "drug problem" in Bolivia is not very good.

Appendixes

Appendix 1: Fieldwork Methods

Fieldwork, an exploratory endeavor, almost always entails a compromise between what one initially sets out to do and what is actually accomplished. I arrived in Cochabamba at the end of August 1982 interested in exploring how and to what extent migration to the Chapare was intertwined with land tenure changes in a migrant highland home community. Migration to the Bolivian lowlands had, of course, been studied before by anthropologists, geographers, and others. Virtually all anthropological research on lowland migration in Bolivia carried out in the late 1970s, heavily influenced by the adaptational approach in ecological and economic anthropology (e.g., Bennett 1969, 1976), emphasized how migrants adapted to novel socioeconomic and ecological conditions in the lowlands (e.g., Hess 1980; J. Weil 1980a; C. Weil 1980; Stearman 1976). I proposed instead to center my attention on whether, how, and to what degree migration to the Chapare was accompanied by changes in the socioeconomic organization of the migrant home communities, especially in modes of accessing land and irrigation water. It was only after I arrived in Bolivia and selected Pampa as my research site did I fully realize the critical importance of the demand for coca, and of coca cultivation in the Chapare, for my research topic. There was simply no way to skirt the coca issue. Pampeños constantly talked about coca and state policies toward its cultivation and eradication, and cultivating coca was the major reason given by all Pampeños for migrating to the Chapare. The major themes in this book, then, arose as I reconceptualized in the field how, why, and under what constraints peasants were migrating, the options they had pursued, and some of the correlates of intense migration to and the spread of commodity production in the Chapare.

I spent part of my first three months in Bolivia acquainting myself with the Department of Cochabamba and in efforts at selecting an appropriate research site. José Blanes, a member of the Centro de La Realidad Económica y Social (CERES), had written to me while I was still in Madison and suggested that I consider selecting a community between the city of Cochabamba and the town of Colomi in the Sacaba Valley area. According to Blanes, large numbers of peasants from many communities in this area, especially those bordering the paved road to the Chapare, were migrating to the Chapare. With the assistance of Eusebio Solís, also of CERES, my wife and I spent many days acquainting ourselves with several of these communities. After some preliminary and informal conversations with their leaders (*dirigentes*), I finally chose Pampa as my research site. Pampa seemed appropriate for several reasons: it bordered the paved road to the Chapare, from which I could easily observe who was traveling to the Chapare, when, and with whom; it was also easily accessible by public transportation from Cochabamba (where my wife and I had rented a small house); I was informed that some Pampeños had had prior experience with other "gringos" and that our presence would therefore generate little resistance from community members; finally, this community was one of the area's largest and best known, and it seemed likely that I could find good historical documentation on it in local and regional archives.

Mr. Solís, fluent in Quechua, subsequently met with some of Pampa's leaders, introduced us to them, informed them of our intentions of "writing a book" on their community, and requested that they ask the *sindicato*'s permission to allow us to move into Pampa. Several weeks later we learned through Mr. Solís that Pampa's *sindicato* had requested our presence at its monthly meeting. When we arrived in Pampa we were escorted to the school amphitheater, where we answered many questions from community members, some genuinely interested in knowing why we wanted to move into Pampa, others deeply suspicious of our intentions altogether. Several weeks later, in yet another meeting with Pampa's leaders, we were told that the *sindicato* had approved our stay in Pampa and that we could sleep in a vacant room in the health station (*posta sanitaria*). The health station, in the pueblo and within easy view of the paved Chapare road, proved an ideal location for learning of important upcoming events and for meeting and greeting those migrating to the Chapare.

Many Pampeños always remained deeply suspicious of my intentions and in many ways avoided answering my questions. Their suspicions (and resentments) heightened during government antidrug operations (e.g., the military occupation of the Chapare) and often surfaced during birthday parties, other ceremonies, or roadblocks, which were often accompanied by heavy drinking. Fictive kin ties that I forged with key Pampeños were important in convincing others that I was not some secret government or drug enforcement agent. My wife and I finally moved into Pampa in mid-January 1983. I carried out fieldwork through May of 1985—intermittently interrupted by illness and other pressing concerns—and left Bolivia in June of that year. I spent most of the last 10 or 11 months of fieldwork gathering archival data and other historical documentation in the town of Sacaba's parish church, and in Bolivian and Argentine archives, for a 200-year study of Pampa's historical demography presently underway.

My fieldwork consisted of informal interviews, participant observation in a variety of informal settings and daily activities (such as potato sowings and harvests, birthday parties, weddings), and the use of semi-structured interview instruments. I consistently avoided depending on a single source or method for obtaining specific types of data on particular themes.

A detailed census of all of Pampa's 253 households (completed with household heads in 90 percent of the cases) yielded data on household composition described in chapter 2. In addition to eliciting standard demographic data on all household members (age, sex, education, place of birth, etc.), this household census provided additional information on primary occupation, ownership of land plots in and/or migration to the Chapare, and length of stays in Pampa and the Chapare. The material on social stratification and land and labor relationships prior to the agrarian reform is based on Pampa's agrarian reform dossier, other archival documents, and lengthy informal interviews with elder Pampeños.

Data on migration to and access to land in the Chapare (chap. 4) was drawn from several sources. A genealogical census (coupled with the household census) centered on each of Pampa's agrarian reform land grantees yielded diachronic data on household composition, migration and residence, and kinship and household linkages. In the Instituto Nacional de Colonización in La Paz I examined documents on the Chapare colonies that Pampeños had been migrating to since the late 1950s. These brief and often incomplete documents yielded data on the names of migrants, the size of their landholdings, and, occasionally, some data on crop production. Since many Pampeños held important *sindicato* positions in the Chapare colonies, I was able to obtain from them detailed and up-to-date lists on all Pampeños with access to Chapare land plots. Data on access to labor in the Chapare was based on detailed interviews.

I traveled to the Chapare four times, always accompanied by fictive kin, to acquaint myself with the colonies to which Pampeños were migrating.

The analyses of land use and the deployment of labor in chapters 5 and 6 are also grounded on different types of data and data collection strategies. I delimited the boundaries of Pampa's crop zones on the basis of their differing potato cultivation cycles and the flow of potato seed from one zone to another. I determined the altitudinal range of each crop zone by taking a total of 26 altitudinal points in the field. The Cochabamba office of meteorology provided me with rainfall and temperature data (see also apps. 2 and 3). A detailed interview schedule provided most of the data on the amount of land sown in potatoes by 42 sample households during the 1984 agricultural season. Estimates of the amount of the land available to each sample household are based on data from the agrarian reform dossier, information on inheritance from informal interviews and the genealogical census, and data on land purchases and rentals from the Registro de Derechos Reales and informal interviews. The amount of cultivable land was estimated by asking each household head for the number of sacks (*cargas*) of potato seed required to plant all his or her cultivable land; this number was then divided by 15, the average number of sacks of potato seed that one hectare of land will absorb.

The material on land tenure and the structure of landholdings presented in chapter 5 is based on informal questioning, an examination of land transaction documents (especially on land purchases) in Cochabamba's office of Derechos Reales, the genealogical census, and Pampa's agrarian reform dossier.

This same interview schedule used to calculate potato sowings and harvests (but supplemented by informal interviews) provided the bulk of the quantitative data in chapter 7 on the amount and type of labor deployed by 47 households in the harvest of the 1983 *huata* potato crop and, during the 1984 crop season, the planting of *huata,* and the sowing and harvest of the *mishka* irrigated crops. I elicited the following categories of data: (1) date of interview; (2) number of potato *cargas* sown or harvested; (3) date of the planting or harvest; (4) crop zone; (5) name of household head undertaking the planting/harvest; (6) number and length of the days that the activity lasted; (7) name, age, and sex; (8) kinship relationship to the household head undertaking the planting and/or harvesting; (9) community membership status; (10) the type of labor contributed by each participant (i.e., *ayuda, ayni,* etc.); and (11) the source of each instance of labor (i.e., from within the household, other kin, or nonkin). I carried out a separate interview for every field planted and harvested by each sample household. Although I attempted to carry out the interviews during or shortly after each planting and harvest, some unfortunately were carried out one to two months later, a delay due primarily to the difficulty of locating migrants who would often leave for the Chapare soon after completing the sowing or harvest. Sometimes I was unable to complete an ongoing interview, and weeks would pass before I would see the household head again. These interviews were always accompanied by informal questioning on difficulties that the household heads had experienced in planting or harvesting (lack of labor, high inputs costs, etc.).

One particularly thorny methodological issue I grappled with was that of quantifying the amount of labor absorbed in the sowing and harvest of Pampa's potato crops. I quickly decided against simply equating the labor contributed by males and females of differing ages into equivalent units, for this approach would have seriously distorted the amount of labor available to and deployed by the sample households. Therefore, following MacFarlane (1976) and Fricke (1984), I decided to express the labor inputs of males and females of varying ages in terms of proportions of a standard unit of measurement—the "production unit." This production unit is equivalent to the labor provided each day by a male between 20 and 45 years old (see table A1). Each proportion was then multiplied by the number of workdays to arrive at the total "person-days" of labor contributed by each worker.

This approach had, admittedly, numerous handicaps. For instance, in many tasks women worked just as hard and produced just as much

TABLE A1.   Work Capacity Scale

Age	Male	Age	Female
0–8	0	0–6	0
9–13	0.2	7–12	0.2
14–16	0.6	13–15	0.4
17–19	0.8	16–17	0.6
20–45	1.0	18–45	0.8
46–60	0.8	46–55	0.8
61–70	0.6	56–70	0.6
70+	0.2	70+	0.2

Source: MacFarlane 1976:114.

as their male counterparts. And in certain key tasks, such as the placing of the seed in the furrows, women were said by male Pampeños to be more adept and efficient. Consequently, their full contribution to their households' livelihood was partly underrepresented. (On the other hand, while children may be as efficient and productive as adults in, say, herding, their productive contribution in the manual harvest of potatoes was no doubt far less.) In addition, my approach was definitely not an emic one: in calculating *ayni* labor contributions, for example, Pampeños considered a woman's daily work equal to that of a male. A further difficulty was that in a few cases Pampeños could not precisely ascertain the exact number of days they or others worked on their fields. (This would have presented problems in any analysis of labor inputs regardless of the methodology employed.) While this hardly represented a problem during sowing (which was, almost without exception, accomplished in one day), it did often present problems during a harvest, when a greater number of workers were involved and when the *mishka* harvest would often be interrupted by heavy rains. A final difficulty of my method for calculating labor inputs resided in reliably ascertaining an individual's age, particularly that of non-Pampeños. Despite these drawbacks, the principal advantage of my methodological approach—the feasibility of determining, to a degree perhaps not otherwise possible, the relative weight of each unit and type of labor in the potato production process— far outweighed its drawbacks. Other Andean ethnographers who have attempted to quantify labor inputs (e.g., Brown 1987) have employed analogous methodological strategies.

My original design called for sampling 20 percent of Pampa's household heads (50 in total). These 50 households were in turn to be divided into 40 migrant and 10 nonmigrant household heads—that is, roughly proportional to the total number of migrant and nonmigrant households in Pampa (see chap. 4). This design was not feasible. Pampeño migrant household heads were extraordinarily mobile: some would unexpectedly arrive in Pampa and remain for several weeks before returning to the Chapare; others remained for just a day or two before quickly heading back to the Chapare and did not reappear in Pampa until several months later; some household heads initially agreed to be interviewed, but I was later unable to locate them and carry out follow-up interviews on other potato plantings; finally, some migrant and nonmigrant household heads provided information on one planting season but refused to answer questions on subsequent ones. For these and other reasons I was able to complete 42 interviews on households sowing potatoes during the 1984 season, and only 47 household heads were interviewed on the deployment of labor.

The analysis of labor inputs excluded some tasks necessary for potato cultivation (such as the different stages of land preparation, weeding, and *aporque*). This was so for a number of reasons. Foremost was the fact that after a preliminary inquiry I realized that many households heads did not accurately recall the labor they expended on all these tasks for each of their *mishka* and *huata* plantings. These difficulties were particularly pronounced in the case of migrant household heads, who often left many of these activities up to other household members or close kinsmen. In addition, since these supplementary labor tasks seemed to fall within the household domain it seemed to me that a focus of labor expended on the sowings and harvests would provide a firmer basis for discussing some of the issues raised by Guillet (1980) and others on the persistence of nonwage labor (see chap. 7). Finally, I was also interested in ascertaining to the extent possible the role that Chapare migrants played in agricultural productive tasks in the home community of Pampa, and early on it became clear to me that many participated only minimally in land preparation, weeding, and similar tasks.

After my original field research ended in 1985 I returned to Pampa in the summers of 1991 and 1992. These short periods of fieldwork are the basis of part of chapter 8.

Appendix 2

Annual Preciptation in Colomi, 1977–81 (in milimeters)

Month	1977	1978	1979	1980	1981	Mean
			Year			
January	75	164	219	157	147	152
February	118	73	137	77	93	100
March	185	55	116	67	55	96
April	0.8	14	46	20	11	18
May	32	7	0	0	0	8
June	0	2	0	2	0	1
July	0.9	12	7	0	0	4
August	33	23	0	18	70	29
September	71	16	8	21	63	36
October	22	19	76	31	21	34
November	50	29	62	4	20	33
December	150	111	119	13	110	100
Totals	741	528	873	413	595	630

Source: Unpublished materials available at the Servicio Nacional de Meteorolgía e Hidrología, Cochabamba. Figures rounded to nearest millimeter.

Appendix 3

Monthly Temperatures in Colomi, 1981–83 (in centigrade)

	Year								
	1981			1982			1983		
Month	Max.	Min.	Med.	Max.	Min.	Med.	Max.	Min.	Med.
January	24	0	13	24	5	13	27	4	14
February	26	0	13	25	4	13	24	5	13
March	29	4	15	25	5	13	27	0	15
April	30	1	13	26	1	12	30	2	14
May	37	− 2	14	33	− 5	12	33	− 3	13
June	33	− 4	12	31	− 4	11	32	− 2	12
July	31	− 5	10	30	− 6	11	31	− 1	12
August	30	− 3	11	30	− 4	12	30	− 2	12
September	27	− 1	11	32	1	12	26	1	12
October	26	3	12	24	3	13	26	1	11
November	25	4	14	23	5	13	23	0	11
December	24	5	13	23	3	13	23	0	11

Source: Unpublished materials available at the Servicio Nacional de Meteorología e Hidrología, Cochabamba. Figures rounded to the nearest degree centigrade.

Notes

Chapter 1

1. By a commodity I mean a good or product produced primarily for exchange and not use or consumption.

2. Modernization theory has not by any means disappeared from academic and policy-making discourse. For example, one recent and polemical attempt to once again explain Latin American poverty and underdevelopment from the vantage point of values, "culture," or "state of mind" is that by Harrison (1985), a former USAID official.

3. The "substantative-formalist" debate mirrored the deep divide within cultural anthropology between proponents of "culture" and advocates of "practical reason" (cf. Sahlins 1976). This theoretical chasm still persists in contemporary anthropology, albeit under different guises.

4. I am referring here to the "world system," "dependency," and "modes of production" approaches. Proponents of these approaches differ on key theoretical and methodological issues (for good reviews, see Nash 1981; Goodman and Redclift 1982; Roseberry 1983; C. Smith 1983; Chilcote 1984; Chilcote and Edelstein 1986). For a recent and fascinating debate on some of these issues from the vantage point of Latin American and Caribbean history, see Stern (1988a, 1988b) and Wallerstein (1988). See also chapter 9.

5. For example, in just two pages Goodman and Redclift (1982:91–92) talk of "peasant commodity producers," "petty commodity producers," "peasant producers," "peasant simple commodity producers," "peasant family-labour enterprises," and "independent family-based peasant enterprises."

6. Peter Reuter of the Rand Corporation has recently illustrated the extraordinary profits obtained by international drug trafficking organizations and how coca leaves account for an insignificant part of cost incurred by traffickers. For example, in 1988 about U.S. $750 worth of coca leaves were needed to manufacture one kilo of cocaine; this same kilo at the retail level (in units of one gram, at 70 percent purity) in Chicago was worth U.S. $135,000 (quoted in United States House of Representatives 1991:26–27).

7. I am grateful to Jim Weil for alerting me to this important point.

8. In a previous publication (Sanabria 1988) I claimed that economic differentiation was indeed taking hold in the Chapare. This conclusion was premature.

9. Hanson's article has generated a considerable amount of controversy among Pacific anthropologists (see, for example, Langdon 1991; Levine 1991; Linnekin

1991; for a response, see Hanson 1991). For other important works on the reinterpretation and recreation of tradition see Thomas (1992) and Keesing (1989).

Chapter 2

1. See *AGN* 13.18.1.1. Jackson (1989:263), however, cites a study based on a 1692 census that claims only 11 haciendas in the Sacaba Valley at the time.

2. Between 1728 and 1748 six landowners related through kinship ties owned at least 14 haciendas and *estancias* in Sacaba—virtually the entire eastern half of the valley floor and its corresponding highlands to the north, east, and south (*ANB* 1748; *DR* 1804; *NE* 1728).

3. In 1881 an agricultural survey carried out in Sacaba listed 2,394 properties (*propiedades*), each owned by a separate owner (*propietario*) of a total of over 15,000 in the entire department of Cochabamba (*El Heraldo* 1883). By 1908 a cadastral survey listed 90 properties with 4,504 owners. The degree of land concentration and fragmentation (roughly corresponding to haciendas and *piquerías*) can be indirectly gauged by the land tax paid by each *propietario*. Ninety-four percent of the *propietarios* paid less than ten *bolivianos,* while just one-half of one percent (representing 26 *propietarios*) paid 100 or more. While the land tax probably varied according to land quality—and the tax was certainly higher for flat and irrigated crop lands—there is little doubt that these 26 *propietarios* owned the largest and most productive haciendas in the *cantón*. Thirteen of these *propiedades,* including Pampa, were listed as owned by only one *propietario* (*TD* 1908).

4. The 1748 survey (*ANB* 1748) fails to mention Pampa, which suggests that it still formed part of a valley floor hacienda. A 1778 *padrón* is the earliest reference I have encountered on Pampa, which is listed as a separate hacienda (*AGN* 13.18.2.1.). A 1792 land transaction, however, unambiguously describes Pampa as an *estancia* of a valley floor hacienda (*DR* 1804). I am unable to explain the apparent contradictory data offered by these two sources.

5. This census was carried out between 1880 and 1881 in all Bolivian departments. For the use of the results of this census in historical research in the departments of Potosí and Chuquisaca, see Platt (1982a) and Langer (1989). The census in manuscript form of Cochabamba has, to my knowledge, never been found by researchers. The Cochabamba newspaper *El Heraldo* (1883) published an abbreviated summary of its results, however, as well as information on production and land value of (presumably) all *propiedades* in previous issues. I was able to find data on only 59 *propiedades,* including Pampa, from the following issues: 1881a, 1881b, 1881c, 1881d, and 1882.

6. The hacienda of Pampa was passed down intact from one generation to another. Moreover, its landowners appear to have been financially solvent and were not, as many of their counterparts, forced to sell off land to peasant tenants. Pampa's landowners were heavily involved in money lending since at least the mid-nineteenth century, and in the process they accumulated many other properties as debtors defaulted on their loans. To take but one example, between

January and March of 1891, Pampa's landowner provided 12 separate loans to fellow landowners, including some kin (*DRD* 1891).

7. Pampa falls within the subtropical, low montane, thorny steepe Holdridge life zone. This ecological zone is characterized by rugged topography with narrow and deep valley floors, annual precipitation between 250 and 500 millimeters, medium annual temperatures from 11 to 12 degree centigrade, and near or below freezing temperatures throughout the winter months (Unzueta 1975:140–1).

8. An interesting example of the prevalence of local histories within each *lugar* is that of the origin myth of the Lake of Parina located in Tuty, Pampa's highest crop zone. According to informants, "long ago" (*unay tiempopi*) a settlement (*llacta*) was located in the middle of what is now Parina. "Evil men" (*malditos*) lived in this settlement. At some point in time a festivity (*agasajo*) was taking place when God (*tata dios*) suddenly appeared. He requested food and drink for he had been long walking from a faraway place (*llacta*). The participants in the *agasajo* did not "recognize" him and refused him his request. Stricken with sadness (*llakiq*) and anger (*p''illaq*) God walked away from Parina in a downward direction away from the festivity. While walking he encountered a young women (*imilla*) grazing sheep and with a baby (*wawa*) in her arms. As God approached he warned her not to turn around and gaze toward the festivity. Not heeding God's warning, she suddenly turned toward Parina. At that very instant the young woman and her baby disappeared, their images suddenly engraved in a nearby boulder. Simultaneously, a period of torrential rain lasting forty days and nights (*jushu p'unllay*) began, drowning all those participating in the festivity, submerging the settlement under water, and giving rise to the lake.

Interestingly enough, it is on the high ridges in the Tuty crop zone where *chullpas,* conical structures built of stone and adobe bricks, are found. The *chullpas,* ancient burial mounds, are where, some Pampeños believe, the "Incas are buried." Similar cultural motifs—cities or settlements submerged under lakes, the end of time, and petrification—surface in other Andean origin myths. See, for instance, Allen (1988:65) and Zuidema (1990:9).

9. In one of the first Aymara dictionaries compiled after the Spanish conquest—that by Bertonio in 1612—*lari lari* referred to "the surroundings of a town or a village where the nonkin, the uncivilized, the lawless people live" (Zuidema 1990:26).

10. The difficulty of delimiting household membership and boundaries in the context of intense migration has been especially acute in Africa, where migrants "can exercise rights and be subject to obligations which are normally thought of as economic beyond the household in which they live" (Guyer 1981:98). How to determine residential propinquity when some Pampa household heads claimed that some of their sons and/or daughters only spent, on an intermittent basis, about half of the year in Pampa or when others stated that when in Pampa their offspring refused to dedicate sufficient time to crop activities are some issues I confronted in Pampa.

11. There were a few exceptions to these criteria. Although the prevailing

postmarital residence rule was virilocality, I encountered two community members living uxorilocally within walking distance from Pampa. They maintained a dwelling in Pampa, attended *sindicato* meetings, fulfilled their communal obligations, and cultivated land in Pampa. For all intents and purposes these Pampeños were "living in" Pampa and were therefore included in the census. On the other hand there were some attempts to inflate the number of persons living in a casa. This was so because the quantity of food staples occasionally distributed in Pampa by foreign assistance programs was contingent on the number of household members; some Pampeños obviously thought that I was affiliated with these programs and that, by providing me with more "members," they would be entitled to more foodstuffs. On two occasions households originally included in the household census were later dropped, for, despite initial claims to the contrary by their kin, members of these two households resided permanently elsewhere, never attended community meetings, nor cultivated land in Pampa.

12. This is a surprisingly low-dependency ratio by Third World standards. There are several possible reasons for this low number. One is that oftentimes many Pampeños could not remember with absolute certainty their correct ages, forcing me to estimate their ages based on those of other household members. The other reason the dependency ratio is low, of course, almost certainly has to do migration: my household census probably did not encompass many others (especially youngsters) who spent a greater part of their time in the Chapare with other kin.

Chapter 3

1. Coca chewing is referred to by various terms in the Andes (e.g., Burchard 1976; Mayer 1988; E. Morales 1989). In Pampa and surrounding areas it is called *aculliku*.

2. I am not suggesting that coca consumption was restricted to the Incan elite, a widely held but incorrect view difficult to defend on logical and empirical grounds. It is unlikely that access to and use of coca—so widespread and with such deep historical roots—could have been so rapidly suppressed by the Incas, and the "Incan monopoloy" thesis rests on chronicler statements conveying an Inca-centered view of the Andean universe. For a discussion of some of these issues, see Murra (1986), Parkerson (1983), and Carter and Mamani (1986:70–71).

3. The practice of taxing coca leaf sales continues in present-day Bolivia.

4. The idea of "tropical frontier," which begins this section, is taken from Larson (1988a).

5. It is important to bear in mind that a *carga* of coca can actually weigh anywhere between 100 and 125 pounds.

6. Yield estimates from *cocales* in the *yungas* of La Paz and in the region of Santa Cruz are invariably lower than the Chapare. One hectare of mature coca plants harvested four times a year can yield between 7,600 and 8,900 kilos; most of this is lost due to humidity, spoilage, etc. (SUBDESAL 1988:19–21).

7. Data from eastern Peru, however, suggest that coca cultivation requires

slightly more than twice as much labor as coffee (J. Collins 1988:72). This difference is probably due to different ways in which labor needs were calculated and perhaps to differing ecological conditions as well.

8. See chapter 5 for a discussion of the issues of labor surplus and scarcity.

9. Large land concessions were also awarded in the Chapare. Studies sponsored in the late 1970s by USAID pointed to the presence of, "more or less," 37 medium to large land concessions in the Chapare totalling some 200,000 hectares (MASI 1979:6; USAID 1981:9). C. Weil (1980:307) claims that by 1975 these concessions, or cooperatives, which she defined as "agribusinesses formed by middle class stockholders," had been alloted 334,940 hectares in the Chapare. Although a detailed social and economic study of these enterprises has yet to be undertaken, some authors (e.g., C. Weil 1980:307; J. Weil 1980a:93; MASI 1979:6; USAID 1981:9) have suggested that these may have evolved by the late 1970s into large enterprises employing wage labor. However, they almost certainly never attained the degree of capitalization and scale achieved by their counterparts in the Department of Santa Cruz. Furthermore, for reasons discussed in chapter 1, it is unlikely that these cooperatives had evolved into large-scale coca-producing plantations. E. Morales is clearly mistaken when he claims that Bolivian coca production is in the hands of "the landed middle and upper class" (1990:634 n.1).

10. Dunkerley and Morales (1986:91) have emphasized that "infant mortality has reached 168 per thousand births; one half of all children are malnourished; only one third of households have access to potable water and one third have no bedroom; sixty per cent of Bolivians earn or cultivate too little to provide themselves with nutritional intake adequate for a healthy life; over 61 per cent of all school-children suffer from goitre."

11. For other interesting contradictions, see Bostwick (1990:112–13) and Rasnake and Painter (1989:14–15).

12. Indeed, intermediaries can often appropriate between 25 and 40 percent of the value of agricultural goods paid for by consumers (see SUBDESAL 1988:85).

13. Much of the early literature on migration to or colonization of the sparsely populated lowlands in Bolivia and elsewhere in Latin America was heavily influenced by modernization theory. As noted in chapter 1, modernization theory places a great deal of attention on psychological or quasipsychological attributes of individuals (often expressed in terms of "values" and "attitudes"). The literature on colonization provides many examples. The work by Wessel (1968) is illustrative. Bolivian highland peasants, who, in spite of their obvious poverty do not migrate to the lowlands, are "shackled with sociological and psychological barriers," while those who do migrate are instilled with an "adventurous spirit" (Wessel 1968:31). A look at so-called psychological attributes informs us little regarding the structural causes of migration. Unless the (dubious) assumption is made that, for instance, periods of intense migration are to a great extent the result of or accompanied by a drastic reorganization in the psychological makeup of the Bolivian peasantry, one is forced to look elsewhere for more viable explanations.

14. What is important here is not necessarily providing indisputable amounts but, rather, pointing to general trends. There is, in fact, considerable disagreement on the amount of land cultivated in coca (and the total coca leaf production) during the 1980s. Estimates from United States and Bolivian government sources tend to be sharply lower (see, e.g., Bureau of International Narcotics Matters 1990:115; United States House of Representatives 1990a:67; SUBDESAL 1988:25, 45).

15. De Franco and Godoy (1990) dispute the claim that an incipient trend toward coca specialization and monocropping was occuring in the Chapare during the early to mid-1980s. For a response, see Sanabria (n.d.).

16. Blanes and Flores (1982:37–38), for example, estimated that some 420,000 individuals traveled to the Chapare between January of 1981 and January of 1982 through the town of Sacaba alone. A more recent study has calculated the Chapare's population at 215,000 (qd. in Rasnake and Painter 1989:33).

17. Bolivia's "coca boom" is, of course, generating vast wealth and capital accumulation elsewhere. Tullis (1987:252–53) estimates that of Bolivia's U.S. $2 billion cocaine industry only U.S. $500 million remain in the country. For other estimates see Doria Medina (1986) and Bostwick (1990). Doria Medina calculated at U.S. $1 billion the dollar value in Bolivia of the coca that enters the illegal black market. This coca can generate U.S. $5.7 billion (at prices prevalent in Bolivia) in coca paste and cocaine hydrochloride, almost all of which escaped Bolivia and which he labeled "capital flight" (1986:72).

Chapter 4

1. Demographic instability and unequal access to productive resources within Pampa's peasant class is also illustrated by what my elder informants called *huata runas*—literally "yearly people." *Huata runa,* a term not employed today, suggests mobility, impermanence, and seasonality. *Huata runas,* at the bottom of the social and economic hierarchy, were poor peasants or households who provided labor or other services to the landowner and/or *pefalero* households. They had tenuous access to land and engaged in a variety of productive roles: agricultural wage labor, payment in kind, and sharecropping of *pefalero* and desmesne land. What critically set apart *huata runa* households was that they lacked independent access to some means of production (such as the lack of oxen to work the land or the minimum amount of labor required to sustain itself and satisfy hacienda labor and other tribute obligations) that would have enabled them to gain long term usufruct rights to desmesne land. In time some *huata runa* households managed to accumulate the necessary productive means to "move" to *pefalero* status. Not one non-Pampeño *huata runa* gained permanent access to land and remained in Pampa after the agrarian reform. Pampa's *huata runas* bore a structural resemblance to the *kantu runas* (literally "people of the margin") described by Platt (1982a:52–54, 1982b:38) in northern Potosí. Godoy, also writing on northern Potosí, states that *kantu runas* were originally landless immigrants, who, during the second half of the nineteenth century, gained tenuous forms of access to land in *ayllu* territories (1984:370–71).

2. Detailed research on hacienda-hacienda and hacienda-*piquería* migration in the Department of Cochabamba prior to the agrarian reform has, to my knowledge, yet to be undertaken. Dandler and Torrico (1986) claim that considerable peasant mobility was present in the province of Ayopaya in the 1940s. They also suggest that peasant spatial mobility was one concrete manifestation of underlying social and political currents sweeping the Cochabamba Valley region at the time.

3. This number excludes those born in Santa Cruz.

4. The drought was the result of meteorological anomalies in the eastern Pacific associated with the warm El Niño current off the Pacific coast of South America (Canby 1984; Philander 1983).

5. However, J. Collins does not provide specific data on the number of migrants from specific highland communities with land titles in Tambopata, how many have secure or insecure land titles (or no titles at all), nor additional data on the amount of time spent by migrants in the Tambopata Valley.

6. This is consistent with more recent data gathered by Blanes and Flores (1982:175) demonstrating that permanent sharecroppers were present in 20 percent of the more coca-specialized colonies. Miguelino's sharecroppers often spent time in Pampa, residing in his large, two-story house, which they were remodeling. One group of three sharecroppers and their spouses and offspring once remained in Pampa for about a month. While in Pampa, they performed a variety of tasks for Miguelino, such as preparing his land for the planting and cleaning the ditches that irrigated his fields.

7. *Los Tiempos* 1983g, 1983h, 1983i, 1983j, 1983k, 1983l, 1984a, 1984b, 1984c, 1984d.

8. Some of Pampa's most successful and wealthy migrants were said to have "found gold" in nearby mountains with which they purchased their vehicles as well as land in nearby areas. Interestingly enough, some Pampeños also claimed that the town of Sacaba's parish priests had discovered gold—"gold of the Incas," it was claimed—in the Tunari Mountains north of Pampa during their frequent trips there to remote villages and that it was with this gold that they were constructing the new church in Pampa. For a similar cultural theme in contemporary Chiapas, Mexico, see Loyola (1988) and Cancian (1989).

9. Many refused to discuss how much cash they had earned over specific periods of time and what exactly they did to obtain it. Moreover, I believed that the statements I elicited could not be accepted at face value.

10. Antidrug raids against coca paste and cocaine operations usually raised the price of coca paste and cocaine but, as a result of the immediate shortfall in the demand for coca leaves, lowered the price of coca leaves.

11. According to local oral tradition, the Virgin appeared in Pampa in the late 1800s. Perhaps not coincidentally, she manifested herself not to poor peasants but to one of Pampa's wealthiest and most powerful *kurakas*. Since then fiestas have commemorated her appearance in Pampa. According to some elder Pampeños, one hacienda administrator did "not love the Virgin" and attempted to forbid these fiestas, arguing that the heavy drinking that invariably accompanied them interfered with hacienda production. He soon thereafter became deaf—a

"punishment," Pampeños stated, by the Virgin. After this incident hacienda owners and administrators apparently never again attempted to interfere with fiestas.

12. I am, of course, alluding here to some of the Mesoamerican literature that interprets the investment of wealth in fiestas and other ceremonies as a way of maintaining relative equality in peasant communities (e.g., Carrasco 1961). For more recent critical perspectives on how sponsorship of fiestas and ceremonies serve to perpetuate socioeconomic inequality, see Cancian 1965 and Wasserstrom and Rus 1981.

Chapter 5

1. For a now classic study of reciprocity, peasant subsistence, and resistance, see Scott (1976). For a critique of Scott's position, see Haggis et al. (1986). Joseph (1990) presents a detailed review of the "moral economy," banditry, and peasant resistance literature, especially pertaining to Latin America. Platt (1982a) has studied *ayllu*-state relationships in northern Potosí from the vantage point of reciprocal rights and obligations (but see Larson 1988c).

2. See Stern (1983) and Wolf (1986) for recent reevaluations of the closed corporate peasant community (CCPC) model.

3. In the early 1980s neither consanguineal kin ties to a community member nor birth in Pampa were in themselves necessary and sufficient conditions for the attainment and maintenance of membership status. Pampeños revalidated their status as community members by residing and maintaining social and productive ties in Pampa and demonstrating a consanguineal link to a community member. Pampeños who had left Pampa and had not returned in many years (e.g., permanent migrants) ran the risk of "disappearing" (*chinkapun*)—severing their social ties to Pampa, not being "remembered" by current Pampeños, and losing their membership status and rights to land. Birth in Pampa did not in itself convey the right to later, as an adult, claim membership status, for, as noted above, a consanguineal link to a Pampeño (father, mother, or both) was also necessary. Offspring of noncommunity members living in the pueblo were barred from claiming membership rights, as were their parents, regardless of the time they had lived in Pampa or how often they participated in community activities. At the same time offspring of Pampeños born elsewhere were not automatically classed as *ajenos*. Children of migrants in Santa Cruz or the Chapare who returned to Pampa could attain membership status as well as children of Pampeñas who moved out of Pampa as a result of virilocal post-marital residence.

4. I analyze *tarpuja* in greater detail in chapter 6.

5. These modes of obtaining access to property rights in turn delimited five categories of land determined by their principal mode of access and differing rights and obligations: (1) agrarian reform land; (2) cultivable former hacienda land bought by Pampeños; (3) cultivable hacienda land still legally owned by the former landowner but sharecropped by Pampeños; (4) land bought from the

landowners but used for the construction of the pueblo; and (5) land suited principally for grazing but from which cultivable land plots were carved out.

6. Several other important inheritance rules are worth briefly mentioning. One is that inheritance cannot lead to the alienation of land to non-Pampeños. The norm that inheritance should not lead to the transfer of usufruct rights to non-Pampeños, or "outsiders," conflicted with the ideology of bilateral inheritance but was consistent with the general principle that access to land be restricted to community members. In a context of virilocal residence, offspring born and raised in another community were not considered Pampeños, and strict adherence to the ideology of bilateral inheritance would have resulted in a permanent alienation of the mother's land to outsiders (e.g., her children). This may be one reason why outmarrying women often lost their inheritance rights. An ideology stressing equality within the sibling group was yet another rule of inheritance transmission in Pampa: agrarian reform grantees could claim inheritance from their father only if they had siblings who did not receive state land grants after the agrarian reform. The last important rule was that kin should strive to keep land within the sibling group. Inheritance of irrigation water usually went hand in hand with that of land. Pampeños with lifelong rights to water from the irrigation lake of Kuyuq Qocha or Pampa's streams (see chap. 6) can transmit rights to water allotments (*mit'as*) to their descendants. Inheritance of irrigated crop land automatically entailed access to a proportional allotment of irrigation water.

7. An illegitimate child (*ilegítimo/natural*) was a child whose mother was unmarried at the time of his birth (regardless of whether she had a spouse and had entered into a consensual union) and who had not been adopted, or "recognized," (*reconocido/legitimado*) by a male adult. Children of a married couple were automatically classed as legitimate. Illegitimate children were said "not to have" a father or that the father was "not known." Legitimate offspring had the right to claim their (socially recognized) father's surname and to inherit land from him (as well as from their mother). Illegitimate descendants had a right to a share of their mother's land, but they had a right to their father's land only after they had been legitimized (legally adopted) by him. (For an identical pattern in a Peruvian peasant community, see Isbell 1978:78.) If an illegitimate child's father died before recognizing him, he then lost all claims to his father's land. Offspring of a *soltera* who at the moment of passing away did not have a spouse had the right to claim their mother's share of the land. A married woman never adopted her spouse's surname. At birth a child born of a married couple inherited both parents' surnames. Paternal surname transmission was cross-generational, while maternal surnames usually changed every other generation. Illegitimate children bore their mother's paternal surname repeated twice (e.g., Sánchez Sánchez). Adoption, or *reconocimiento,* inevitably entailed a corresponding change in the surnames of the newly adopted children. Finally, it is important to note that the transmission of birth status, surnames, and property rights go hand in hand and no doubt predate the agrarian reform.

8. To bury referred not merely to the physical act of entombing a deceased relative or neighbor but also participation in a constellation of obligatory and

costly funerary rituals on behalf of the deceased and his or her close kin. Members of the deceased's household and his or her immediate consanguineal and affinal kin were expected to partake of these rituals and to share in their costs. The washing of the body and clothes of the deceased, the purchase of the casket, and the marshaling of large quantities of coca, food, and drink for the all-night wake were interrelated activities that had to be quickly coordinated without hesitation, as was the burial in the local cemetery. In Pampa this ritual complex included sponsoring four masses within the year (after nine days, one month, six months, and the last after one year). For an almost identical cultural pattern in southern Bolivia, see Harris (1983).

9. The former landlord's two hectares of irrigated land were divided into 13 sharecropped plots. After the agrarian reform her sharecroppers were guaranteed lifelong access to her land. The former landowner could not arbitrarily dislodge her sharecroppers, who had the right to transmit usufruct rights to the land they sharecropped to their offspring. Only if a sharecropper failed to work the land or turn over to the landlord half of the harvest could he be deprived of his usufruct rights. If the sharecropper became ill, too old to work, or died, his usufruct rights were passed to his offspring (or, in the absence of offspring, to his siblings). Despite legal ownership, any attempt by the landlord to strip a sharecropper of his usufruct rights had to be unanimously upheld by the *sindicato*. Even then the landlord was not a free agent as she had to first offer rights to her land to sharecropper's siblings. Under no circumstances could non-Pampeños sharecrop this land.

10. Land-based Chapare migrants also expressed fears of losing their land to sharecroppers (see chap. 4).

11. Highland-lowland *canje* exchanges were not the only mode of accessing land drastically altered by high coca prices and runaway inflation. Land rentals, far more prevalent in the past, were virtually nonexistent during my research. With prices and wages sometimes doubling overnight it made little sense to enter into a binding agreement in a fixed amount of local currency.

12. Unfortunately, not all land purchases that took place in Pampa were recorded in *Derechos Reales*. Sometimes a simple oral agreement temporarily sufficed for a transaction, and only years later would this transaction be duly registered in *Derechos Reales*.

13. There were no restrictions on *ajenos* (e.g., Chapare migrants) renting dwellings in the pueblo. The *corregidor,* however, had to be notified, and the owner of the house was responsible for his tenants' behavior while in Pampa.

Chapter 6

1. It should be noted that *serranías* are not necessarily uncultivable lands. Very rocky, but potentially cultivable, land in the *serranías* is called *firushanka.* The term probably derives from the Spanish word *hierro* (iron) and the Quechua term *chanka* (high rock), suggesting the need of appropriate tools and a heavy deployment of labor to clear the terrain of rocks and small boulders. A *firushanka* cleared of rocks and placed under cultivation is called by Pampeños a *p''urma,*

while in other parts of Cochabamba it is called a *puruma,* a Quechua word denoting virgin land (Herrero and Sanchez de Losada 1979:298). In Pampa the term *q"akqa* refers to totally useless land subject to severe gully erosion.

2. There is another lake northwest of Kuyuq Qocha called Parina, which, due to topographical conditions, is unsuited for irrigation.

3. Four neighboring, lower-level communities have exclusive rights to the water of one major stream, and during the dry season they will send an observer (*yacu q"awaq*) to insure its water is not being diverted by Pampeños for their own use. The irrigation network is the direct responsibility of the 157 member irrigation association (Asociación Pro-Riego), which is headed by an elected water master (*juez de aguas*). In 1964 Pampeños, with technical and financial assistance from USAID, improved Kuyuq Qocha's irrigation capacity by building new and higher walls and installing new floodgates. Only Pampeños who contributed either labor or money (*socios*) were guaranteed life long access to this water (see also chap. 4). Access to Kuyuq Qocha's water follows a rigid weekly schedule with specific days reserved for Pampa's different neighborhoods. The irrigation canals are cleaned once a year, between the second and third week of April. All community members with access to this water are required to participate by cleaning the parts of the canals that irrigate their fields. Those who fail to do so are fined. For comparable data from Peru, see Mitchell (1977).

4. Household access to Pampa's vertically arranged crop or production zones corresponded to the type Salomon (1985:513) has labeled as "mechanisms which achieve direct access to multiple resources without central control." For a detailed analysis of diseases and pests that afflict potato crops, see Sage (1990:235–38).

5. At least 23 potato varieties were cultivated in Pampa immediately prior to the agrarian reform, mostly for consumption. Of these five are no longer cultivated in Pampa, and only miniscule amounts of the other varieties are sometimes sown for consumption but not for sale. For comparable data on crop varieties in Peru, see Browman (1987:173) and Franquemont et al. (1990:20–21).

6. The production of barley—traditionally sold almost exclusively to Taquiña, Cochabamba's only brewery—was declining due to unfavorable market conditions. One of Pampa's largest barley producers in the *lugar* of Condor claimed to have cut back on his production of barley, adducing that one *quintal* (hundredweight) of barley would only fetch him one and a half bottles of beer.

7. Although infrequent, land can also be prepared by using a tractor. Only twice did I observe tractors preparing land. Both cases involved large tracts of level land in the Tuty crop zone, and in both cases the tractors were employed by wealthy peasants.

8. One sack of *mishka* seed will yield from five to eight 225 pound sacks of potatoes. Since one hectare will absorb 15 sacks (*cargas*) of seed, total production will often oscillate between 7,670 and 12,272 kilos (i.e., 3.4–5.5 metric tons). It should be noted that Cochabamba potato yields are higher than that of other major potatoproducing departments such as La Paz and Potosí (Jones 1980:82–86; Ministerio de Asuntos Campesinos y Agropecuarios 1990:92).

9. Chemical fertilizers were introduced in Pampa in 1954, while the expansion of Cochabamba's poultry industry in the early 1970s has made chicken

dung, though expensive, available for purchase. Sage (1990:238) has labeled the intensive use of chemical fertilizers throughout Cochabamba's potato-producing areas as "chemical fetishism."

10. My objective has not been to calculate actual amounts harvested and sold (an exceedingly difficult undertaking, given the great variability in planting strategies and the rapid changing economic context in the mid-1980s). Rather, my intent has been to simply illustrate the enormous gap between coca and potato returns during this period.

11. Of Bolivia's nine departments all but Beni and Pando produce potatoes.

12. In 1983–84 a new agrarian reform law was being drafted by the Bolivian Congress. According to Pampeños, the new law would have awarded share-croppers permanent rights to the land they cropped, and some wealthy migrants with numerous sharecroppers in the Chapare viewed such a possibility with alarm. For instance one prominent migrant nicknamed "the lieutenant" (*el teniente*), because of his former army service and large labor force at his disposal in the Chapare, had 12 sharecroppers working for him on his coca fields at any given moment. He claimed to replace his sharecroppers every three or four years lest they attempted to lay permanent claim to his land. A strikingly similar pattern has been documented in southern Peru by Guillet (1987:218), who writes that "retaining land, even abandoned land, in Lari is a form of insurance should one have to return to the village from failure to adjust to city life. Paradoxically, while some land might be expected to be sharecropped by the nonresident land-owner under these circumstances, outmigrants often prefer to abandon land rather than cultivate it under an indirect arrangement such as sharecropping; under Peruvian law, if land is sharecropped for more than five consecutive years, the tenant can claim right of ownership."

13. Weatherford (1987:414) has recently underscored a similar situation in the valley of Pocona. Guillet (1987) also claims that labor migration was leading to agricultural deintensification in Lari, a community in the Colca Valley of Peru. Yet he attached far more importance to local ecological factors than migration patterns and availability of labor in explaining land abandonment. Appleby (1982) emphasizes that high inflation in Peru during the late 1970s created "increasingly unfavorable terms of trade for rural producers" and that farmers [in Puno] kept "more of their staples for domestic use" (1982:3–4).

14. The onset of the coca boom, however, led to coca cultivation in parts of Santa Cruz, including Yapacaní. For recent estimates of coca cultivation in Yapacaní, see Bureau of International Narcotics Matters 1991:84–85.

Chapter 7

1. In the previous chapter I examined Pampeño production strategies during the 1984 agricultural season. This chapter is based on the labor deployed in the harvest of the 1983 *huata* crop and, during the 1984 crop season, the planting of huata and the sowing and harvest of the *mishka*-irrigated crop. In addition, while the present discussion rests on a 47 household sample, the analysis of sowing and harvest patterns in chapter 5 was based on 42 households. The reason

for this difference is that reliable data could not be obtained on the amount of land held by five households, and they were therefore excluded from the analysis. A detailed account of rationale and methods employed in calculating labor inputs appears in appendix 1.

2. An exchange of irrigation water between owners of adjacent crop fields is also called *ayni*. This exchange occurs when the *mit'a* water allocation exceeds the needs of the field being irrigated; to avoid unnecessary loss of water and topsoil the person with access to water on that day will loan out part of that water to neighbors whose nearby fields are also in need of irrigation. They, in turn, will reciprocate with an equal amount of water at a future date.

3. Non-Pampeño lowland sharecroppers or wage laborers could also form part of this system of exchanges as long as the ones responsible for the reciprocal *ayni* labor were Pampeños.

4. In Guillet's (1980) classification of forms of labor recruitment, *ayuda* would be classed as "familial," *paga* and *jornal* as "contractual," and *ayni* as "reciprocal" labor. The terminology varies greatly throughout the Andes: *paga* is called *mink'a* in parts of Peru (Sánchez 1982:159,167), while what is known in Pampa as *mink'a* (cooperative work parties engaged in nonagricultural work such as in the building and or completion of dwellings) is referred to as *jornal,* or wage, labor (Bradby 1982:113). Elsewhere in the Andes *mink'a* labor is reportedly deployed in the cultivation of land as well as in nonagricultural pursuits (H. Skar 1982:215–16).

5. *Ajenos* could form part of the kin category through marriage, adoption, or *compadrazgo* (Mintz and Wolf 1950), of which the most important and prestigious was the one established by sponsoring a child's baptism. Pampa lacked *ayllu* kinship groupings, moiety divisions, communal controls on land use and sectoral fallowing (i.e., the *laymi* system), and civil-religious hierarchies, some of the most noteworthy features of the socioeconomic organization of "traditional" Andean communities (see Orlove and Godoy 1986; de la Cadena 1986; Izko 1986; Isbell 1978; H. Skar 1982; Carter 1964; Platt 1982a). Ethnographic research has shown that, by and large, Peruvian *ayllus* consist of bilateral kindreds in which access to communally-held land is of little import in their definition and perpetuation (Isbell 1978; H. Skar 1982; but cf. Allen 1988:117–202). In southern Bolivia, by contrast, *ayllus* primarily loom as corporate kin groups pivoting on access to communal land (e.g., Godoy 1984, 1985, 1986; Harris 1985; Platt 1982a; West 1981; Rasnake 1988:49–92). Although in Pampa the term *ayllu* never spontaneously surfaced in everyday conversations, most Pampeños recognized it as broadly denoting "family." Moreoever, the structure of kinship in Pampa (e.g., egocentered, bilateral kindred with a third cousin range) was strikingly similar to that reported in other Andean communities in Peru (cf. Isbell 1978; H. Skar 1982).

6. Labor recruitment patterns in the Chapare during the mid-1970s paralleled those present in Pampa a decade later. J. Weil (1980a, 1989:235) has clearly demonstrated the critical role of *ayni* labor for agricultural production on the frontier, where it accounted for a full 43 percent of all agricultural exchange labor. It should nevertheless be stressed that the importance of wage (and other

forms of monetary payments) almost certainly increased by the mid-1980s. At the same time the coca "bust" has probably been accompanied by a corresponding rise in the importance of *ayni* (and perhaps sharecropping as well).

7. That the wage labor market developed in response to the incredible rise in the demand for coca leaves is clear from the detailed data provided by J. Weil (1989:324–26) of work inputs during 1976 in one Chapare community. At that time the daily wage did not exceed the equivalent of U.S. $1.50 and the proportion of all forms of monetary payment for agricultural labor remained well below that of *ayni* alone (35 and 43 percent, respectively).

8. Bergad (1983), for instance, has suggested such a functional equivalence between cash wages and payment in kind in nineteenth-century Puerto Rican coffee haciendas.

9. The fact that the Peruvian hacienda landowners were often unsuccessful in converting tenants into wage-earning laborers or in evicting them from the hacienda after meeting their obligations to the landowners points, of course, to the strong degree of autonomy that peasant tenants exercised within hacienda estates (see chap. 5). For an analogous example of the strong reluctance of Guatemalan peasants to engage in plantation wage labor, see Swetnam (1989). The examples could be multiplied many times over. For comparative materials from Southeast Asia see, Scott's landmark book on reciprocity and resistance (1976) and his more recent analyses of domination and resistance (1985, 1986, 1991). See also chap. 9.

10. Ekstrom (1979:104) has written on a similar pattern of highland-lowland labor exchanges in contemporary Ecuador.

Chapter 8

1. Despite the wealth of studies on the multifaceted dimensions of coca use in the Andes (see chap. 3), amazingly enough coca chewing is still viewed by powerful policymakers—as it was decades ago—as virtually identical to cocaine addiction and, consequently, as a "habit" detrimental to Andeans. In 1984, for example, the influential House Select Committee on Narcotics Abuse and Control urged that the United States "begin eliminating coca chewing in Bolivia by December 1989," for, it claimed, "the chewing of [the] coca leaf is a primitive, antiquated, debilitating practice, harmful to the individuals and the public health and has considerable genocidal overtones" (cited by Henman 1985:188).

2. Mintz (1989:32) has stated that "what makes cocaine truly sinful, even for those who can't just say no, is not its toxicity: It is produced, bought and sold under circumstances that prevent the state from taxing it, or even from taxing the investments made with the profit it yields. In the modern world, cocaine sins thrice: It interferes with labor productivity; the profits it garners are not made by 'respectable' capitalists, and the state has trouble claiming its share."

3. For instance, the mayor of the city of Cochabamba was quoted a few years back as saying, "I am interested in resources coming in, not where they come from. If it is cocaine, it is a question for the police. I don't ask a person

who pays taxes to City Hall where the money comes from" (*New York Times* 1989).

4. In the mid-nineteenth century opiates were widely consumed by members of all social classes in the United States and England, but especially in the countryside and among the urban working class. Coca and cocaine sooned joined this complex of widely used substances. In about 50 years—from about the latter half of the 1800s to the first decades of the 1900s—the consumption of coca, cocaine, and opiates in the United States and England underwent a substantial change. From relatively widespread use and tolerance, opiate, cocaine, and coca consumption faced increasing official intolerance and growing restrictions on use. Intolerance of and restrictions on the use of these substances—and, more specifically, the social construction of consumption as an "addiction problem"—mirrored important economic and political transformations. Dominant trends against the consumption of opiates and cocaine in England surfaced against a backdrop of the expansion of industry and the rise of pharmaceutical concerns and the professionalization of medicine. For example, opiate and cocaine use spread from the English countryside—where consumption was legal, socially sanctioned, and widespread in health practices—to urban areas, such as Manchester, with emerging concentrations of factory workers of rural background. As this shift occurred—one paralleled by increasing industrial discipline and regimentation of work—the use of both substances began to be frowned upon and construed as a societal "problem." In contrast to England, dominant concerns on the use of opiates, coca, and cocaine the United States during this era of "social Darwinism" (Hofstadter 1959 [1944]) were more closely linked, as in many respects they are today, with immigration, fears of foreigners and minorities, racial intolerance, and labor agitation: opium-smoking Chinese on the West Coast, marijuana-smoking Mexican Americans in the Southwest, the socalled cocaine-crazed African Americans in the South, and union organizers—many of them immigrants—in cities and factories (see esp. Musto 1973; 1987; Helmer and Vietorisz 1974; Berridge and Edwards 1981; Morgan 1981; Kinder 1988). Not unexpectedly, drug consumption as a "problem" in England partly overlapped with the widespread use of sugar, particularly among the emerging proletariat in England's factories (Mintz 1985). The professionalization of medicine in the United States, which entailed growing political and economic power by the fledgling American Medical Association to diagnose, treat, and shape illness discourse, also led to growing medical control over abortion in the United States (cf. Ginsberg 1989:23–42).

5. International agreements to limit the cultivation of coca have included, among others, the 1925 International Convention on Narcotics Traffic; the 1949 United Nations Commission of Enquiry on the Coca Leaf; the 1962 decree limiting new coca fields, followed by a similar decree in 1966; the 1973 agreement calling for a coca crop eradication program; the 1977 National Narcotics Control Law, which outlawed new coca plantings in unregistered lands; and the 1983 accord with the United States that called for control on the production and commerce of coca leaves and the suppression of coca paste and cocaine operations (e.g., Figueras 1978:2–3; USAID 1978; Henkel 1988).

6. By January 3, 1987 "no important cocaine boss ha[d] been jailed here or elsewhere in Bolivia" (*New York Times* 1987). Roberto Suárez, an agroindustrial entrepreneur and landowner believed at the time to be the most important of Bolivia's cocaine kingpins, was, however, arrested in July of 1988. Nevertheless, the exact circumstances of his "arrest" remain shrouded in mystery. It may very well be that Suárez, like former former dictator and notorious drug trafficker General García Meza (United States House of Representatives 1991:17), enjoys considerable freedom despite his "incarceration."

7. The most vigorous and violent United States efforts at eradicating coca plantings in the Andes, including the use of toxic herbicides, have centered on eastern Peru (Andean Focus 1988; Kawell 1989; E. Morales 1989). In Bolivia the use of toxic herbicides to destroy coca plants has been opposed by past and present governments.

8. The decline in Bolivian coca leaf prices was paralleled by, but was only partly responsible for, a rise in streetlevel cocaine prices in the United States (United States House of Representatives 1990:34–35; Uprimny 1990:2).

9. Between January and August 1989 the price of a hundredweight (*carga*) rose from 154 to 241 *bolivianos,* and yet by December of that year the price had dipped to a low of 55 *bolivianos.* Average monthly leaf prices continued to plunge during the early 1990, reaching a low of 32.8 *bolivianos* in April. By September 12, 1990 the price had shot up again to 192 *bolivianos* (Ministerio de Asuntos Campesinos y Agropecuarios 1989, 1990 [n.p.].

10. There are a variety of reasons why many Pampeños in the Chapare did not, in fact, receive the total amount of cash promised them for each hectare taken out of production (for details, see Sanabria 1992). Given longstanding agricultural and credit policies, it should come as no surprise that no Pampeños (or, I suspect, any smallscale colonists in the Chapare) received loans. It is more likely that "farmers" in neighboring Santa Cruz were the primary beneficiaries of these loans.

11. An analogous situation has occurred in Colombia. According to Peter Reuter of the Rand Corporation, "the senior Medellín traffickers are being offered the opportunity of becoming respectable at a time when they probably have enough money to enjoy respectability" (qd. in United States House of Representatives 1991:54).

12. For example, in May 28, 1987, at least three persons died as army troops confronted peasants who protested eradication plans by blocking roads to the city of Cochabamba, while in late June 1988 seven peasants and one soldier died when thousands of Chapare migrants overran a narcotics police post in Villa Tunari (*Latin American Weekly Report* 1987a, 1987b, 1988b, 1988c, 1988d, 1988e; see also Healy 1988).

13. The rising levels of coca- and cocaine-related consumption has been labeled by E. Morales (1989) as "cosmetic development."

Chapter 9

1. Adherents of these approaches remain deeply divided along a number of key theoretical and methodological issues. There is, for example, the question

of ascertaining the precise mechanisms by means of which the decapitalization of and the transfer of surplus from the periphery and semiperiphery to the core actually takes place. Perhaps a more critical and hotly contested issue, however, concerns the primacy of relations of exchange or of production in defining capitalism itself. Seemingly unending debates about when "capitalism" appeared; whether or not all local, regional, and national economies are capitalist and, in the event that they are not, the manner in which non- or precapitalist economies articulate with capitalist ones; and the question of whether the impact of the spread of capitalism worldwide is uniform or is contingent on local political and socioeconomic conditions, all stem from the contrasting views on how capitalism is conceptualized. In addition, the propensity to reify global processes and to view capitalism as a thing in itself with its own goals and purposes has been criticized at length. For example, Foster-Clark's (1978:232) talks of "bland talk of 'capitalism' doing or being this and that." Reification not only makes it extremely difficult to identify actors in concrete and constantly shifting sociopolitical arenas but also conveys a false impression of homogeneous goals and interests. As C. Smith (1983:346) has emphasized: "Capitalism per se does not want anything. Some capitalists want cheap labor, some capitalists want expanding markets, some capitalists want the state out of their affairs, and some other capitalists want the state to help them."

2. Andean research has characteristically displayed a convergence of anthropological and social historical interests, methods, and perspectives (e.g., Stern 1982; Spalding 1984; Murra, Wachtel, and Revel 1986; Harris, Larson, and Tandeter 1987; Larson 1988a; Rasnake 1988). This convergence has been particularly prominent in Bolivia, where, as the historian Larson has recently emphasized, a fruitful overlap of anthropological and historical methods and research questions has led to the emergence of important studies in "historical anthropology or anthropological history" (1988b:84–85). For a recent and comprehensive overview of historical approaches within anthropology, see Kellog (1991).

3. Samaniego (1984:225–27) provides an overview of analogous urban food price policies in Peru. For comparative materials from other Latin America countries, see Wright (1985).

Glossary

Abono: Chemical fertilizer.

Abuso: Literally "abuse"; unfair treatment by others.

Aculliku (Quechua): The chewing of coca leaves.

Afiliado: Household head with permanent usufruct rights to land.

Ajeno: Noncommunity members; also nonkin.

Altiplano: High plateau between the eastern and western Andean mountain chains.

Aporque: The loosening of the soil between furrows.

Aqa (Quechua): Corn beer (see also *chicha*).

Aqa huasi (Quechua): Place where corn beer is sold (see also *chichería*).

Arroba: Fifty pounds of potatoes; also the amount of land required to sow 50 pounds of potato seed.

Asambleas: Monthly communal gatherings.

Asociación Pro-Riego: Pampa's irrigation association.

Ayllu (Quechua): Corporate Indian community; also a kinship category.

Ayni (Quechua): Reciprocal obligation. Denotes primarily reciprocal labor exchanges.

Ayuda: Reciprocal exchange of labor primarily between household members.

Campesino: Peasant.

Caminante: Drifter; without ties to a community.

Cantón: Smallest administrative unit into which Bolivia is divided.

Canje: Exchange or permutation of usufruct rights over land and irrigation water.

Carga: Sack of potatoes weighing 225 pounds; the amount of land sown with one sack of potato seed; 100 pounds of coca leaves.

Casa: House or dwelling.

Cato: Plot of coca land measuring 1,600 meters.

Ch'akitaclla (Quechua): Andean foot plow.

Ch'alla (Quechua): Celebration marking a special occasion; festivity.

Chankaka (Quechua): Unrefined blocks of sugar.

Chapara (Quechua): A very large potato.

Chaupi Mishka (Quechua): Potato crop sown on irrigated fields.

Chicha: Corn beer (see also *Aqa*).

Chichería: Place where corn beer is sold.

Ch'ili (Quechua): Tiny (potato).

Ch'uño (Quechua): Freeze-dried potato.

Cocal: Coca field.

Colono: Former estate tenant.
Compadrazgo: Fictive kinship.
Compadre: Literally "coparent"; fictive kin.
Concertación: An arrangement whereby a peasant in the Chapare destroys part or all of his or her coca and receives monetary payment to offset labor costs.
Concubinado/a: Male or female in a consensual union.
Cordillera Occidental: Western Andean mountain chain.
Cordillera Oriental: Eastern Andean mountain chain.
Corregidor: Justice secretary in the local community.
Criado: Literally "servant." Also children adopted into a household and to laborers permanently attached to a household.
Descanso: Fallow; literally "to rest."
Derechos Reales: Land registration office.
Dirigente: Person with authority in the community.
Día del Indio: Anniversary date of the agrarian reform.
Dotado: Household head who obtained a land grant after the agrarian reform.
Dotación: State land grant.
Empanto: First irrigation of soil before planting.
Entenado/a: Offspring of unmarried female.
Escritura: Legally binding document.
Estalla: Disease that afflicts coca plants.
Estancia: High-altitude grazing area.
Fiesta: Religious celebration.
Forastero: Literally "stranger"; noncommunity member (see also *ajeno*).
Guano (Quechua): Dung.
Guaniru (Quechua): Worker who deposits dung into furrows.
Haba: Broad bean.
Hacendado: Estate landowner.
Hacienda: Rural estate worked by tenants.
Huasi (Quechua): House or dwelling.
Huata (Quechua): Literally "year"; potato crop sown on rain-fed fields.
Huata Runa (Quechua): Literally "yearly people"; poor landless peasants attached to *pefalero* households before the agrarian reform.
Ichu (Quechua): Coarse Andean grass.
Imilla blanca (Quechua): Potato variety similar to a russet potato.
Indio: Indian; pejorative term for nonacculturated Andean.
Jatun tarpuy (Quechua): Winter potato sowing.
Jornal: Wage labor.
Juez de aguas: Water master; irrigation judge.
Kuraka (Quechua): Loyal peasant recruited to assist hacienda landowner.
K'uyuna (Quechua): Homemade cigarrette.
Lari (Quechua): Disparaging term for *altiplano* dweller.
Legítimo/a: Offspring of a married couple or legally adopted by mother's spouse.
Leopardos: Narcotics police.
Lote: Plot of land.

Lugar: Geographical neighborhood in Pampa.

Maestro: Skilled artisan.

Media Lata: Five liters (of corn beer).

Mestizo/a: Ethnic label that denotes acculturated Andeans; non-Indian; of mixed cultural heritage.

Minka (Quechua): Festive work party.

Minifundia: Tiny landholdings.

Mishka (Quechua): "Early" potatoes sown on irrigated fields.

Mit'a (Quechua): Irrigation water allotments.

Mujiru (Quechua): Worker who deposits potato seed into furrow.

Multa: Fine.

Narcotráfico: Drug trafficking.

Oca (Oxalis tuberosa): Andean tuber.

Oriente: The eastern lowlands.

Paga: Payment in kind for a day's work in agriculture.

Papalisa (Ullucus tuberosus): Andean tuber.

Pasante: Sponsor of a fiesta.

Patrón: Estate landowner; also *hacendado*. See also *propietaria*.

Pefal (Quechua): In pre-reform times desmesne land to which a tenant had usufruct rights.

Pefalero (Quechua): In pre-reform times a tenant with usufruct rights to desmesne land.

Peón: Wage of contractual laborer.

Piquería: Independent freeholding peasant community.

Piquero: Peasant with land rights in a *piquería*.

Pisacocas (also *pisadores*): Coca stompers.

Plaza: Town square.

Propietaria: Pampa's (female) landowner at the moment of the agrarian reform.

Pueblo: Literally town. In Pampa the dense settlement bordering the Cochabamba-Chapare road.

Q''apaq Runas (Quechua): Wealthy persons.

Quinoa (Chenopodium quinoa): A native Andean grain.

Rescatista: Wholesale merchant who purchases agricultural products.

Reconocimiento: Legal adoption.

Rosca: Pre-reform landed elite.

Runa (Quechua): Person; also variety of potato similar to an Idaho potato.

Runakuna (Quechua): People.

Serranías: Small mountain chain; also high-altitude uncultivated slopes.

Sindicato: Peasant union or political organization at the community level.

Socios: Members of Pampa's Irrigation Association.

Soltera: Unmarried female.

Soltero: Unmarried male.

Surco: Furrow of land.

Taller: Technical shop in Pampa's pueblo.

Tarpuja (Quechua): Exchange of the harvest of one furrow of land for labor.

Titulo: Property title.

Trago: Cane alcohol.

Tranca: Roadblock.

Uk''upi (Quechua): Literally "inside"; in the Chapare.

Valles: Valleys; also intermontane valley zone between the *altiplano* and the eastern lowlands.

Valle Alto: One of the three major intermontane valleys of the department of Cochabamba.

Valle Central (Bajo): One of the three major intermontane valleys of the department of Cochabamba.

Vocal: A neighborhood representative of Pampa's *sindicato.*

Yacu Q''awaq (Quechua): Literally "water observer"; community member responsible for ensuring that irrigation water is not diverted to neighboring communities.

Yungas (Quechua): Steep subtropical valleys east of La Paz.

Yuntas: Pair of oxen used in sowing and harvest.

Bibliography

Manuscript Sources

Archivo General de la Nacion (AGN), Buenos Aires, Argentina. 13.18.1.1. Padrones-Cochabamba, 1683. "Padrón de los Indios Forasteros que residen en las haciendas de la jurisdicción del curato de Sacaba."
———. 13.18.2.1. Padrones-Cochabamba, 1771–1786. "Matrícula de Sacaba." Carried out in 1778.
Archivo Nacional de Bolivia (ANB), Sucre, Bolivia. 1748. "Composición y amparos de haciendas, tierras y estancias de esta Provincia de Cochabamba, actuados por Don José Antonio de Závala," Tierras e Indios, no. 100.
Registro de Derechos Reales (DR), Cochabamba, Bolivia. 1804. "Libro de Hipotecas que corresponden al Partido de Sacaba," 1804 tomo 6, folios 10–12.
Registro de Derechos Reales, Registros Reales, Documentos (DRD), Cochabamba, Bolivia. 1891. Comprobantes 15, 19, 35, 36, 38, 41, 44, 60, 62, 63, 76, 80.
Notaría Eclesiástica del Arzobispado de Cochabamba (NE), Cochabamba, Bolivia. 1728. "Imposición de 40 pesos de principal por Don Clemente de Apodaca y su mujer María Fernández Barbeito en su hacienda de Sangangoche," Legajo 3, no. 50.
Tesoro Departamental (TD), Prefectura Departamental de Cochabamba, Bolivia. 1908. "Padrón Catastral Rústico de la Provincia del Chapare, Cantón Sacaba."

Published Sources

Abegglen, R., J. Mantilla, and R. Belmonte. 1987. *Diferenciación, pobreza y campesinado.* La Paz: UNICEF.
Aguirre, A., J. L. Perez, and Carlos Villegas. 1990. *NPE: Recesión económica.* La Paz: CEDLA.
Alberti, G., and Enrique Mayer. 1974. Reciprocidad andina: ayer y hoy. In *Reciprocidad e intercambio en los Andes Peruanos,* ed. G. Alberti, and E. Mayer, 13–33. Lima: Instituto de Estudios Peruanos.
Albó, Javier. 1981. *Lenguaje y sociedad en Bolivia, 1976.* La Paz: Instituto Nacional de Estadística.
Allen, C. 1988. *The hold life has: Coca and cultural identity in an Andean community.* Washington, D.C.: Smithsonian Institution Press.

Andean Focus. 1988. Peru: Coca eradication or genocide? *Andean Focus* 5 (3): 4–6.

Antezana, O. R. 1990. *Bolivia: Exito macroeconómico, deficiencias microeconómicas.* La Paz: Los Amigos del Libro.

Appleby, G. 1982. Price policy and peasant production in Peru: Regional disintegration during inflation. *Culture and Agriculture* 15:1–6.

Arnould, E. 1989. Anthropology and West African development: A political-economic critique and auto-critique. *Human Organization* 48 (2): 135–48.

Arriaga, P. J. 1967 [1621]. *The extirpation of idolatry in Peru.* Trans. and ed. L. Clark Keating. Lexington: University of Kentucky Press.

Arrieta, M., G. Abrego, A. Castillo, and M. de la Fuente. 1990. *Agricultura en Santa Cruz: De la encomienda colonial a la empresa modernizada (1559–1985).* La Paz: EDOBOL.

Aquí. 1991. Mininterior contra productores de coca: Los vinculará con el narcotráfico. July 5.

Bailey, J. L., and T. Knutsen. 1987. Surgery without anaesthesia: Bolivia's response to economic chaos. *World Today* 43: 47–51.

Barlett, P. F. 1980. Adaptive strategies in peasant agricultural production. *Annual Review of Anthropology* 9:545–73.

Bascopé, R. 1982. *La veta blanca: Coca y cocaína en Bolivia.* La Paz: Ediciones "Aquí."

Bennett, J. W. 1969. *Northern plainsmen: Adaptive strategy and agrarian life.* Chicago: Aldine.

———. 1976. *The ecological transition: Cultural anthropology and human adaptation.* New York and London: Pergamon Press.

Bergad, L. W. 1983. *Coffee and the growth of agrarian capitalism in nineteenth-century Puerto Rico.* Princeton: Princeton University Press.

Bernstein, H. 1982. Notes on capital and peasantry. In *Rural development: Theories of peasant economy and agrarian change,* ed. J. Harris, 160–77. London: Hutchinson University Library.

Berridge, V., and G. Edwards. 1981. *Opium and the people: Opiate use in nineteenth-century England.* London: Allen Lane.

Blanes, J., and G. Flores. 1982. *Campesino, migrante y "colonizador": Reproducción de la economía familiar en el Chapare tropical.* La Paz: CERES.

Bostwick, D. 1990. *Evaluation of the Chapare Regional Development Project* (draft of September 1990). Arlington, Va.: Pragma Corporation.

Bourgois, P. 1989. In search of Horatio Alger: Culture and Ideology in the Crack Economy. *Contemporary Drug Problems* 16 (34): 619–49.

Bradby, B. 1982. Resistance to capitalism in the Peruvian Andes. In *Ecology and exchange in the Andes,* ed. D. Lehmann, 97–122. Cambridge: Cambridge University Press.

Brass, T. 1983. Of human bondage: Campesinos, coffee, and capitalism on the Peruvian frontier. *Journal of Peasant Studies* 11 (1): 76–88.

Bray, W., and C. Dollery. 1983. Coca chewing and high-altitude stress: A spurious correlation. *Current Anthropology* 24 (3): 269–82.

Brooner, W. 1981. *Bolivian coca: Technical evaluations of recent aerial survey projects in the Chapare of Bolivia.* Berkeley: Earth Satellite Corporation.

Browman, D. L. 1987. Agro-pastoral risk management in the Central Andes. *Research in Economic Anthropology* 12: 139–87.

Brown, P. F. 1987. Population growth and the disappearance of reciprocal labor in a highland Peruvian community. *Research in Economic Anthropology* 8:225–45.

Brush, S. 1977a. The myth of the idle peasant: Employment in a subsistence economy. In *Peasant livelihood: Studies in economic anthropology and cultural ecology,* ed. R. Halperin and J. Dow, 60–78. New York: St. Martin's Press.

———. 1977b. *Mountain, field, and family: The economy and human ecology of an Andean village.* Philadelphia: University of Philadelphia Press.

———. 1987. Diversity and change in Andean agriculture. In *Lands at risk in the Third World: Local-level perspectives,* ed. P. D. Little and M. Horowitz (with A. Endre Nyerges), 271–89. Boulder: Westview Press.

Bunker, S. 1985. *Underdeveloping the Amazon: Extraction, unequal exchange and the failure of the modern state.* Urbana: University of Illinois Press.

Burchard, R. E. 1976. Myths of the sacred leaf: Ecological perspectives on coca and peasant biocultural adaptation in Peru. Ph.D. diss., Department of Anthropology, Indiana University.

———. 1992. Coca chewing and diet. *Current Anthropology* 33 (1): 1–24.

Bureau of International Narcotics Matters. 1988. *International Narcotics Control Strategy Report.* Washington, D.C.: United States Department of State. Bureau of International Narcotics Matters.

———. 1989. *International Narcotics Control Strategy Report* (midyear update). Washington, D.C.: United States Department of State. Bureau of International Narcotics Matters.

———. 1990. *International Narcotics Control Strategy Report.* Washington, D.C.: United States Department of State. Bureau of International Narcotics Matters.

———. 1991. *International Narcotics Control Strategy Report.* Washington, D.C.: United States Department of State. Bureau of International Narcotics Matters.

———. 1992. *International Narcotics Control Strategy Report.* Washington, D.C.: United States Department of State. Bureau of International Narcotics Matters.

Caballero, J. M. 1984. Agriculture and the peasantry under industrialization pressures: Lessons from the Peruvian experience. *Latin American Research Review* 19 (2): 3–41.

Canak, W. L. 1989. Debt, austerity, and Latin America in the new international division of labor. In *Lost promises: Debt, austerity, and development in Latin America,* ed. W. Canak, 9–27. Boulder: Westview Press.

Canby, T. Y. 1984. El Niño's ill wind. *National Geographic* 165 (2): 145–83.

Cancian, F. 1965. *Economics and prestige in a Maya community.* Stanford: Stanford University Press.

————. 1980. Risk and uncertainty in agricultural decision making. In *Agricultural decision making: Anthropological contributions to rural development,* ed. P. F. Barlett, 161–76. New York: Academic Press.

————. 1989. Economic behavior in peasant communities. In *Economic anthropology,* ed. S. Plattner, 127–70. Stanford: Stanford University Press.

Canedo-Arguelles F. 1988. Efectos de Potosí sobre la población indígena del Alto Perú: Pacajes a mediados del siglo XVII. *Revista de Indias* 48 (182–83): 237–55.

Canelas, A., and J. C. Canelas. 1983. *Bolivia, coca cocaína: Subdesarollo y poder político.* Cochabamba: Los Amigos del Libro.

Cardoso, F. 1977. The consumption of dependency theory in the United States. *Latin American Research Review* 12 (3): 7–24.

Carrasco, P. 1961. The civil-religious and political hierarchy in Mesoamerican communities. *American Anthropologist* 63: 483–97.

Carter, W. 1964. *Aymara communities and the Bolivian agrarian reform.* Gainesville: University of Florida Press.

————. 1977. Trial marriage in the Andes? In *Andean kinship and marriage.* ed. R. Bolton and E. Mayer, 177–218. Washington, D.C.: American Anthropological Association.

Carter, W., and M. Mamani. 1986. *Coca en Bolivia.* La Paz: Editorial Juventud.

Carter, W., J. Morales, and M. Mamani. 1981. Medicinal uses of coca in Bolivia. In *Health in the Andes,* ed. J. W. Bastien and J. M. Donahue, 119–50. Washington: American Anthropological Association.

Centro de Investigación y Desarollo Regional. 1990. *Monografía del trópico del Departamento de Cochabamba.* Cochabamba: Centro de Investigación y Desarollo Regional.

Centro de Investigación y Promoción del Campesinado (CIPCA). 1979. *Estudio de la situación socio-económica de los productores de papa del Departamento de Cochabamba.* Cochabamba: Centro de Investigación y Promoción del Campesinado y Asociación de Productores de Papa del Departamento de Cochabamba.

Chayanov, A.V. 1986 [1966]. *The theory of peasant economy* (with a new intro. by Teodor Shanin). Madison: University of Wisconsin Press.

Chibnik, M. 1990. Double-edged risks and uncertainties: Choices about rice loans in the Peruvian Amazon. In *Risk and uncertainty in tribal and peasant economies,* ed. E. Cashdan, 279–302. Boulder: Westview Press.

Chibnik, M., and W. de Jong. 1989. Agricultural labor organization in Ribereño communities of the Peruvian Amazon. *Ethnology* 28 (1): 75–95.

Chilcote, R. H. 1984. *Theories of development and underdevelopment.* Boulder: Westview Press.

Chilcote, R. H., and J. C. Edelstein. 1986. *Latin America: Capitalist and socialist perspectives of development and underdevelopment.* Boulder: Westview Press.

Cohen, A. 1969. *Custom and politics in urban Africa: A study of Hausa migrants in Yoruba towns.* Berkeley: University of California Press.

Cole, J. 1987. *Latin American inflation: Theoretical interpretations and empirical results.* New York: Praeger.

Coleman, J. S. 1986. Social theory, social research, and a theory of action. *American Journal of Sociology* 91 (6): 1309–35.

Collins, J. L. 1984. The maintenance of peasant coffee production in a Peruvian valley. *American Ethnologist* 11 (3): 413–37.

——. 1986a. The household and relations of production in southern Peru. *Comparative Studies in Society and History* 28 (4): 651–71.

——. 1986b. Smallholder settlement of tropical South America: The social causes of ecological destruction. *Human Organization* 45 (1): 1–10.

——. 1987. Labor scarcity and ecological change. In *Lands at risk in the Third World: Local-level perspectives,* ed. P. D. Little and M. Horowitz (with A. Endre Nyerges), 19–37. Boulder: Westview Press.

——. 1988. *Unseasonal migrations: The effects of rural labor scarcity in Peru.* Princeton: Princeton University Press.

——. 1990. Unwaged labor in comparative perspective: Recent theories and unanswered questions. In *Work without wages: Domestic labor and self-employment within capitalism,* ed. J. L. Collins and M. Giménez, 3–24. Albany: State University of New York Press.

Collins, J. L., and M. Painter. 1986. *Settlement and deforestation in Central America: A discussion of development issues.* Binghamton, N.Y.: Institute for Development Anthropology. Cooperative Agreement on Human Settlements and Natural Resource Systems Analysis. Working Paper no. 31.

Collins, R. 1981. On the micro-foundations of macro-sociology. *American Journal of Sociology* 86:984–1014.

Conaghan, C. M. 1991. Hot money and hegemony: Andean capitalists in the 1980s. Paper presented at the Sixteenth International Congress of the Latin American Studies Association.

Conaghan, C. M., J. M. Malloy, and L. A. Abugattas. 1990. Business and the "boys": The politics of neoliberalism in the central Andes. *Latin American Research Review* 25 (2): 3–31.

Cook, S. 1982. *Zapotec stoneworkers: The dynamics of rural simple commodity production in modern Mexican capitalism.* Washington: University Press of America.

——. 1986. The "managerial" vs. the "labor" function, capital accumulation, and the dynamics of simple commodity production in rural Oaxaca, Mexico. In *Entrepreneurship and social change,* ed. S. Greenfield and A. Strickon, 54–95. Washington: University Press of America.

Cook, S., and L. Binford. 1990. *Obliging need: Rural petty industry in Mexican capitalism.* Austin: University of Texas Press.

Crabtree, J., G. Duffy, and J. Pearce. 1987. *The great tin crash: Bolivia and the world tin market.* London: Latin American Bureau.

Dandler, J. 1982. Household diversification and labor processes: Some anthropological perspectives on Andean peasantry. Paper presented at the Social Science Research Council Conference on Demographic Research in Latin America (Linking individual, household and societal variables).

————. 1983 [1971]. Sindicalismo campesino en Bolivia: Cambios estructurales en Ucureña, 1935–52. Trans., 1971 Ph.D. diss., University of Wisconsin-Madison. La Paz: CERES.

————. 1984. El desarollo de la agricultura, políticas estatales y el proceso de acumulación en Bolivia. *Estudios Rurales Latinoamericanos* 7 (2): 81–149.

Dandler, J., B. Anderson, R. León, C. Sage, and J. Torrico. 1982. *Economía campesina en los valles y serranías de Cochabamba: procesos de diversificación y trabajo.* Cochabamba: CERES.

Dandler, J., and C. Sage. 1985. What is happening to Andean potatoes? A view from the grass roots. *Development Dialogue* 1: 125–38.

Dandler, J., and J. Torrico. 1986. El congreso nacional indígena de 1945 y la rebelión de Ayopaya (1947). In *Bolivia: la fuerza histórica del campesinado,* 2d ed., ed. F. Calderón and J. Dandler, 135–204. Geneva and La Paz: Instituto de Investigaciones de la Naciones Unidas para el Desarollo Social/ Centro de Estudios de la Realidad Económica y Social.

Deere, C. D. 1990. *Household and class relations: Peasants and landlords in northern Peru.* Berkeley: University of California Press.

de Franco, M., and R. Godoy. 1990. The economic consequences of cocaine production in Bolivia: Historical, local, and macroeconomic perspectives. Ms.

de Janvry, A. 1981. *The agrarian question and reformism in Latin America.* Baltimore and London: Johns Hopkins University Press.

de la Cadena, M. 1986. Cooperación y mercado en la organización comunal andina. *Revista Andina* 4 (1): 31–58.

Delaine, B. 1979. Coca farming in the Chapare, Bolivia: A form of collective innovation. Ph.D. diss., Department of Sociology, St. Louis University.

Denzin, Norman K. 1986. The death of sociology in the 1980s: Comment on Collins. *American Journal of Sociology* 86:984–1014.

DeWalt, B. R. and P. J. Pelto. 1985. Microlevel/macrolevel linkages: An introduction to the issues and a framework for analysis. In *Micro and macro levels of analysis in anthropology: Issues in theory and research,* ed. B. R. Dewalt and P. Pelto, 1–22. Boulder: Westview Press.

Doria Medina, S. 1986. *La economía informal en Bolivia.* La Paz: Editorial Offset.

Dorsey, J. 1975. A case study of ex-hacienda Toralapa in the Tiraque region of the Upper Cochabamba Valley. Madison: University of Wisconsin Land Tenure Center. Research Paper no. 65.

Doughty, P. L. 1991. The food game in Latin America. In *Anthropology and food policy: Human dimensions in Africa and Latin America,* ed. D. E. McMillan, 145–66. Athens and London: University of Georgia Press.

Duke, J. A. 1976. Crop diversification in lowland Bolivian hills. In *Hill lands,* ed. J. Luchok, D. J. Cawthon, M. J. Breslin, 331–35. Morgantown, W.Va.: University Books.

Duke, J. A., D. Aulik, and T. Plowman. 1983 [1975]. El valor nutritivo de la coca. In *Ensayos científicos sobre la coca,* ed. W. Carter, 71–8. La Paz: Editorial Juventud.

Dunkerley, J. 1984. *Rebellion in the veins: Political struggle in Bolivia, 1952–1982*. London: Verso.

Dunkerley, J., and R. Morales. 1986. The crisis in Bolivia. *New Left Review* 155:86–104.

Duviols, P. 1977 [1971]. *La destrucción de las religiones andinas*. Mexico: Universidad Nacional Autónoma.

Eastwood, D. A., and H. J. Pollard. 1987. Colonisation and coca in the Chapare, Bolivia: A development paradox for colonisation theory. *Tijdschrift Voor Economische en Sociale Geographie* 77 (4): 258–68.

Eckstein, S. 1983. Transformation of a "revolution from below": Bolivia and international capital. *Comparative Studies in Society and History* 25 (1): 105–35.

Economist Intelligence Unit. 1986. *Country report: Peru, Bolivia*. London: Economist Intelligence Unit.

———. 1986–87. *Country profile: Bolivia*. London: Economist Intelligence Unit.

———. 1990. *Latin America: Economic structure and analysis: Argentina, Bolivia, Brazil, Chile, Colombia, Ecuador, Mexico, Peru, Venezuela*. New York: Economist Intelligence Unit.

Ekstrom, J. 1979. Colonization east of the Andes: Responding to a new ecology. Ph.D. diss., Department of Anthropology, University of Illinois–Urbana.

El Diario. 1991a. Fuerzas Armadas: Aguardan estructuración de organismo único de lucha contra el narcotráfico. July 8, 1.

———. 1991b. Asistencia técnica y económica de USAID en el desarollo alternativo. July 7, 5.

El Heraldo. 1881a. Catastro: provincia del Chapare. Cantón Sacaba, sec. A. July 20.

———. 1881b. Catastro: Provincia del Chapare. Cantón Sacaba, Sec. B. November 20.

———. 1881c. Catastro: Provincia del Chapare. Cantón Sacaba, Sec. B. December 16.

———. 1881d. Catastro: Provincia del Chapare. Cantón Sacaba, Sec. B. December 28.

———. 1882. Catastro: Provincia del Chapare. Cantón Sacaba, Sec. C. February 3.

———. 1883. Cuadro jeneral del catastro departamental de Cochabamba. July 1.

Erasmus, C. 1956. Culture, structure and process: The occurrence and disappearance of reciprocal farm labor. *Southwestern Journal of Anthropology* 12:444–69.

Europa Yearbook. 1986. Bolivia: Introductory survey. In *The Europa Yearbook*, 1:508–22. London: Europa Publications.

Evans, B. M. 1990. Migration processes in upper Peru in the seventeenth century. In *Migration in colonial Spanish America*, ed. D. J. Robinson, 62–85. New York and Cambridge: Cambridge University Press.

Figueras, J. A. 1978. *El Chapare: Sus recursos y sus usos*. La Paz: USAID Universidad de Florida, Misión Agrícola en Bolivia.

Figueroa, A. 1984. *Capitalist development and the peasant economy in Peru*. New York and Cambridge: Cambridge University Press.

Firth, R. 1961 [1951]. *Elements of social organization*. Boston: Beacon Press.

Foster-Clark, A. 1978. Can we articulate "articulation"? In *The new economic anthropology*, ed. J. Clammer, 210–49. New York: St. Martin's Press.

Foweraker, J. 1981. *The struggle for land: A political economy of the pioneer frontier in Brazil From 1930 to the present day*. Cambridge: Cambridge University Press.

Fox, D. J. 1986. Bolivian mining, a crisis in the making. In *Miners and mining in the Americas*, ed. T. Greaves and W. Culver, 108–35. Manchester: Manchester University Press.

Frank, A. G. 1988. American roulette in the globonomic casino: Retrospect and prospect on the world economic crisis today. *Research in Political Economy* 11:3–43.

Franquemont, C., T. Plowman., E. Franquemont., S. R. King., C. Niezgoda., W. Davis., C. R. Sperling. 1990. *The ethnobotany of Chinchero, an Andean community in southern Peru*. Chicago: Field Museum of Natural History.

Fricke, T. E. 1984. And another to plough the fields . . . economy, demography, and the household in a Tamang village of north central Nepal. Ph.D. diss., Department of Anthropology, University of Wisconsin–Madison.

Friedmann, H. 1980. Household production and the national economy: Concepts for the analysis of agrarian formations. *Journal of Peasant Studies* 7 (2): 158–84.

———. 1986. Postcript: Small commodity production. *Labour, Capital and Society* 19 (1): 117–26.

Fuchs, A. 1978. Coca chewing and high-altitude stress: Possible effects of coca alkaloids on erythropoiesis. *Current Anthropology* 19 (2): 277–91.

Gade, D. W. 1979. Inca and colonial settlement, coca cultivation and endemic disease in the tropical forest. *Journal of Historical Geography* 5 (3): 262–79.

Gagliano, J. 1963. The coca debate in colonial Peru. *Americas* 20 (1): 43–63.

———. 1978. La medicina popular y la coca en el Perú: Un análisis histórico de actitudes. *América Indígena* 38 (4): 789–835.

Galloway, J. F., and M. Vélez de Berliner. 1988. The cocaine trade, state autonomy and world political economy. Paper presented at the 1988 Annual Meeting of the American Political Science Association.

Gill, L. 1987. *Peasants, entrepreneurs, and social change: frontier development in lowland Bolivia*. Boulder: Westview Press.

Ginsberg, Faye D. 1989. *Contested lives: The abortion debate in an American community*. Berkely: University of California Press.

Glave, L. M. 1983. Trajines: Un capítulo en la formación del mercado interno colonial. *Revista Andina* 1 (1): 1–67.

———. 1985. La producción de los trajines: coca y mercado interno colonial. *HISLA: Revista Latinoamericana de Historia Económica y Social* 6:21–42.

Godoy, R. 1984. Ecological degradation and agricultural intensification in the Andean highlands. *Human Ecology* 12 (4): 359–83.

———. 1985. The fiscal role of the Andean ayllu. *Man* 21 (2): 723–41.

———. 1986. State, ayllu, and ethnicity in northern Potosí, Bolivia. *Anthropos* 80: 53–65.

Golte, J. 1980. *La racionalidad de la organización andina.* Lima: Instituto de Estudios Peruanos.

Goode, E. 1989. The American drug panic of the 1980s: Social construction or objective threat? *Violence, Aggression and Terrorism* 33 (34): 327–48.

Goodman, D., and M. Redclift. 1982. *From peasant to proletarian: Capitalist development and agrarian transitions.* New York: St. Martin's Press.

Goody, J. 1958. The fission of domestic groups among the LoDagaba. In *The developmental cycle in domestic groups,* ed. J. Goody, 53–91. Cambridge: Cambridge University Press.

Graeff, P. 1974. *The effects of continued landlord presence in the Bolivian countryside during the post-reform era: Lessons to be learned.* Madison: University of Wisconsin Land Tenure Center. Reprint no. 103.

Grupo de Estudios Andrés Ibáñez. 1983. *Tierra, estructura productiva y poder en Santa Cruz.* La Paz: Centro de Estudios Andrés Ibáñez.

Gudeman, S. 1986. *Economics as culture: Models and metaphors of livelihood.* London: Routledge and Kegan Paul.

Guillet, D. 1978. Toward an analytical model of the Andean peasant economy. Paper presented at the Tenth International Congress of Anthropological and Ethnological Sciences.

———. 1980. Reciprocal labor and peripheral capitalism in the central Andes. *Ethnology* 19 (2): 151–67.

———. 1983. Toward a cultural ecology of mountains: The central Andes and the Himalayas compared. *Current Anthropology* 24 (5): 561–74.

———. 1987. Agricultural intensification and deintensification in Lari, Colca Valley, Southern Peru. *Research in Economic Anthropology* 8: 201–24.

Guyer, J. 1981. Household and community in African studies. *African Studies Review* 24: 87–137.

Haggis, J., S. Jarrett, D. Taylor, and P. Mayer. 1986. By the teeth: A critical examination of James Scott's *The moral economy of the peasant. World Development* 14 (12): 1435–55.

Hanna, J. M. 1983 [1974]. El uso de la hoja de la coca en el sur del Perú: algunos aspectos bio-sociales. In *Ensayos científicos sobre la coca,* ed. W. Carter 43–66. La Paz: Editorial Juventud.

Hanson, A. 1989. The making of the Maori: Cultural invention and its logic. *American Anthropologist* 91 (4): 890–902.

———. 1991. Reply to Langdon, Levine, and Linnekin. *American Anthropologist* 93 (2): 449–50.

Harris, O. 1982. Labour and produce in an ethnic economy, northern Potosí, Bolivia. In *Ecology and exchange in the Andes,* ed. D. Lehmann, 70–96. Cambridge: Cambridge University Press.

———. 1983. Los muertos y los diablos entre los Laymi de Bolivia. *Chungará* 11: 135–52.

———. 1985. Ecological duality and the role of the center: Northern Potosí. In *Andean ecology and civilization: An interdisciplinary perspective on Andean ecological complementarity,* ed. S. Masuda, I. Shimada and C. Morris, 311–35. Tokyo: University of Tokyo Press.

Harris, O., B. Larson, and E. Tandeter, eds. 1987. *La participación indígena en los mercados surandinos: Estrategias y reproducción social, siglos XVI a XX.* La Paz: CERES.

Harrison, L. E. 1985. *Underdevelopment is a state of mind.* Lanham, Md.: University Press of America.

Havet, J. 1985. *The diffusion of power: Rural elites in a Bolivian province.* Ottawa: University of Ottawa Press.

Hazelrigg, L .E. 1991. The Problem of micro-macro linkage: rethinking questions of the individual, social structure, and autonomy of action. *Current Perspectives in Social Theory* 11:229–54.

Healy, K. 1979. Power, class, and rural development in southern Bolivia. Ph.D. diss., Department of Sociology, Cornell University.

———. 1986. The boom within the crisis: Some recent effects of foreign cocaine markets on Bolivian rural society and economy. In *Coca and cocaine: Effects on people and policy in Latin America,* ed. D. Pacini and C. Franquemont, 101–44. Cambridge, Mass. and Ithaca, N.Y.: Cultural Survival and Latin American Studies Program, Cornell University.

———. 1988. Coca, the state, and the peasantry in Bolivia, 1982–1988. *Journal of Interamerican Studies and World Affairs* 2–3:105–25.

———. 1991a. Structural adjustment, peasant agriculture, and coca in Bolivia. Paper presented at the Sixteenth International Congress of the Latin American Studies Association.

———. 1991b. The political ascent of Bolivia's peasant coca leaf producers. *Journal of Interamerican Studies and World Affairs* 33:87–121.

Hecht, S. B. 1989. Murder at the margins of the world. *NACLA Report on the Americas* 23 (1): 36–8.

Heilman, L. C. 1982. U.S. development assistance to rural Bolivia, 1941–1974: The search for a development strategy. Ph.D. diss., Department of History, American University.

Helmer, J., and T. Vietorisz. 1974. *Drug use, the labor market, and class conflict.* Washington, D.C.: The Drug Abuse Council.

Henkel, R. 1971. The Chapare of Bolivia: A study of tropical agriculture in transition. Ph.D. diss., Department of Geography, University of Wisconsin–Madison.

———. 1986. Regional analysis of the Latin American cocaine industry. Paper presented at the Conference of Applied Geographers, West Point, New York.

———. 1988. The Bolivian cocaine industry. In *Drugs In Latin America,* ed. E. Morales, 53–81. Williamsburg, Va.: Department of Anthropology, College of William and Mary. Studies in Third World Societies, Publication no. 37.

Henman, A. 1985. Cocaine futures. In *Big deal: The politics of the illicit drugs business,* ed. A. Henman, R. Lewis, and T. Malyon (with B. Ettore and L. O'Bryon), 118–89. London: Pluto Press.

Hernández Príncipe, R. 1923 [1622]. Mitología andina. *Inca* 1:25–78.

Herrero, J., and F. Sánchez de Losada. 1979. *Diccionario Quechua: Estructura semántica del Quechua Cochabambino contemporáneo.* Sucre: C.E.F. Co.

Hess, D. W. 1980. Pioneering in San Julián: A study of adaptive strategy formation by migrant farmers in eastern Bolivia. Ph.D. diss., Department of Anthropology, University of Pittsburgh.

Hiraoka, M. 1974. Pioneer settlements in eastern Bolivia. Ph.D. diss., Department of Anthropology, University of Wisconsin-Milwaukee.

Hobsbawm, E. 1983. Introduction: Inventing traditions. In *The invention of tradition,* ed. E. Hobsbawm and T. Ranger, 1-14. Cambridge: Cambridge University Press.

Hofstadter, R. 1959 [1944]. *Social darwinism in American thought.* New York: George Braziller.

Hoopes, R. W., and C. Sage. 1982. *Overview of potato production and consumption in Bolivia.* La Paz: Consortium for International Development.

Horton, S. 1991. Labour markets and the shock treatment in Bolivia. Paper presented at the Sixteenth International Congress of the Latin American Studies Association.

Hoy. 1991. Tropa de casi 700 soldados lista para la lucha antidroga. June 24, 5.

Hulshof, J. 1978. La coca en la medicina tradicional andina. *América Indígena* 38 (4): 837-48.

Inciardi, J. A. 1986. *The war on drugs: Heroin, cocaine, crime, and public policy.* Palo Alto, Calif.: Mayfield Publishing Company.

Instituto Nacional de Estadística. 1978. *Resultados del censo nacional de población y vivienda 1976.* La Paz: Instituto Nacional de Estadística.

———. 1982. *Atlas censal de Bolivia.* La Paz: Instituto Nacional de Estadística.

———. 1990a. *Encuesta nacional agropecuaria: resultados de la producción agrícola, 1988-1989.* La Paz: Instituto Nacional de Estadística.

———. 1990b. *Resultados departamentales: il Censo nacional agropecuario 1984.* La Paz: Instituto Nacional de Estadística.

Isbell, B. J. 1978. *To defend ourselves: Ecology and ritual in an Andean village.* Austin: University of Texas Press.

Izko, X. 1986. Comunidad andina: persistencia y cambio. *Revista Andina* 4 (1): 59-99.

Jackson, R. H. 1988. Land and economic policy and the transformation of the rural sector of the Bolivian economy: The case of Cochabamba, 1860-1929. Ph.D. diss., Department of History, University of California-Berkeley.

———. 1989. The decline of the hacienda in Cochabamba, Bolivia: The Case of the Sacaba Valley, 1870-1929. *Hispanic American Historical Review* 69 (2): 259-81.

Jameson, K. P. 1989. Austerity programs under conditions of political instability and economic depression: The case of Bolivia. In *Paying the costs of austerity in Latin America,* ed. H. Handelman and W. Baer, 81-103. Boulder: Westview Press.

Jencks, C., and P. E. Peterson, eds. 1991. *The urban underclass.* Washington, D.C.: Brookings Institution.

Johnson, A. 1971. Security and risk taking among poor peasants: A Brazilian case study. In *Studies in economic anthropology,* ed. G. Dalton, 144–52 Washington, D.C.: American Anthropological Association.

Johnson, B. D., T. Williams, K. Dei, and H. Sanabria. 1990. Drug abuse in the inner city: Impact on hard drug users and the community. In *Drugs and crime,* ed. M. Tonry and J. Q. Wilson, 9–67. Chicago: University of Chicago Press.

Johnson, B. D., A. Hamid, and H. Sanabria. 1992. Emerging models of crack distribution. In *Drugs, crime, and social policy: Research, issues, and Concerns,* ed. T. Mieczkowski, 56–78. Boston: Allyn and Bacon.

Jones, J. R. 1980. Technological change and market organization in Cochabamba, Bolivia: Problems of agricultural development among potato producing small farmers. Ph.D. diss., Department of History, University of California–Los Angeles.

Joseph, G. M. 1990. On the trail of Latin American bandits: A reexamination of peasant resistance. *Latin American Research Review* 25 (3): 7–54.

Kahn, J. 1980. *Minangkabau social formations.* Cambridge: Cambridge University Press.

———. 1986. Problems in the analysis of peasant ideology. *Labour, Capital and Class* 19 (1): 36–69.

Kawell, J. Ann. 1989. The addict economies. *NACLA Report on the Americas* 12 (6): 33–40.

Kearney, M. 1986. From the invisible hand to visible feet: Anthropological studies of migration and development. *Annual Review of Anthropology* 15: 331-61.

Keesing, R. M. 1989 Creating the past: Custom and identity in the contemporary Pacific. *Pacific Anthropologist* 1 (1–2): 19–42.

Kellog, Susan. 1991. Histories for anthropology: Ten years of historical research and writing by anthropologists, 1980–1990. *Social Science History* 15 (4): 418–55.

Kertzer, D. I., S. Silverman, D. B. Rutman, and A. Plakans. 1986. History and anthropology: A dialogue. *Historical Methods* 19 (3): 119–28.

Kinder, D. C. 1988. Nativism, cultural conflict, drug control: United States and Latin American antinarcotics diplomacy through 1965. In *The Latin American narcotics trade and U.S. national security,* ed. D. J. Mabry, 11–26. New York and Westport, Conn.: Greenwood Press.

Klarén, P. F., and T.J. Bossert. 1986. Lost promise: Explaining Latin American underdevelopment. In *Promise of development: theories of change in Latin America,* ed. P. F. Klarén, and T. J. Bossert, 3–38. Boulder: Westview Press.

Klein, H. 1982. *Bolivia: The evolution of a multi-ethnic society.* Oxford: Oxford University Press.

———. 1986. Coca production in the Bolivian yungas in the colonial and early national periods. In *Coca and cocaine: effects on people and policy in Latin America,* ed. D. Pacini and C. Franquemont, 53–64. Cambridge, Mass. and Ithaca, N.Y.: Cultural Survival and Latin American Studies Program, Cornell University.

Knorr-Cetina, K. 1981. Introduction. In *Advances in social theory and methodology: Toward an integration of micro and macro sociologies,* ed. K.

Knorr-Cetina, and A. V. Cicourel, 1-47. Boston and London: Routledge and Kegan Paul.

Lagos, M. L. 1988. Pathways to autonomy, roads to power: Peasant-elite relations in Tiraque, Cochabamba (Bolivia), 1900-1985. Ph.D. diss., Department of Anthropology, Columbia University.

Langer, E. D. 1985. Labor strikes and reciprocity on Chuquisaca haciendas. *Hispanic American Historical Review* 65 (2): 255-77.

———. 1989. *Economic change and rural resistance in southern Bolivia, 1889-1930.* Stanford: Stanford University Press.

———. 1990. Rituals of rebellion: The Chayanta revolt of 1927. *Ethnohistory* 37 (3): 227-53.

Langdon, R. 1991. Caucasian Maoris: 16th-century Spaniards in New Zealand. *American Anthropologist* 93 (2): 440-44.

Larson, B. 1980. Maize, markets, and mines: Potosí and agrarian social relations in 16th century Cochabamba. Paper presented at the Ninth Annual Meeting of the Latin American Studies Association.

———. 1982. *Explotación agraria y resistencia campesina en Cochabamba.* Cochabamba: CERES.

———. 1988a. *Colonialism and agrarian transformation in Bolivia: Cochabamba, 1550-1900.* Princeton: Princeton University Press.

———. 1988b. Bolivia revisited: New directions in North American research in history and anthropology. *Latin American Research Review* 23 (1): 63-90.

———. 1988c. *Exploitation and moral economy in the southern Andes: A Critical Reconsideration.* New York: Consortium of Columbia University Institute of Latin American and Iberian Studies.

Laserna, R. 1984. *Espacio y sociedad regional.* Cochabamba: CERES.

Laserna, R., and R. Valdivieso. 1979. *La tenencia de la tierra en el valle central de Cochabamba.* Cochabamba: Universidad Mayor de San Simón. Instituto de Estudios Sociales y Económicos.

Lassen, C. 1980. *Landlessness and rural poverty in Latin America: Conditions, trends and policies affecting income and employment.* Ithaca: Cornell University. Rural Development Committee.

Latin American Bureau. 1982. *Narcotráfico y política: militarismo y mafia en Bolivia.* London: IEPALA.

Latin American Weekly Report. 1985. Narcos wary of bank offer: They prefer to launder funds in anonymity. November 8.

———. 1987a. Peasants protests at coca plan: Thousands block roads to protect their livelihood. June 11.

———. 1987b. Coca eradication plan is modified. June 25.

———. 1987c. COB demands Paz's ouster: Government must put "human face" on economic policy. June 4.

———. 1988a. COB prepares to stage protests: Talks over wages break down; Oil workers lose battle. March 24.

———. 1988b. Violence greets eradication plan: Seven dead as peasants in Chapare clash with police. July 14.

————. 1988c. Left allies with coca producers: New law to eradicate crop and suppress trafficking. July 21.

————. 1988d. Government seeks U.S. $380m in funds. September 1.

————. 1988e. Team clinches IMF, World Bank loans. June 2.

Layder, D. 1989. The macro/micro distinction, social relations and methodological bracketing: Unresolved issues in structuration theory. *Current Perspectives in Social Theory* 9:123–41.

Leacock, E. 1985. Individuals and society in anthropological theory. *Critique of Anthropology* 10 (1–2): 69–91.

Lee, R. W. 1989. *The white labyrinth: Cocaine and political power.* New Brunswick and London: Transaction Publishers.

Lehmann, D. 1982. After Chayanov and Lenin: New paths of agrarian capitalism. *Journal of Development Economics* 11:133–61.

————. 1986a. Two paths of agrarian capitalism, or a critique of Chayanovian Marxism. *Comparative Studies in Society and History* 28 (4): 601–27.

————. 1986b. Sharecropping and the capitalist transition in agriculture: Some evidence from the highlands of Ecuador. *Journal of Development Economics* 23 (2): 333–54.

Leons, M. B. 1986. Prospering in times of crisis. Paper presented at the Annual Meeting of the American Anthropological Association.

Levine, H. B. 1991. Comment on Hanson's "The making of the Maori." *American Anthropologist* 93 (2): 444–46.

Levitsky, M. 1990. *The Andean strategy to control cocaine.* Washington, D.C.: U.S. Department of State, Bureau of Public Affairs.

Linnekin, J. 1991. Cultural invention and the dilemma of authenticity. *American Anthropologist* 93 (2): 449–50.

Long, N. 1984. Introduction. In *Family and work in rural societies: Perspectives on non-wage labor,* ed. N. Long, 1–28. London and New York: Tavistock.

Long, N., and B. Roberts. 1978. Peasant cooperation and underdevelopment in central Peru. In *Peasant cooperation and capitalist expansion in central Peru,* ed. N. Long and B. Roberts, 297–328. Austin: University of Texas Press.

————. 1984. *Miners, peasants and entrepreneurs: Regional development in the central highlands of Peru.* Cambridge: Cambridge University Press.

Los Tiempos (Cochabamba). 1983a. Habrá campaña de solidaridad por la grave sequía en Potosí. April 1.

————. 1983b. Pérdida considerable en agricultura origina la sequía en Potosí y Oruro. March 27.

————. 1983c. Grupo de 600 familias campesinas será enviado al norte de Potosí. December 18.

————. 1983d. La COD alienta operación retorno de campesinos del Norte de Potosí. December 18.

————. 1983e. Los campesinos de Potosí: un símbolo de la tragedia. December 13.

————. 1983f. Aseguradora pagara 30 millones por daños que provocó la sequía. May 21.

―――. 1983g. Colonizadores del Chapare exigen solución al problema de terrenos. December 11.

―――. 1983h. Empresarios privados del trópico retomaran sus terrenos invadidos. December 9.

―――. 1983i. Disponen desalojo de tierras ocupadas en forma arbitraria. October 30.

―――. 1983j. Campesinos del Chapare denuncian nuevas ocupaciones de propiedades. July 23.

―――. 1983k. Una nueva invasión de campesinos se produjo a terrenos del Chapare. May 12.

―――. 1983l. Campesinos declaran emergencia ante invasión de sus terrenos. May 24.

―――. 1984a. Los campesinos del Chapare piden reversión de tierras. January 14.

―――. 1984b. Ocupación de tierras en el Chapare origina inmoralidad de dirigentes. July 19.

―――. 1984c. Veinte campesinos heridos en disputa entre dos grupos. July 6.

―――. 1984d. Colonizadores defenderán sus tierras si se repiten hechos vandálicos. July 11.

―――. 1991a. Donan 120 millones de dólares para el desarollo alternativo. July 2.

―――. 1991b. Marcha de cocaleros fué disuelta por la fuerza: Un herido, principales dirigentes detenidos y una veintena de desaparecidos. July 2.

Loyola, L. 1988. Brokerage, capital accumulation, and development: Transporters in the process of economic and political change in Chiapas, Mexico. Ph.D. diss., Department of Anthropology, City University of New York.

MacFarlane, A. 1976. *Resources and population: A study of the Gurungs of Nepal.* Cambridge: Cambridge University Press.

Maletta, H. 1988. Agricultura y política económica en Bolivia, 1985–1987. *Debate Agrario* 2:87–130.

Mallon, F. 1983. *The defense of community in Peru's central highlands: Peasant struggle and capitalist transition, 1860–1940.* Princeton: Princeton University Press.

Malloy, J. M. 1970. *Bolivia: The uncompleted revolution.* Pittsburgh: University of Pittsburgh Press.

Malloy, J. M., and E. Gamarra. 1988. *Revolution and reaction: Bolivia, 1964–1985.* New Brunswick: Transaction Books.

Mann, A., and M. Pastor. 1990. Orthodox and heterodox stabilization policies in Bolivia and Peru: 1985–1988. Paper presented at the Fifteenth International Congress of the Latin American Studies Association.

Mannarelli, M. E. 1985. Inquisición y mujeres: las hechiceras en el Perú durante el siglo XVII. *Revista Andina* 3 (1): 141–55.

Marcus, G. E. 1986. Contemporary problems of ethnography in the modern world system. In *Writing culture: The poetics and politics of ethnography,* ed. J. Clifford and G. E. Marcus, 165–93. Berkeley: University of California Press.

Marcus, G. E. and M. J. Fischer. 1986. *Anthropology as cultural critique: An experimental moment in the human sciences.* Chicago and London: University of Chicago Press.

Masuda, S., I. Shimada, and C. Morris, eds. 1985. *Andean ecology and civilization: An interdisciplinary perspective on Andean ecological complementarity.* Tokyo: University of Tokyo Press.

Martínez-Alier, J. 1973. *Los huacchilleros del Perú.* Lima: Instituto de Estudios Peruanos.

Mayer, E. 1985. Production Zones. In *Andean ecology and civilization: An interdisciplinary perspective on Andean ecological complementarity,* ed. S. Masuda, I. Shimada, and C. Morris, 45–84. Tokyo: University of Tokyo Press.

————. 1988. Coca use in the Andes. In *Drugs In Latin America,* ed. E. Morales, 1–24. Williamsburg, Va.: Department of Anthropology, College of William and Mary. Studies in Third World Societies, Publication no. 37.

Ministerio de Asuntos Campesinos y Agropecuarios. 1965. *Costos de producción de arroz, papa, maíz, trigo, maní y ají.* La Paz: Servicio Agrícola Interamericano.

————. 1983. *Estudio de costos de producción y comercialización de productos agrícolas y precios a nivel productor, intermediarios y consumidor.* Cochabamba: Ministerio de Asuntos Campesinos y Agropecuarios.

————. 1989. *Informe anual de actividades, 1989.* La Paz: Ministerio de Asuntos Campesinos y Agropecuarios. Dirección Nacional de Reconversión Agrícola (DIRECO).

————. 1990a. *Resumé de reducciones del 2-ene-90 al 12-sep-90.* La Paz: Ministerio de Asuntos Campesinos y Agropecuarios. Dirección Nacional de Reconversión Agrícola (DIRECO).

————. 1990b. *Estadísticas agropecuarias 1980–1990.* La Paz: Ministerio de Asuntos Campesinos y Agropecuarios. Dirección Nacional de Información y Estadística Sectorial.

Ministerio de Hacienda y Estadística. 1950. *Censo Demográfico 1950.* La Paz: Ministerio de Hacienda y Estadística.

Mintz, S. W. 1973. A note on the definition of peasantries. *Journal of Peasant Studies* 1:91–106.

————. 1985. *Sweetness and power: The place of sugar in modern history.* New York: Penguin.

————. 1989. The forefathers of crack. *NACLA Report on the Americas* 12 (6): 31–33.

Mintz, S. W. and E. Wolf. 1950. An analysis of ritual co-parenthood (Compadrazgo). *Southwestern Journal of Anthropology* 6: 341–68.

Mitchell, W. P. 1977. Irrigation farming in the Andes: Evolutionary implications. In *Peasant livelihood: Studies in economic anthropology and cultural ecology,* ed. R. Halperin and J. Dow, 36–59. New York: St. Martin's Press.

Mitchell, W. P. 1991. *Peasants on the edge: Crop, cult, and crisis in the Andes.* Austin: University of Texas Press.

Monte de Oca, I. 1982. *Geografía y recursos naturales de Bolivia.* La Paz: Banco Central de Bolivia.

Moore, K. M. 1984. The household allocation of farm-based families in Wisconsin. Ph.D. diss., Department of Sociology, University of Wisconsin-Madison.

Moore, W. 1990. Capital accumulation and revolutionary nationalism in Bolivia, 1952–85. In *The state and capital accumulation in Latin America volume 2: Argentina, Bolivia, Colombia, Ecuador, Peru, Uruguay, Venezuela,* ed. C. Anglade and C. Fortin, 32–53. Pittsburgh: University of Pittsburgh Press.

Morales, E. 1989. *Cocaine: White gold rush in Peru.* Tuscon: University of Arizona Press.

————. 1990. Comprehensive economic development: An alternative measure to reduce cocaine supply. *The Journal of Drug Issues* 20 (4): 629–637.

Morales, J. A. 1990. Impacto de los ajustes estructurales en la agricultura campesina Boliviana. In *El impacto de la NPE en el sector agropecuario,* 9–70. La Paz: Ministerio de Asuntos Campesinos y Agropecuarios.

Morgan, H. W. 1981. *Drugs in America: A social history, 1800–1980.* Syracuse, N.Y.: Syracuse University Press.

Mujica, E. 1985. Altiplano-coast relationships in the south-central Andes: From indirect to direct complementarity. In *Andean ecology and civilization: An interdisciplinary perspective on Andean ecological complementarity,* ed. S. Masuda, I. Shimada, and C. Morris, 103–40. Tokyo: University of Tokyo Press.

Multinational Agribusiness Systems, Inc. (MASI). 1979. *Regional development of the tropical Chapare of Bolivia.* La Paz: MASI and USAID.

Munck, R. 1984. *Politics and dependency in the Third World: The case of Latin America.* London: Zed Books.

Murra, J. V. 1975. *Formaciones económicas y políticas del mundo andino.* Lima: Instituto de Estudios Peruanos.

————. 1980. *La organización económica del estado Inca.* Mexico: Siglo Veintiuno, 2d ed., trans. 1955 Ph.D diss., Department of Anthropology, University of Chicago.

————. 1986. Notes on pre-Columbian cultivation of coca leaf. In *Coca and cocaine: Effects on people and policy in Latin America,* ed. D. Pacini and C. Franquemont, 49–52. Cambridge, Mass. and Ithaca, N.Y.: Cultural Survival and Latin American Studies Program, Cornell University.

Murra, J. V., N. Wachtel, and J. Revel, ed. 1986. *Anthropological history of Andean polities.* Cambridge: Cambridge University Press.

Musto, D. 1973. *The American disease: Origins of narcotics control.* New Haven, Conn.: Yale University Press.

————. 1987. The history of legislative control over opium, cocaine, and their derivatives. In *Dealing With drugs: Consequences of government control,* ed. R. Hamowy, 37–71. Lexington, Mass.: D. C. Heath.

Naciones Unidas. 1982. *Campesinado y desarrollo agrícola en Bolivia.* Santiago: Comisión Económica para América Latina.

———. 1983. *Los desastres naturales de 1982–1983 en Bolivia, Ecuador y Perú.* La Paz: Comisión Económica para América Latina.

Nash, J. 1979. *We eat the mines and the mines eat us.* New York: Columbia University Press.

———. 1981. Ethnographic aspects of the world capitalist system. *Annual Review of Anthropology* 10: 393–423.

———. 1992. Interpreting social movements: Bolivian resistance to economic conditions imposed by the International Monetary Fund. *American Ethnologist* 19 (2): 275–93.

Netherley, P. J. 1988. From event to process: The recovery of late Andean organizational structure by means of Spanish colonial written records. In *Peruvian Prehistory*, ed. R. W. Keatinge, 257–75. Cambridge: Cambridge University Press.

Netting, R. McC., R. Wilk, and E. Arnould, eds. 1984. *Households: Comparative and historical studies of the domestic group.* Berkeley: University of California Press.

New York Times. 1987. Bolivia cocaine trade revives after G.I.'s go. January 3.

———. 1989. A nice place to live (just ask the drug barons). May 23.

O'Brien, J., and W. Roseberry, eds. 1991. *Golden ages, dark ages: Imagining the past in anthropology and history.* Berkeley: University of California Press.

Oficina Nacional de Inmigración, Estadística, y Propaganda Geográfica. 1903. *Sinópsis estadística y geográfica de la Republica de Bolivia.* La Paz.

Opinión. 1991a. Gigantesco despliegue militar-policial neutraliza efectos de bloqueo campesino: medio centenar de cocaleros detenidos por fuerzas combinadas. June 18.

———. 1991b. Ejército desbarató marcha de campesinos productores de coca. July 1.

———. 1991c. Oficial: gobierno propone amplia discusión sobre Anexos II y III: marcha de la "Soberanía y dignidad" llegó a la zona de El Palmar a 60 kilómetros de Villa Tunari. June 30.

———. 1991d. Productores de coca exigen presencia de Min. Interior y Asuntos Campesinos: reiteran disposición de dialogar con una comisión de alto nivel del gobierno tema de militarización. June 29.

Organization of American States (OAS). 1984. *Bolivia: Magnitude and origin of the economic crisis of 1982 and the economic policies of the constitutional government.* Washington, D.C.: Organization of American States. General Secretariat. Executive Secretariat for Economic and Social Affairs. Short-term Economic Reports, vol. 9.

Orlove, B. 1977a. Inequality among peasants: The forms and uses of reciprocal exchange in Andean Peru. In *Peasant livelihood: Studies in economic anthropology and cultural ecology*, ed. R. Halperin and J. Dow, 201–14. New York: St. Martin's Press.

———. 1977b. *Alpacas, sheep, and men: The wool export economy and regional society in southern Peru.* New York: Academic Press.

Orlove, B., and G. Custred. 1980. The alternative model of agrarian society in the Andes: Households, networks and corporate groups. In *Land and power in Latin America: Agrarian economies and social processes in the Andes*, ed. B. Orlove and G. Custred, 31–53. New York: Holmes and Meir.

Orlove, B., and R. Godoy. 1986. Sectoral farming systems in the central Andes. *Journal of Ethnobiology* 6:169–204.

Ortiz, Sutti. 1980. Forecasts, decisions, and the farmer's response to uncertain environments. In *Agricultural decision making: Anthropological contributions to rural development*, ed. Peggy F. Barlett, 177–202. New York: Academic Press.

Ortner, S. B. 1984. Theory in anthropology since the sixties. *Comparative Studies in Society and History* 26 (1): 126–66.

Painter, M. 1984. Changing relations of production and rural underdevelopment. *Journal of Anthropological Research* 40 (2): 271–92.

———. 1985. Reconstructing reciprocity in an Andean peasant society. Paper presented at the Annual Meeting of the American Anthropological Association.

———. 1986. The value of peasant labour power in a prolonged transition to capitalism. *Journal of Peasant Studies* 13 (4): 221–39.

———. 1991. Re-creating peasant economy in southern Peru. In *Golden ages, dark ages: Imagining the past in anthropology and history*, ed. J. O'Brien, and W. Roseberry, 81–106. Berkeley: University of California Press.

Parkerson, P. T. 1983. The Incan coca monopoly: Fact or legal fiction? *Proceedings of the American Philosophical Society* 127 (1): 107–23.

———. 1989. Neither "green gold" nor "the devil's leaf": Coca farming in Bolivia. In *State, capital, and rural society: Anthropological perspectives on political economy in Mexico and the Andes*, ed. B. S. Orlove, M. W. Foley, and T. F. Love, 267–97. Boulder: Westview Press.

Pattie, P. S. 1988. *Agriculture sector assessment for Bolivia*. Washington, D.C.: Chemonics International Consulting Division.

Philander, S. G. H. 1983. El Niño southern oscillation phenomena. *Nature* 302 (March 24): 295–301.

Platt, T. 1982a. *Estado boliviano y ayllu andino*. Lima: Instituto de Estudios Peruanos.

———. 1982b. The role of the Andean Ayllu in the reproduction of the petty commodity regime in northern Potosí (Bolivia). In *Ecology and Exchange in the Andes*, ed. D. Lehmann, 27–69. Cambridge: Cambridge University Press.

———. 1983. Conciencia andina y conciencia proletaria: Qhuyaruan y ayllu en el Norte de Potosí. *HISLA: Revista Latinoamericana de Historia Económica y Social* 2: 47–73.

Plowman, T. 1984a. The origin, evolution, and diffusion of coca, erythoxylum spp., in south and central America. In *Pre-Columbian Plant Migration*, ed. D. Stone, 126–63. Cambridge, Mass: Papers of the Peabody Museum of Archaeology and Ethnology, vol. 76.

———. 1984b. The ethnobotany of coca (erthroxylum spp., erythroxylacae). *Advances in Economic Botany* 1:62–111.

———. 1986. Coca chewing and the botanical origins of coca (erythroxyluum spp.) in South America. *In Coca and cocaine: Effects on people and policy in Latin America*, ed. D. Pacini and C. Franquemont, 5–34. Cambridge, Mass. and Ithaca, N.Y.: Cultural Survival and Latin American Studies Program, Cornell University.

Presencia. 1983a Miles de camélidos murieron a consequencia de la sequía. October 5.

———. 1983b. Campesinos de Potosí afectados por la sequía no reciben ayuda-Exodo hacia Chile es cada vez mayor. October 4.

———. 1991a. Elecciones municipales y operaciones militares antidroga. October 7.

———. 1991b. Oscar Roca y Moisés Flores serán los próximos en entregarse a la justicia. September 17.

———. 1991c. Hugo Rivera V. se entregó a la DEA en Santa Ana de Yacuma. September 16.

———. 1991d. Estados Unidos concretó ayuda de $US 120 millones para Bolivia. July 6.

———. 1991e. A raíz de enfrentamientos con DIRECO y UMOPAR: Campesinos del Chapare en estado de apronte y tensión.

———. 1991f. Bertero culpa al narcotráfico de los incidentes del Chapare. 2nd.

Prudencio, J. 1984. La sequía en Bolivia, 1982–1983. Paper presented at the seminar "El impacto socio-económico y ambiental de los catástrofes naturales en las economías regionales y en sus centros urbanos." Santa Cruz, July 30–August 1.

Prudencio, J., and M. Velasco. 1987. *La defensa del consumo: crisis de abastecimiento alimentario y estrategias de sobrevivencia.* La Paz: CERES.

Rasnake, R. 1988. *Domination and cultural resistance: Authority and power among an Andean people.* Durham and London: Duke University Press.

Rasnake, R., and M. Painter. 1989. *Rural development and crop substitution in Bolivia: USAID and the Chapare Regional Development Project.* Binghamton, N.Y.: Institute for Development Anthropology. Working Paper no. 45.

Reinarman, C., and H. G. Levine. 1989a. The crack attack: Politics and media in America's latest drug scare. In *Images of Issues: Typifying Contemporary Social Problems*, ed. J. Best, 115–37. Hawthorne, N.Y.: Aldine de Gruyter.

———. 1989b. Crack in context: Politics and media in the making of a drug scare. *Contemporary Drug Problems* 16 (34): 535–77.

Riester, B., J. Riester, B. Simón, and B. Schuchard. 1979. *Me vendí, me compraron: análisis socio-económico, en base a testimonios, de la zafra de caña en Santa Cruz de la Sierra.* Santa Cruz.

Reye, U. 1970. *Política de desarollo regional en el Oriente Boliviano.* Bilbao, Spain: Ediciones Deusto.

Roberts, R. 1975. Migration and colonization in Colombian Amazonia: Agrarian reform or neo-latufundismo? Ph.D. diss., Department of Anthropology, Syracuse University.

Romano, R., and G. Tranchand. 1983. Una encomienda coquera en los yungas de La Paz (1560–1566). *HISLA: Revista Latinoamericana de Historia Económica y Social* 1:57–88.

Roseberry, W. 1983. *Coffee and capitalism in the Venezuelan Andes.* Austin: University of Texas Press.

———. 1986. The ideology of domestic production. *Labour, Capital and Society* 19 (1): 70–93.

———. 1988. Political economy. *Annual Review of Anthropology* 17: 161–85.

———. 1989a. *Anthropologies and histories: Essays in culture, history, and political economy.* New Brunswick and London: Rutgers University Press.

———. 1989b. Peasants and the world. In *Economic anthropology*, ed. S. Plattner, 108–26. Stanford: Stanford University Press.

Rostworoski de Diez Canseco, M. 1970. Mercaderes del valle de Chincha en la época prehispánica: un documento y unos comentarios. *Revista Española de Antropología Americana* 5:135–78.

———. 1973. Plantaciones prehispánicas de coca en la vertiente del Pacífico. *Revista del Museo Nacional* (Lima) 39:193–224.

———. 1988. Conflicts Over coca fields in XVIth century Peru. *Memoirs of the Museum of Anthropology* (Ann Arbor) 21.

Sachs, J. 1987. The Bolivian hyperinflation and stabilization. *American Economic Review* 77 (2): 279–83.

Sage, C. 1984. Intensification of commodity relations: Agricultural specialization and differentiation in the Cochabamba Serranía, Bolivia. *Bulletin of Latin American Research* 3 (1): 81–97.

———. 1990. Petty producers, potatoes and land: A case study of agrarian change in the Cochabamba Serranía, Bolivia. Ph.D. diss., Department of Geography, University of Durham.

Sahlins, M. 1972. *Stone Age Economics.* Hawthorne, N.Y.: Aldine.

———. 1976. *Culture and practical reason.* Chicago: University of Chicago Press.

Saignés, T. 1985. *Los andes orientales: historia de un olvido.* Cochabamba: CERES.

———. 1988. Capoche, Potosí y la coca: el consumo popular de estimulantes en el siglo XVII. *Revista de Indias* 47: (182–83): 207–35.

Salomon, F. 1985. The Dynamic Potential of the Complementarity Concept. In *Andean Ecology and Civilization: An Interdisciplinary Perspective on Andean Ecological Complementarity*, ed. S. Masuda, I. Shimada, and C. Morris, 511–31. Tokyo: University of Tokyo Press.

———. 1986. *Ethnic lords of Quito in the age of the Incas: The political economy of north Andean chiefdoms.* Cambridge: Cambridge University Press.

Samaniego, C. 1984. Estado, acumulación y agricultura en el Perú. *Estudios Rurales Latinoamericanos* 7 (3): 200–62.

Sanabria, H. 1988. Migration, coca, and social differentiation in the Bolivian lowlands. In *Drugs In Latin America*, ed. E. Morales, 81–124. Williamsburg, Va.: Department of Anthropology, College of William and Mary. Studies in Third World Societies, Publication no. 37.

———. 1991. Review of "The cocaine kids: The inside story of a teenage drug ring." *Qualitative Sociology* 13 (4): 393–96.

————. 1992. Holding their ground: Crop eradication, repression, and peasant resistance in the Chapare of Bolivia. Paper presented at the Seventeenth International Congress of the Latin American Studies Association.

————. n.d. Subsistence agriculture, crop specialization, and labor availability: Some perspectives from Bolivia. Ms.

Sánchez-Albornoz, N. 1978. *Indios y tributos en el Alto Perú*. Lima: Instituto de Estudios Peruanos.

————. 1982. Migraciones internas en el Alto Perú: el saldo acumulativo en 1645. *Historia Boliviana* 2 (1): 11–19.

————. 1983a. Migración rural en los Andes: Sipe Sipe (Cochabamba), 1645. *Revista de Historia Económica* 1 (1): 13–36.

————. 1983b. Mita, migraciones y pueblos. Variaciones en el espacio y en el tiempo: Alto Perú, 1573–1692. *Historia Boliviana* 3 (1): 31–59.

Sánchez, R. 1982. The andean economic system and capitalism. In *Ecology and Exchange in the Andes*, ed. D. Lehmann, 157–90. Cambridge: Cambridge University Press.

Santamaría, D. J. 1987. La participación indígena en la producción y comercio de coca, Alto Perú 1780–1810. In *La participación indígena en los mercados surandinos: estrategias y reproducción social, siglos XVI a XX*, ed. O. Harris, B. Larson, and E. Tandeter, 425–44. La Paz: CERES.

Scheffler, H. 1985. Filiation and affiliation. *Man* 20 (1): 1–20.

————. 1986. The descent of rights and the descent of persons. *American Anthropologist* 88 (2): 339–50.

Schmink, M. 1981. *A case study of the closing frontier in Brazil*. Gainesville: University of Florida. Amazon Research and Training Program. Research Paper no.1.

————. 1984. Household economic strategies: Review and research agenda. *Latin American Research Review* 19 (3): 87–101.

Scott, J. C. 1976. *The moral economy of the peasant: Rebellion and subsistence in Southeast Asia*. New Haven and London: Yale University Press.

————. 1985. *Weapons of the weak: Everyday forms of peasant resistance*. New Haven: Yale University Press.

————. 1986. Everyday forms of peasant resistance. *Journal of Peasant Studies* 13 (2): 5–35.

————. 1991. *Domination and the arts of resistance: Hidden transcripts*. New Haven: Yale University Press.

Sewell, W. H. 1987. Theory of action, dialectic, and history: Comment on Coleman. *American Journal of Sociology* 93: 166–72.

Shanin, T. 1986. Chayanov's message: Illuminations, miscomprehensions, and the contemporary "Development Theory." In *The Theory of Peasant Economy*, By A. V. Chayanov (with a new intro. by T. Shanin.), 1–24. Madison: University of Wisconsin Press.

Shoemaker, R. 1981. *The peasants of El Dorado: Conflict and contradiction in a Peruvian frontier settlement*. Ithaca: Cornell University Press.

Silverblatt, I. 1987. *Moon, sun, and witches: Gender ideologies and class in Inca and colonial Peru*. Princeton: Princeton University Press.

Silverman, S. 1979. The peasant concept in anthropology. *Journal of Peasant Studies* 7 (1): 49–69.

Skar, H. 1982. *The warm valley people: Duality and land reform among the Quechua Indians of highland Peru.* Oslo: Universitetsforlaget.

Skar, S. L. 1984. Interhousehold co-operation in Peru's southern Andes: A case of multiple sibling-group marriage. In *Family and work in rural societies: Perspectives on non-wage labor*, ed. N. Long, 83–98. London and New York: Tavistock.

Smith, C. 1983. Regional analysis in world-system perspective: A critique of three structural theories of uneven development. In *Economic anthropology: Topics and theories*, ed. S. Ortiz, 307–60. Lanham, Md.: University Press of America.

———. 1984. Does a commodity economy enrich the few while ruining the masses? Differentiation among petty commodity producers in Guatemala. *Journal of Peasant Studies* 11 (3): 60–95.

Smith, C. L. 1991. Patterns of wealth concentration. *Human Organization* 50 (1): 50–60.

Spalding, K. 1982. Exploitation as an economic system: The state and the extraction of surplus in colonial Peru. In *The Inca and Aztec States, 1400–1800: Anthropology and History*, G. A. Collier, R. Rosaldo, and J. D. Wirth, 321–44. New York: Academic Press.

———. 1984. *Huarochirí: An Andean society under Inca and Spanish rule.* Stanford: Stanford University Press.

Spiegel, A. D. 1989. Towards an understanding of tradition: Uses of tradition(al) in apartheid South Africa. *Critique of Anthropology* 9 (1): 49–74.

Stearman, A. M. 1976. The highland migrant in lowland Bolivia: Regional migration and the department of Santa Cruz. Ph.D. diss., Department of Anthropology, University of Florida.

———. 1985. *Camba and Kolla: Migration and development in Santa Cruz, Bolivia.* Gainesville: University Presses of Florida.

Stein, W. 1984. How are peasants exploited? The extraction of unpaid labor in rural Peru. *Research in Economic Anthropology* 6:273–308.

Stern, S. 1982. *Peru's Indian peoples and the challenge of Spanish conquest: Huamanga to 1640.* Madison: University of Wisconsin Press.

———. 1983. Struggle for solidarity: Class, culture, and community in highland Indian America. *Radical History Review* 27:21–45.

———. 1988a. Feudalism, capitalism, and the world system in the perspective of Latin America and the Caribbean. *American Historical Review* 93 (4): 829–72.

———. 1988b. Reply: "Ever more solitary." *American Historical Review* 93 (4): 886–97.

Subsecretaría de Desarollo Alternativo y Sustitución de Cultivos de Coca (SUB-DESAL). 1988. *DIRECO: Programa de reconversión agrícola.* La Paz: Ministerio de Asuntos Campesinos y Agropecuarios. Subsecretaría de Desarollo Alternativo y Sustitución de Cultivos de Coca.

Swetnam, J. 1989. What else did Indians have to do with their time? Alternatives to labor migration in prerevolutionary Guatemala. *Economic Development and Cultural Change* 38 (1): 89–112.

Thiesenhusen, W. 1977. Current development patterns in Latin America with special reference to agrarian policy. Madison: University of Wisconsin Land Tenure Center. Ms.

———. 1984. The illusory goal of equity in Latin American agrarian reform. In *International dimensions of land reform*, ed. J. D. Mont, 31–62. Boulder: Westview Press.

———. 1987. Rural development questions in Latin America. *Latin American Research Review* 12 (1): 171–203.

Thomas, N. 1992. The inversion of tradition. *American Ethnologist* 19 (2): 231–32.

Thompson, E.P. 1976. The grid of inheritance: A comment. In *Family and inheritance: Western Europe, 1200–1800*, ed. J. Goody, J. Thirsk, and E. P. Thompson, 328–60. Cambridge: Cambridge University Press.

Thorn, R. S. 1971. The economic transformation. In *Beyond the revolution: Bolivia since 1952*, ed. J. M. Malloy and R. S. Thorn, 157–216. Pittsburgh: University of Pittsburgh Press.

Tienda, M. 1989. Puerto Ricans and the underclass debate. *Annals, AAPSS* 501:105–19.

Tienda, M., R. Schurman, and K. Booth. 1987. *Cycles of boom and bust in Latin America: A quarter century profile of social and economic inequality.* Madison: University of Wisconsin Center for Demography and Ecology. Working Paper no. 87-27.

Tipps, D. C. 1973. Modernization theory and the comparative study of societies: A critical perspective. *Comparative Studies in Society and History* 15 (2): 199–226.

Tolisano, J. 1989. *Environmental assessment of the Chapare Regional Development Project, Bolivia.* Washington, D.C.: Development Alternatives.

Tosi, J. 1983. *Análisis ecológico y capacidad de uso de la tierra en el area del proyecto Chapare.* Report prepared for the U.S. Agency for International Development.

Troll, C. 1968. The cordilleras of the tropical Americas: Aspects of climatic, phytogeographical, and agrarian ecology. In *Geo-ecology of the mountainous regions of the tropical Americas*, 13–65. Bonn: Ferd. Dummlers Verlag (Colloquim Geographicum, bd. 9).

Tullis, F. L. 1987. Cocaine and food: Likely effects of a burgeoning transnational industry on food production in Bolivia and Peru. In *Pursuing food security: Strategies and obstacles in Africa, Asia, Latin America, and the Middle East*, ed. W. Ladd Hollist and F. LaMond Tullis, 247–283. Boulder: Lynne Rienner.

Turovsky, P. 1980. Bolivian haciendas: Before and after the revolution. Ph.D. diss., Department of History, University of California–Los Angeles.

Ultima Hora. 1991. Campesinos inician marcha contra militarización del Chapare a La Paz. June 24.

Unidad de Análisis de Politicas Económicas (UDAPE). 1990. Análisis del impacto de las políticas macroeconómicas y factores externos en el sector agrícola. In *El impacto de la NPE en el sector agropecuario*, 71–178. La Paz: Ministerio de Asuntos Campesinos y Agropecuarios.

United Nations. *See* Naciones Unidas.

United States Agency for International Development (USAID). 1978. Narcotics strategy paper for Bolivia. La Paz: USAID. Mimeo.

———. 1981. Chapare development–Project paper outline. La Paz: USAID. Mimeo.

———. 1988. Review of USAID/Bolivia development assistance support for coca eradication. La Paz: USAID. Mimeo.

United States House of Representatives. 1990a. United States anti-narcotics activities in the Andean region. *Thirty-Eighth Report by the Committee on Government Operations.* Washington, D.C.: U.S. Government Printing Office.

———. 1990b. Review of Bolivian soybeans, U.S. drug policy, and the food for peace program. Joint hearing before the Subcommittee on Wheat, Research, and Foreign Agriculture. Washington, D.C.: U.S. Government Printing Office.

———. 1991. Andean drug strategy. Hearing before the Subcommittee on Western Hemispheric Affairs. Washington, D.C.: U.S. Government Printing Office.

Unzueta, O. 1975. *Mapa ecológico de Bolivia.* La Paz: Ministerio de Asuntos Campesinos y Agropecuarios.

Uprimny, R. 1990. The U.S. War on drugs: Addicted to repression? Washington, D.C.: Washington Office on Latin America. Issue Brief no. 1.

Urioste, M. 1987. *Segunda reforma agraria: campesinos, tierra y educación popular.* La Paz: Talleres CEDLA.

Urquidi, J. M. 1949. *El origen de la Noble Villa de Oropesa.* Cochabamba: Imprenta Universitaria.

Urquidi, G. 1954. *Monografía del departamento de Cochabamba.* Cochabamba: Imprenta Tunari.

Vandergeest, P. 1989. Peasant strategies in a world context: Contingencies in the transformation of rice and palm sugar economies in Thailand. *Human Organization* 48 (2): 117–25.

Vargas, C., W. Mendoza, and H. Céspedes. 1979. *El potencial agropecuario de los valles de Cochabamba.* Cochabamba: Corporación Regional de Desarollo de Cochabamba. Documento de Trabajo no. 7.

Wachtel, N. 1982. The mitimas of the Cochabamba Valley: The colonization policy of Huayna Capac. In *The Inca and Aztec States, 1400–1800: Anthropology and History*, ed. George A. Collier, R. Rosaldo. and J. D. Wirth, 199–235. New York and London: Academic Press.

Wacquant, L., and W. J. Wilson. 1989. The cost of racial and class exclusion in the inner city. *Annals, AAPSS* 501:8–25.

Wallace, B. C. 1990. Crack addiction: Treatment and recovery issues. *Contemporary Drug Problems* 17 (1): 79–119.

Wallerstein, I. 1988. Comments on Stern's critical tests. *The American Historical Review* 93 (4): 873–85.

Walton, J. 1988. Debt, protest, and the state in Latin America. In *Power and popular protest: Latin American social movements*, ed. Susan Eckstein, 299–328. Berkeley: University of California Press.

Walton, J., and C. Ragin. 1988. Austerity and dissent: Social bases of popular struggle in Latin America. In *Debt, austerity, and development in Latin America*, ed. W. Canak, 216–32. Berkeley: University of California Press.

Wasserstrom, R., and J. Rus. 1981. Civil-religious hierarchies in central Chiapas: A critical perspective. *American Ethnologist* 7:466–78.

Weatherford, J. M. 1987. Cocaine and the economic deterioration of Bolivia. In *Conformity and conflict: Readings in cultural anthropology*, ed. J. P. Spradley and D. W. McCurdy, 412–423. Boston: Little, Brown.

Webster, S. 1981. Interpretation of an Andean social and economic formation. *Man* 16 (4): 616–33.

Weil, C. 1980. The adaptiveness of tropical settlement in the Chapare of Bolivia. Ph.D. diss., Department of Geography, Columbia University.

———. 1983. Migration among landholdings by Bolivian campesinos. *Geographical Review* 73:182–97.

Weil, J. 1980a. The organization of work in a Quechua pioneer settlement: Adaptation of highland tradition in the lowlands of eastern Bolivia. Ph.D. diss., Department of Anthropology, Columbia University.

———. 1980b. Coca and tropical colonization in Bolivia: The adaptiveness of a cash crop. *Central Issues in Anthropology* 2 (1): 15–25.

———. 1989. Cooperative labor as an adaptive strategy among homesteaders in a tropical colonization zone: Chapare, Bolivia. In *The human ecology of tropical land settlement in Latin America*, ed. D. A. Schumann and W. L. Partridge, 298–339. Boulder: Westview Press.

Wennergren, E. B., and M. D. Whitaker. 1975. *The status of Bolivian agriculture*. New York: Praeger.

Werge, R. 1981. *The agricultural strategy of rural households in three ecological zones of the central highlands*. Lima: International Potato Center.

Wessel, K. 1968. An economic assessment of pioneer settlements in the Bolivian lowlands. Ph.D. diss., Department of Agricultural Economics, Cornell University.

West, T. L. 1981. Sufriendo nos vamos: From a subsistence to a market economy in an Aymara community of Bolivia. Ph.D. diss., Department of Anthropology, New School for Social Research.

Wharton, C. R. 1971. Risk, uncertainty, and the subsistence farmer: Technological innovation and resistance to change in the context of survival. In *Studies in economic anthropology*, ed. G. Dalton, 144–52. Washington, D.C.: American Anthropological Association.

Wightman, A. M. 1990. *Indigenous migration and social change: The Forasteros of Cuzco, 1570–1720*. Durham and London: Duke University Press.

Wilk, R. R. 1989. Decision-making and resource flows within the household:

beyond the black box. In *The household economy: reconsidering the domestic mode of production*, ed. R. R. Wilk, 23–54. Boulder: Westview Press.

Wilk, R. R., and R. McNetting. 1984. Households: changing forms and functions. In *Households: comparative studies of the domestic group*, ed. R. McNetting, R. Wilk and E. Arnould, 1–28. Berkeley: University of California Press.

Williams, R. G. 1986. *Export agriculture and the crisis in Central America*. Chapel Hill: University of North Carolina Press.

Williams, T. 1989. *The cocaine kids: The inside story of a teenage drug ring*. Reading, Mass.: Addison-Wesley.

Wilson, W. J. 1989. The underclass: Issues, perspectives, and public policy. *Annals, AAPSS* 501:182–192.

Wolf, E. 1957. Closed corporate peasant communities in Mesoamerica and central Java. *Southwestern Journal of Anthropology* 13 (1): 1–18.

———. 1982. *Europe and the people without history*. Berkeley: University of California Press.

———. 1986. The vicissitudes of the closed corporate peasant community. *American Ethnologist* 13 (2): 325–29.

———. 1990. Distinguished lecture: Facing power-old insights, new questions. *American Anthropologist* 92 (3): 586–96.

World Bank. 1984. *Bolivia: agricultural pricing and investment policies*. Washington, D.C.: International Bank for Reconstruction and Development.

Wright, T. C. 1985. The politics of urban provisioning in Latin American history. In *Food, politics, and society in Latin America*, ed. J. C. Super and T. C. Wright, 24–45. Lincoln and London: University of Nebraska Press.

Yanagisako, S. J. 1979. Family and household: The analysis of domestic groups. *Annual Review of Anthropology* 8:161–205.

Zeballos-Hurtado, H. 1975. From the uplands to the lowlands: An economic analysis of Bolivian rural-rural migration. Ph.D. diss., Department of Agricultural Economics, University of Wisconsin–Madison.

Zinn, M. B. 1989. Family, race, and poverty in the eighties. *Signs* 14 (4): 856–74.

Zuidema, R. T. 1990. *Inca civilization in Cuzco*. Austin: University of Texas Press.

Zulawski, A. 1987. Wages, ore sharing, and peasant agriculture: Labor in Oruro's silver mines, 1607–1720. *Hispanic American Historical Review* 67 (3): 405–430.

———. 1990. Frontier workers and social change: Pilaya and Paspaya (Bolivia) in the early eighteenth century. In *Migration in colonial Spanish America*, ed. D. J. Robinson, 112–127. New York and Cambridge: Cambridge University Press.

Index

Agrarian reform: and agri-business enterprises in eastern lowlands, 50; and bias against small-scale agriculturalists, 51–52; and colonization, 43; decline in nutritional and health standards after, 53; decline in terms of trade after, 53; and distribution of land in Pampa, 93–94; economic development polices after, 50–51, 199; limitations of, 50. *See also* Colonization; Economic crisis; Terms of trade

Ajenos, 32, 83, 111–12, 154, 190–91

Allen, Catherine J., 38, 163

Andean Initiative, 174–75

Ayni, 78–80, 106, 125, 149–50, 152–57, 160, 162, 164. *See also* Nonwage and reciprocal labor

Ayuda, 152–56, 160. *See also* Nonwage and reciprocal labor

Beni, 51, 54, 173, 191

Bernstein, Henry, 129

Bolivia, major geographic regions, 21

Burchard, Roderick E., 38, 172

Bureau of International Narcotics Matters, 13, 45, 61, 175–76, 178–79, 181, 183–84, 188

Canje: defined, 100; and migration to the Chapare, 105–6; and usufruct rights to land in Pampa, 105. *See also* Nonwage and reciprocal labor

Chapare: agricultural development and, 15; coca production compared to Yungas of La Paz, 41; competition over land in, 80–81; expansion of agricultural frontier in, 28; hectares sown in coca in, 59; land area and ecology of, 28; migrant categories and access to land and labor, 76; militarization of, 177; Pampeños affiliated with colonies in, 68–69; repression in, 177, 182; soils and crop production, 28. *See also* Coca cultivation; Resistance

Chapare Rural Development Project, 175–76

Chayanov, A. V., 7–8, 12

Coca: adaptability to eastern tropics, 44; and alternative development programs, 172–73; conflict and competition over, 38–39, 198; decline in prices and income to peasants, 174; domesticated species of, 37; early colonial debate over eradication of, 39–40; and economic crisis, 171; and economic development policies, 199; economic roles of, 38; and medicinal practices, 38; and migrant life careers, 90–91; production and consumption after the Spanish conquest, 39; production and trade by Aymara ayllus, 41; and purchase of vehicles, 84–86; and repression by police and military, 4, 172; and silver mining in Potosí, 40–41; social and cultural dimensions of, 38; and symbolic display of wealth in ceremonies, 86–89; vitamin and mineral content of, 37. *See also* Coca cultivation; Coca eradication; Economic crisis

Coca chewing, 38, 40, 172

273